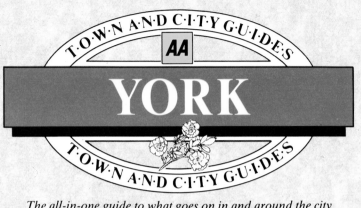

T·O·W·N A·N·D C·I·T·Y G·U·I·D·E·S

AA

YORK

T·O·W·N A·N·D C·I·T·Y G·U·I·D·E·S

The all-in-one guide to what goes on in and around the city

*Tourist information,
maps, walks, tours,
eating out, where to stay,
PLUS
the Royal connection*

Produced by the Publishing Division of the Auto...

*Cover Picture: York Minster, viewed from the narrow
confines of Kleisers Court – one of many fascinating little
alleys criss-crossing the City's ancient heart*

*Introductory Picture, pages 4 & 5: Building styles and
materials separated by centuries are seen close together
in complementary harmony within York*

Editors: Roland Weisz, Russell P O Beach
Art Editor: Dave Austin
Design Assistant: K A G Design
Original Photography: Richard Newton
Editorial contributors: Ivan Broadhead (The City's Rivers and
Bridges), Charles Kightley (The Dukes and Duchesses of York,
Traditions and Ceremonies), Mark Jones (A Spider's Web of
Alleyways), A L Laishley (York Minster), Rachel Semlyen
(Cultural Heritage), Peter Semmens (A City and its Railways),
William Taylor (York – and chocolate), Ronald Willis (The
history of York).

York Gazetteer and Walks researched and written by Colin Park

District Gazetteer, Drives and Index prepared by the Editorial
Research Unit of the Automobile Association

Maps produced by the Cartographic Department of the
Automobile Association.

Phototypeset, printed and bound by W S Cowell Ltd,
Butter Market, Ipswich

The contents of this publication are believed correct at the time
of printing. Nevertheless, the Publishers cannot accept
responsibility for errors or omissions, or for changes in details
given.

Produced and distributed in the United Kingdom by the
Publishing Division of the Automobile Association,
Fanum House, Basingstoke, Hampshire, RG21 2EA.

ISBN 0 86145 510 X
AA Reference 59255

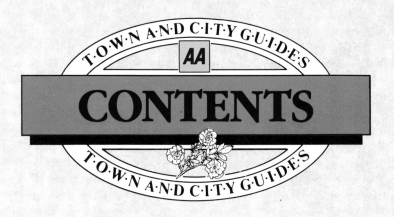

TOWN AND CITY GUIDES

AA

CONTENTS

TOWN AND CITY GUIDES

City of York

*T*his AA guide is part of a series designed to be a comprehensive 'potted' introduction to Britain's historic cities. The quality of the information and its production is a fitting tribute to York, whose ancient Royal connections were brought to the attention of the world when Prince Andrew became the 14th Duke of York in July 1986.

Two separate, detailed gazetteers list and describe places of interest in and around York, each location being shown on a clear and easy-to-use town plan. Other AA maps support planned City walks and out-of-town drives – all cross-referenced to the gazetteers – and show York in the context of its surrounding area.

Important features of the Guide are the Directory and Index, both of which are packed with touring information. Essential services, with attractions, shopping opportunities, places to stay, places to eat, and various other amenities, with addresses and phone numbers, are listed in the Directory, while the Index includes admission charges and opening times for locations accessible to the public.

Written by local experts, a comprehensive range of articles at the beginning of the book provides background, colour and depth to the fine detail, which follows in later sections. The subjects are wide ranging, from the history of York and its superb Minster to the impact of railways and the chocolate industry. *AA York*, illustrated throughout with colour photographs, is a Guide showing the many facets of the City. The book offers a concise introduction to the geography around York, and routes by which to explore it. As such it is as valuable to the city resident as it is to the visitor.

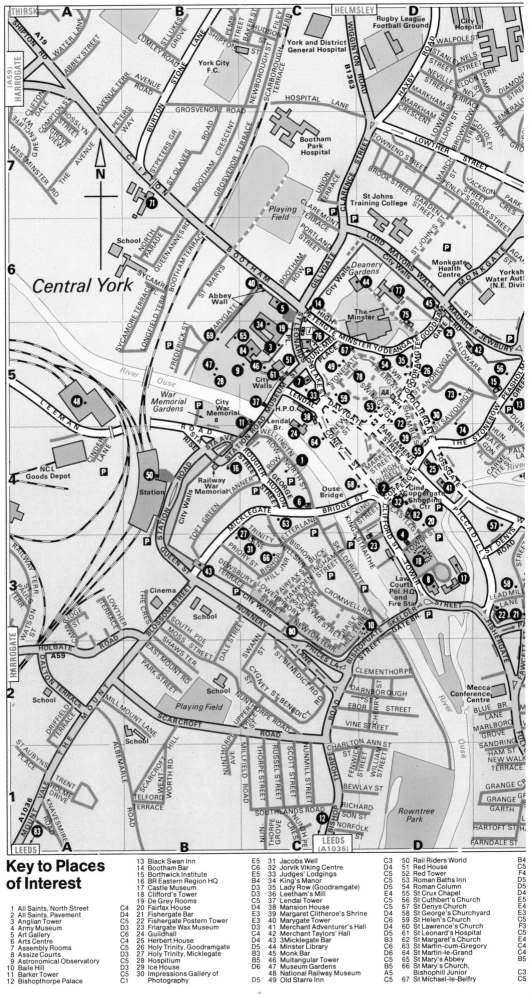

Key to Places of Interest

1 All Saints, North Street	C4	
2 All Saints, Pavement	D4	
3 Anglian Tower	C5	
4 Army Museum	D3	
5 Art Gallery	C6	
6 Arts Centre	C4	
7 Assembly Rooms	C5	
8 Assize Courts	D3	
9 Astronomical Observatory	C5	
10 Baile Hill	D3	
11 Barker Tower	C5	
12 Bishopthorpe Palace	C1	

13 Black Swan Inn	E5	
14 Bootham Bar	C6	
15 Borthwick Institute	E5	
16 BR Eastern Region HQ	B4	
17 Castle Museum	D3	
18 Clifford's Tower	D3	
19 De Grey Rooms	C5	
20 Fairfax House	D4	
21 Fishergate Bar	E3	
22 Fishergate Postern Tower	E3	
23 Friargate Wax Museum	D3	
24 Guildhall	C4	
25 Herbert House	D4	
26 Holy Trinity, Goodramgate	D5	
27 Holy Trinity, Micklegate	B3	
28 Hospitium	B5	
29 Ice House	D6	
30 Impressions Gallery of Photography	D5	

31 Jacobs Well	C3	
32 Jorvik Viking Centre	D4	
33 Judges' Lodgings	C5	
34 King's Manor	C5	
35 Lady Row (Goodramgate)	D5	
36 Leetham's Mill	E4	
37 Lendal Tower	C5	
38 Mansion House	D4	
39 Margaret Clitheroe's Shrine	D4	
40 Marygate Tower	C5	
41 Merchant Adventurer's Hall	D4	
42 Merchant Taylors' Hall	D5	
43 3Micklegate Bar	B3	
44 Minster Library	C5	
45 Monk Bar	D6	
46 Multangular Tower	C5	
47 Museum Gardens	B5	
48 National Railway Museum	A5	
49 Old Starre Inn	C5	

50 Rail Riders World	B4	
51 Red House	C5	
52 Red Tower	F4	
53 Roman Baths Inn	D5	
54 Roman Column	D5	
55 St Crux Chapel	D4	
56 St Cuthbert's Church	E5	
57 St Denys Church	E4	
58 St George's Churchyard	E3	
59 St Helen's Church	C5	
60 St Lawrence's Church	F3	
61 St Leonard's Hospital	C5	
62 St Margaret's Church	E4	
63 St Martin-cum-Gregory	C4	
64 St Martin-le-Grand	C4	
65 St Mary's Abbey	B5	
66 St Mary's Church, Bishophill Junior	C3	
67 St Michael-le-Belfry	C5	

6

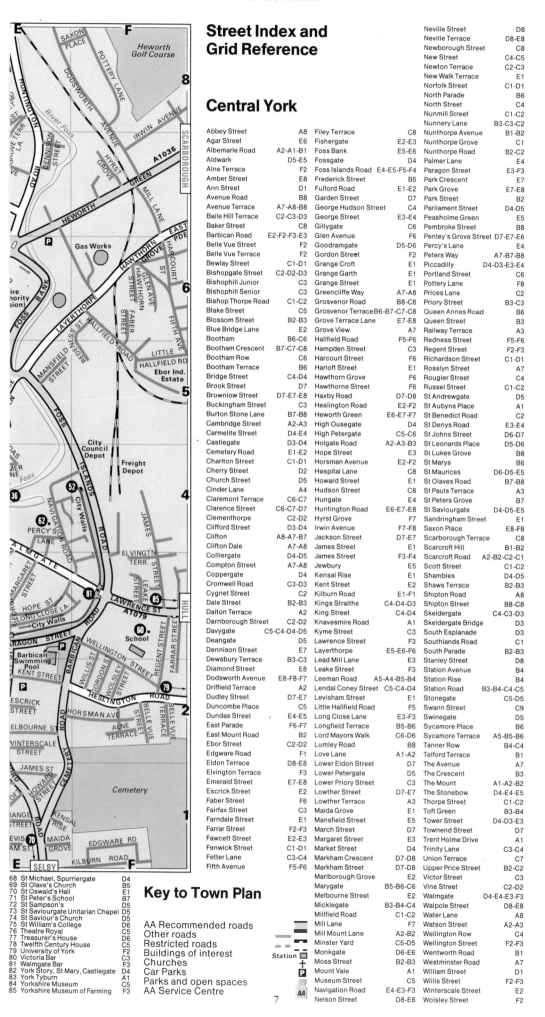

Street Index and Grid Reference

Central York

Street	Grid
Abbey Street	A8
Agar Street	E6
Albemarle Road	A2-A1-B1
Aldwark	D5-E5
Alne Terrace	F2
Amber Street	E8
Ann Street	D1
Avenue Road	B8
Avenue Terrace	A7-A8-B8
Baile Hill Terrace	C2-C3-D3
Baker Street	C8
Barbican Road	E2-F2-F3-E3
Belle Vue Street	F2
Belle Vue Terrace	F2
Bewlay Street	C1-D1
Bishopgate Street	C2-D2-D3
Bishophill Junior	C3
Bishophill Senior	C3
Bishop Thorpe Road	C1-C2
Blake Street	C5
Blossom Street	B2-B3
Blue Bridge Lane	E2
Bootham	B6-C6
Bootham Crescent	B7-C7-C8
Bootham Row	C6
Bootham Terrace	B6
Bridge Street	C4-D4
Brook Street	D7
Brownlow Street	D7-E7-E8
Buckingham Street	C3
Burton Stone Lane	B7-B8
Cambridge Street	A2-A3
Carmelite Street	D4-E4
Castlegate	D3-D4
Cemetery Road	E1-E2
Charlton Street	C1-D1
Cherry Street	D2
Church Street	D5
Cinder Lane	A4
Claremont Terrace	C6-C7
Clarence Street	C6-C7-D7
Clementhorpe	C2-D2
Clifford Street	D3-D4
Clifton	A8-A7-B7
Clifton Dale	A7-A8
Colliergate	D4-D5
Compton Street	A7-A8
Coppergate	D4
Cromwell Road	C3-D3
Cygnet Street	C2
Dale Street	B2-B3
Dalton Terrace	A2
Darnborough Street	C2-D2
Davygate	C5-C4-D4-D5
Deangate	D5
Dennison Street	E7
Dewsbury Terrace	B3-C3
Diamond Street	E8
Dodsworth Avenue	E8-F8-F7
Driffield Terrace	A2
Dudley Street	D7-E7
Duncombe Place	C5
Dundas Street	E4-E5
East Parade	F6-F7
East Mount Road	B2
Ebor Street	C2-D2
Edgware Road	F1
Eldon Terrace	D8-E8
Elvington Terrace	F3
Emerald Street	E7-E8
Escrick Street	E2
Faber Street	F6
Fairfax Street	C3
Farndale Street	E1
Farrar Street	F2-F3
Fawcett Street	E2-E3
Fenwick Street	C1-D1
Fetter Lane	C3-C4
Fifth Avenue	F5-F6
Filey Terrace	C8
Fishergate	E2-E3
Foss Bank	E5-E6
Fossgate	D4
Foss Islands Road	E4-E5-F5-F4
Frederick Street	B5
Fulford Road	E1-E2
Garden Street	D7
George Hudson Street	C4
George Street	E3-E4
Gillygate	C6
Glen Avenue	F6
Goodramgate	D5-D6
Gordon Street	F2
Grange Croft	E1
Grange Garth	E1
Grange Street	E1
Greencliffe Way	A7-A8
Grosvenor Road	B8-C8
Grosvenor Terrace	B6-B7-C7-C8
Grove Terrace Lane	E7-E8
Grove View	A7
Hallfield Road	F5-F6
Hampden Street	C3
Harcourt Street	F6
Harlott Street	E1
Hawthorn Grove	F6
Hawthorne Street	F6
Haxby Road	D7-D8
Heslington Road	E2-F2
Heworth Green	E6-E7-F7
High Ousegate	D4
High Petergate	C5-C6
Holgate Road	A2-A3-B3
Hope Street	E3
Horsman Avenue	E2-F2
Hospital Lane	C8
Howard Street	E1
Hudson Street	C8
Hungate	E4
Huntington Road	E6-E7-E8
Hyrst Grove	F7
Irwin Avenue	F7-F8
Jackson Street	D7-E7
James Street	E1
James Street	F3-F4
Jewbury	E5
Kensal Rise	E1
Kent Street	E2
Kilburn Road	E1-F1
Kings Straithe	C4-D4-D3
King Street	C4-D4
Knavesmire Road	A1
Kyme Street	C3
Lawrence Street	F3
Layerthorpe	E5-E6-F6
Lead Mill Lane	E3
Leake Street	F3
Leeman Road	A5-A4-B5-B4
Lendal Coney Street	C5-C4-D4
Levisham Street	E1
Little Hallfield Road	F5
Long Close Lane	E3-F3
Longfield Terrace	B5-B6
Lord Mayors Walk	C6-D6
Lumley Road	B8
Love Lane	A1-A2
Lower Eldon Street	D7
Lower Petergate	D5
Lower Priory Street	C3
Lowther Street	D7-E7
Lowther Terrace	A3
Maida Grove	E1
Mansfield Street	E5
March Street	D7
Margaret Street	E3
Market Street	D4
Markham Crescent	D7-D8
Markham Street	D7-D8
Marlborough Grove	E2
Marygate	B5-B6-C6
Melbourne Street	E2
Micklegate	B3-B4-C4
Millfield Road	C1-C2
Mill Lane	F7
Mill Mount Lane	A2-B2
Minster Yard	C5-D5
Monkgate	D6-E6
Moss Street	B2-B3
Mount Vale	A1
Museum Street	C5
Navigation Road	E4-E3-F3
Nelson Street	D8-E8
Neville Street	D8
Neville Terrace	D8-E8
Newborough Street	C8
New Street	C4-C5
Newton Terrace	C2-C3
New Walk Terrace	E1
Norfolk Street	C1-D1
North Parade	B6
North Street	C4
Nunmill Street	C1-C2
Nunnery Lane	B3-C3-C2
Nunthorpe Avenue	B1-B2
Nunthorpe Grove	C1
Nunthorpe Road	B2-C2
Palmer Lane	E4
Paragon Street	E3-F3
Park Crescent	E7
Park Grove	E7-E8
Park Street	B2
Parliament Street	D4-D5
Peasholme Green	E5
Pembroke Street	B8
Penley's Grove Street	D7-E7-E6
Percy's Lane	E4
Peters Way	A7-B7-B8
Piccadilly	D4-D3-E3-E4
Portland Street	C6
Pottery Lane	F8
Prices Lane	C2
Priory Street	B3-C3
Queen Annes Road	B6
Queen Street	B3
Railway Terrace	A3
Redness Street	F5-F6
Regent Street	F2-F3
Richardson Street	C1-D1
Rosslyn Street	A7
Rougier Street	C4
Russel Street	C1-C2
St Andrewgate	D5
St Aubyns Place	A1
St Benedict Road	C2
St Denys Road	E3-E4
St Johns Street	D6-D7
St Leonards Place	D5-D6
St Lukes Grove	B8
St Marys	B6
St Maurices	D6-D5-E5
St Olaves Road	B7-B8
St Pauls Terrace	A3
St Peters Grove	B7
St Saviourgate	D4-D5-E5
Sandringham Street	E1
Saxon Place	E8-F8
Scarborough Terrace	C8
Scarcroft Hill	B1-B2
Scarcroft Road	A2-B2-C2-C1
Scott Street	C1-C2
Shambles	D4-D5
Shaws Terrace	B2-B3
Shipton Road	A8
Shipton Street	B8-C8
Skeldergate	C4-C3-D3
Skeldergate Bridge	D3
South Esplanade	D3
Southlands Road	C1
South Parade	B2-B3
Stanley Street	D8
Station Avenue	B4
Station Rise	B4
Station Road	B3-B4-C4-C5
Stonegate	C5-D5
Swann Street	C9
Swinegate	D5
Sycamore Place	B6
Sycamore Terrace	A5-B5-B6
Tanner Row	B4-C4
Telford Terrace	B1
The Avenue	A7
The Crescent	B3
The Mount	A1-A2-B2
The Stonebow	D4-E4-E5
Thorpe Street	C1-C2
Toft Green	B3-B4
Tower Street	D4-D3-E3
Townend Street	D7
Trent Holme Drive	A1
Trinity Lane	C3-C4
Union Terrace	C7
Upper Price Street	B2-C2
Victor Street	C3
Vine Street	C2-D2
Walmgate	D4-E4-E3-F3
Walpole Street	D8-E8
Water Lane	A8
Watson Street	A2-A3
Wellington Row	C4
Wellington Street	F2-F3
Wentworth Road	B1
Westminster Road	A7
William Street	D1
Willis Street	F2-F3
Winterscale Street	E2
Wolsley Street	F2

68 St Michael, Spurriergate — D4
69 St Olave's Church — B5
70 St Oswald's Hall — E1
71 St Peter's School — B7
72 St Sampson's — D5
73 St Saviourgate Unitarian Chapel — D5
74 St Saviour's Church — D5
75 St William's College — D6
76 Theatre Royal — C5
77 Treasurer's House — D6
78 Twelfth Century House — C5
79 University of York — F2
80 Victoria Bar — C3
81 Walmgate Bar — F3
82 York Story, St Mary, Castlegate — D4
83 York Tyburn — A1
84 Yorkshire Museum — C5
85 Yorkshire Museum of Farming — F3

Key to Town Plan

AA Recommended roads
Other roads
Restricted roads
Buildings of interest
Churches
Car Parks
Parks and open spaces
AA Service Centre
Station

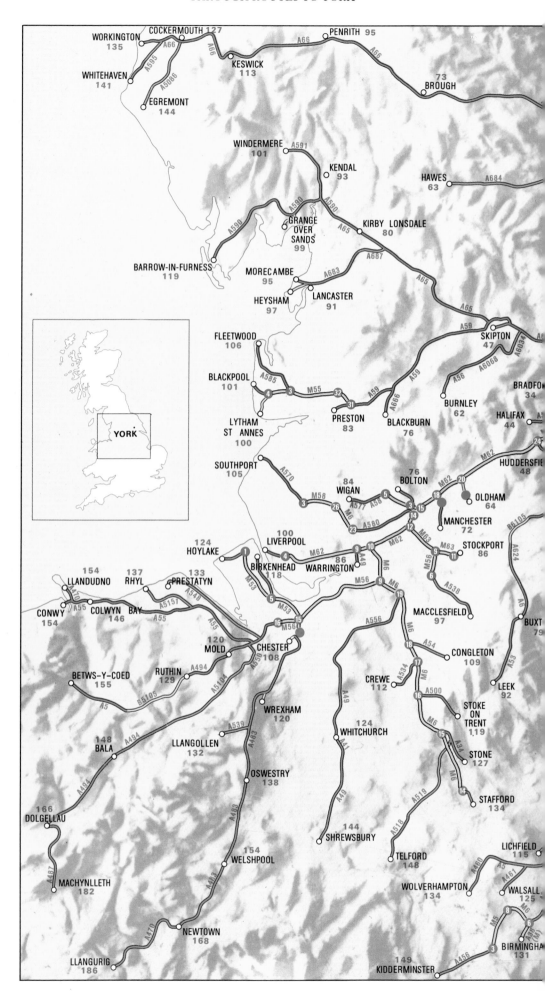

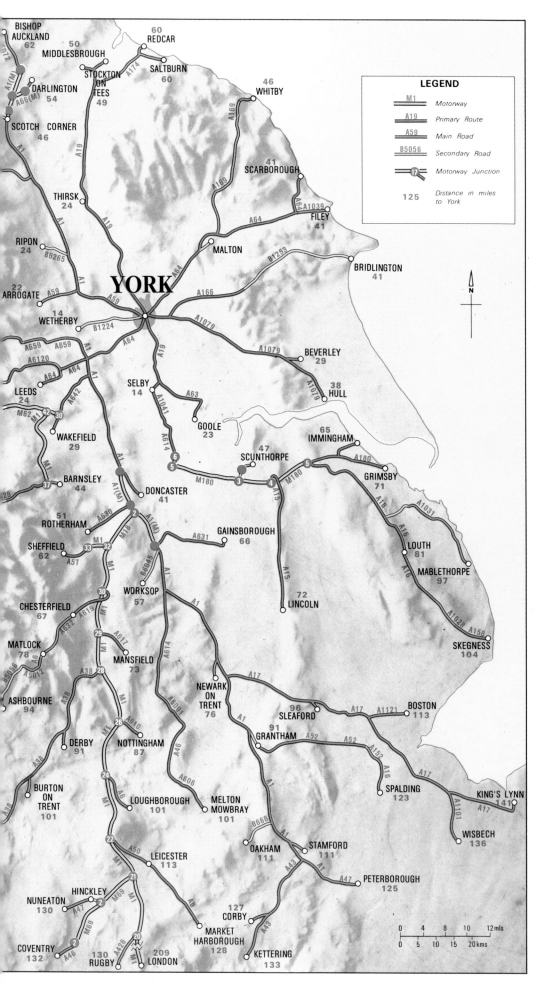

LEGEND

M1	Motorway
A19	Primary Route
A59	Main Road
B5056	Secondary Road
17	Motorway Junction
125	Distance in miles to York

BISHOP AUCKLAND 62
MIDDLESBROUGH 50
REDCAR 60
STOCKTON ON TEES 49
SALTBURN 60
WHITBY 46
DARLINGTON 54
SCOTCH CORNER 46
SCARBOROUGH 41
THIRSK 24
FILEY 41
RIPON 24
MALTON
BRIDLINGTON 41
ARROGATE 22
YORK
WETHERBY 14
BEVERLEY 29
LEEDS 24
SELBY 14
HULL 38
GOOLE 23
IMMINGHAM 65
WAKEFIELD 29
SCUNTHORPE 47
GRIMSBY 71
BARNSLEY 44
DONCASTER 41
ROTHERHAM
GAINSBOROUGH 66
LOUTH 81
SHEFFIELD 62
MABLETHORPE 97
WORKSOP 57
LINCOLN 72
CHESTERFIELD 67
MATLOCK 78
MANSFIELD 73
SKEGNESS 104
ASHBOURNE 94
NEWARK ON TRENT 76
SLEAFORD 96
BOSTON 113
DERBY 91
NOTTINGHAM 87
GRANTHAM 91
BURTON ON TRENT 101
LOUGHBOROUGH 101
MELTON MOWBRAY 101
SPALDING 123
KING'S LYNN 141
WISBECH 136
LEICESTER 113
OAKHAM 111
STAMFORD 111
PETERBOROUGH 125
NUNEATON 130
HINCKLEY
CORBY 127
MARKET HARBOROUGH 128
COVENTRY 132
RUGBY 130
LONDON 209
KETTERING 133

9

From Settlement
-to-
City

CITY SEAL
York's 14th-century second seal, showing on the obverse St Peter – the Minster's patron saint – with his keys

K ing George VI commented that 'The history of York is the history of England', and the City's ancient alleys, well-appointed museums, romantic ruins and splendid buildings provide plenty of picturesque evidence to support his perceptive observation.

A stone, brick and timber pattern of winding streets, courtyards, churches and guildhalls, York has at its heart one of the greatest Gothic cathedrals in the country. Behind its battlemented parapet, the limestone ribbon of the Medieval wall offers a natural history trail across the city.

Four great gates — or Bars — each with its own brooding personality, pierce the defences, which change mood with every stretch, sometimes breezily exposed but often overhung by mature trees which lean from secluded gardens to screen the inner face. The turrets, towers and posterns, glinting with heraldry and carved figures, make up a scene which could have been the inspiration for an illuminated manuscript.

Though the Vale of York was heavily wooded and boggy in prehistoric times, it is possible that an Iron Age settlement already existed when the Roman 9th Legion marched north from Lincoln in AD 71 to invade the territory of the Brigantes, a confederation of Celtic tribes who occupied the region. This

significant date was chosen in 1971 to celebrate the city's 1,900th anniversary, looking back to the days when the site, at the meeting place of a major and minor river, was known as *Eboracum* or *Eburacum*.

The Roman fortress, a rectangular 50 acres with rounded corners, was to remain a principal bulwark of the Empire until the withdrawal of the Legions from Britain. In time, the power of this provincial centre was so great that it created a white-walled, towered and gated settlement on the east bank of the River Ouse. Possibly no other fortification in the Empire could better it.

The presence of a large bath-house in the forepart of the fortress at York is unusual and today its remains, preserved in the basement of a public house in St Sampson's Square, form one of the visible links with the Roman past. Away from the civic grandeur and the religious life of the fortress, the Roman presence may be equated with small personal possessions . . . the ivory handles of a folding

fan, a glass mirror, a soap-stone stamp for marking cakes of eye ointment, parasol ribs with traces of silver sheathing, a little bronze mouse.

Today, parts of the 4th-century fortifications are still above ground. The Multangular Tower, though capped by a Medieval superstructure, stands 19 feet above the grass of the Museum Gardens, displaying the distinctive red tile facings between the small limestone blocks. Running from it is a 25-yard stretch of the 4th-century wall. The tower's south angle counterpart was found in Feasegate in the heart of the city's shopping centre in 1832.

A historic 10-acre site in the City centre, just off the main route to the west front of the Minster, the Museum Gardens also hold the ruins of St Mary's Abbey and the popular Yorkshire Museum where, in the Roman collection, may be seen the mosaic floor taken from a house in the best part of the civil town — the colonia. In the corners are the symbolic bird of spring, the hay-rake of summer, the grapes of autumn and the bare bough of winter.

Two of the modern City's most attractive streets, Stonegate and Petergate, closely follow the lines of the *Via Praetoria* and the *Via Principalis*.

A secluded lane, Chapter House Street, to the north of the Minster and running beside the Treasurer's House, represents the *Via Decumana*.

In the cellars of the Treasurer's House, a National Trust property of various architectural styles, is a Roman column base of yellow gritstone. A second base was uncovered 15 feet away showing that the

pillars had stood parallel to the Roman street.

The site of the *Principia*, or headquarters building, is now occupied by the Minster. During the £2,000,000 restoration scheme of 1967–72 a substantial part of the headquarters wall was found. A Roman column, discovered under the south transept, has been re-erected on a site opposite the south door. Paintings from a 4th-century room added to the building were found under the east end of the nave and the pastel colours which have survived 16 centuries are to be seen in the Minster's Undercroft Museum created during the restoration.

Large-scale excavations by the York Archaeological Trust have lifted the veil from life in post-Roman York, revealing the Anglo-Saxon *Eoforwic* on the site of a demolished Fishergate glassworks, and the Viking *Jorvik* on a spectacularly developed piece of riverside land in Coppergate. On the cleared industrial site was found not only a Medieval Gilbertine priory but part of the lost Anglian city. Pottery from continental Europe indicated that it was the trading area of the town.

CENTURIES OF BUILDING
Excellent reconstruction of a Roman kitchen, one of many fine displays at the Yorkshire Museum, in Museum Street

South-east prospect of the ancient City of York, executed around 1718 and packed with historical detail ranging from architectural features to agricultural practices

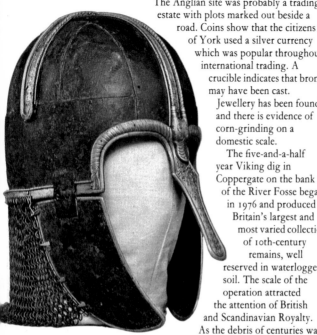

**SAXONS TO
THE VIKINGS**
*One of the finest Saxon
finds ever made, this superb
helmet dates from around
750 AD and came from the
rich dig at Coppergate*

*Reconstruction at the
Jorvik Centre of a Viking
jeweller's market stall,
with potential customers*

The Anglian site was probably a trading estate with plots marked out beside a road. Coins show that the citizens of York used a silver currency which was popular throughout international trading. A crucible indicates that bronze may have been cast.

Jewellery has been found and there is evidence of corn-grinding on a domestic scale.

The five-and-a-half year Viking dig in Coppergate on the bank of the River Fosse began in 1976 and produced Britain's largest and most varied collection of 10th-century remains, well reserved in waterlogged soil. The scale of the operation attracted the attention of British and Scandinavian Royalty. As the debris of centuries was removed to reveal a Viking layer up to six feet deep, archaeologists found houses and workshops still containing shoes, tools, jewellery and cooking utensils. Some 15,000 small and delicate treasures were found.

It was decided to reconstruct the Viking street and houses on the very site where they were found and to display the original timbers and artefacts in an authentic reconstruction of the excavation.

All lies underground in the heart of the new Coppergate shopping complex. The journey back through time is made in small cars fitted with internal speakers for transmitting a commentary and electronically guided along a track laid in the floor. Visitors find themselves in a full-scale reconstruction of 10th-century Coppergate. They see the workshops and houses and experience the sights, sounds and even the smells of *Jorvik*. Two soundtracks were recorded by local people who were specially coached in Old Norse and these were interspersed with the commentary.

Medieval York inherited many of the City's curious street names from the 9th and 10th centuries. The fact that many of the names are compounded with the word 'gate' links them with the old Scandinavian word for street — *gata*. York's most photographed street nameplate is attached to the City's shortest street. Whip-ma-Whop-ma-Gate is little more than a corner site between Colliergate and Pavement and could have been the spot chosen for the local custom of dog-whipping on St Luke's Day, but the name is more likely to refer to the whipping post and pillory which stood near by.

The parish churches which rose over the tangled lanes of the Medieval City have been whittled down by decay and demolition to about half the original number. One of the City centre's best loved churches is approached through a brick arch of 1766 hung with iron gates made in the year of Waterloo. Holy Trinity, Goodramgate, stands in a grassy plot, a 15th-century church with an unspoiled 18th-century interior which suffered no major restoration in the last century, and still retains its high-sided, draught-proof pews.

A 250-year building programme which ended in 1472 gave the city the Minster as it is seen today, and this time-span also saw the development of the walls and Bars, posterns, hospitals, Guildhall, merchant's halls, priories, friaries and St Mary's Abbey, now scene of the periodic production of the Medieval cycle of Mystery Plays.

The five-year rescue operation on the Minster which ended in a thanksgiving service in 1972 was followed by work on a

**BUILDINGS OF
THEIR TIME**
*Left: austere, classical lines
of the old Debtor's Prison,
now a part of the
comprehensive Castle
Museum*

heroic scale to rebuild the south transept roof, destroyed by fire in July 1984.

Medieval York was one of the major English centres of glass painting and today the York Glaziers' Trust is a storehouse of scholarly and practical expertise in the restoration and replacement of historic glass. The Minster's north transept holds one of the most famous stained glass windows in the world, known as the 'Five Sisters', five slim lancets dating from about 1260. This window inspired a tale told by Charles Dickens in *Nicholas Nickleby* (see feature on Minster (page 17)) and fired in the young Sir Basil Spence, architect of Coventry Cathedral, a desire to build in this mould. The 'Five Sisters' are remote, beautiful and a little mysterious, their colouring dominated by the greyish-green grisaille glass. At the other end of the scale, in the small Zouche Chapel, curious creatures enliven the tiny glass panes, none more appealing than the bird which, for more than 500 years, has cocked its head quizzically at a spider in its web.

The City Wall runs for about two-and-a-half miles on a green mound embroidered in spring with daffodils. The great gates of the City punctuate the almost complete circle. Micklegate Bar, once bristling with severed heads; Monk Bar, the tallest of all, carrying figures in the act of hurling stones into the street; Bootham Bar, on the site of the Roman north-west gate; Walmgate Bar, still bearing the cannonball and bullet scars of the Civil War. The 13th-century Clifford's Tower stands on the Conqueror's original mound and was damaged in the Civil War siege of 1644.

Within the walls, the Shambles, the former street of the butchers and the only street in the City to be mentioned in *Domesday*, offers nodding half-timbered gables to tourists' cameras. Though it may be a tourist attraction, the street is also a centre of Roman Catholic pilgrimage, as a house has been set aside as an oratory in memory of the city's own saint, St Margaret Clitherow, wife of a 16th-century Shambles butcher. She was tried at the Common Hall (now Guildhall) for harbouring priests. Refusing to plead,

she was condemned to be pressed to death, and the sentence was carried out at 8 am on 25 March, 1586, at the Tollbooth on Ouse Bridge.

Among the city's other historic personalities, the names of Fawkes and Turpin are outstanding. The register of the Church of St Michael le Belfrey on the south side of the Minster, contains the record of the baptism on 16 April, 1570 of Guy Fawkes whose family lived close by. The condemned cell occupied by Dick Turpin before his execution at the York Tyburn on 7 April, 1739, may be seen virtually unchanged in the Debtors' Prison section of the Castle Museum. His grave is in the garden on the site of St George's Church, just inside the walls, near Fishergate Postern.

Across the City, carved doorways, interlocking courtyards and gabled roofs combine to create one of the City's most romantic buildings, the King's Manor, once the home of the Abbot of St Mary's and later the headquarters of the Council in the North.

The city's finest half-timbered buildings are the Merchant Adventurers' Hall, dating from the mid 14th century, and St William's College built in the 1460s.

The great hall of the Merchant Adventurers has so much exposed timber that it has a ship-like quality, its gently undulating floor having the look of a main gundeck in a ship of Nelson's navy. It is easy to see how in one year alone, 1358, 100 standing trees were bought for its construction.

St William's College was built for the Minster's chantry priests who were 'cathedral freelances' living like laymen in city lodgings before the college was built. They were not, it seems, always well behaved: it is recorded that in 1490, during an argument at one of the gates to the Minster Close, a priest hit a citizen on the head with the blunt side of an axe.

The city's fortifications played an important part in the Civil War of the 17th century, particularly during the siege by the Parliamentary army in 1644 after the Royalist defeat at Marston Moor, now a tract of

*City gates, from the top:
Monk Bar, Bootham Bar
and Micklegate Bar, on the
latter of which the heads of
traitors were once exposed*

farmland just a few miles west of York.

In September 1642 York was put in a
'posture of defence' and cannon were
mounted on the Bars. Deserted remains of
earthworks thrown up during this period
of feverish activity were still to be seen in the
following century and were recorded by
Daniel Defoe during his tour of England in
1724–6.

The 18th century was an age of rebuilding,
giving the city its Assembly Rooms, Mansion
House, Assize Courts and many elegant town
houses. Built in the 1730s, debased during
the last war and splendidly restored by 1951,
Lord Burlington's Palladian Assembly
Rooms were described in Tobias Smollett's
novel *The Expedition of Humphrey Clinker*.
The architect John Carr, though born near
Wakefield, was twice Lord Mayor of York
in 1770 and 1785. He designed two attractive
buildings on the east and west sides of the Eye
of Yorkshire, the circular green plot in the
centre of the castle yard. The Assize Courts
of 1773–7 (now the Crown Court) face the
former Female Prison of 1780, now the
principal building of York Castle Museum.
Between them, facing north, is the former
Debtor's Prison of 1705, also occupied by
the museum. The Mansion House is the
major feature of St Helen's Square. The
foundation stone was laid in 1725 and the
names of the master craftsmen are to be found
in the accounts of the City Chamberlain.

Sometimes, interior splendour of this
quality was more than matched by well-
placed citizens who wanted the best in
Georgian design. Proof is to be found in
Fairfax House, Castlegate, originally the
home of the 9th Viscount Fairfax, and the
scene of one of the most remarkable
restoration stories of recent times.

York Civic Trust's inspired rescue
operation on the near-derelict house,
awakening this nationally important building
from its long sleep, took place between 1982
and October 1984 when the Duchess of Kent
declared it open. Now carpeted, wallpapered,

painted, lavishly furnished and warmly lit,
the house opens a door on the graceful side
of life in the Georgian City.

The century also saw the origin of the
City's delightful Theatre Royal. A travelling
company of actors gave performances at the
Bootham Cockpit House and were so well
received that in 1730 they opened a theatre
in Minster Yard. In 1744 the cloisters of the
Medieval St Leonard's Hospital were leased
and the City's first permanent theatre was
built on this site.

Two of the City's leading manufacturers
have roots in the 18th century. Mary Tuke
opened a grocer's shop in 1725. William
Tuke, a Quaker philanthropist, inherited
it in 1752 and his son Henry joined him in
1785. From then on the Tukes made cocoa
and chocolate at the rear of their shop in
Castlegate. In 1862 the business was
transferred to Henry Rowntree who, with
his brother Joseph, took over an old foundry
in Tanner's Moat. The nucleus of today's
vast Rowntree Mackintosh complex took
shape at the turn of the last century on land
between the Haxby and Wigginton roads.

In 1767 a confectionery business was
established in St Helen's Square, later to
become J Terry & Sons Ltd, though the firm
has now ceased trading on this site and is
concentrated on the Bishopthorpe Road
factory. In time, the founders were to send
their cakes, biscuits, pickles, anchovies, acid
drops, mint cakes, coltsfoot rock, horehound

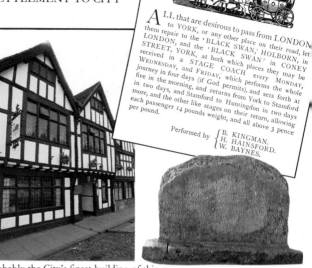

lozenges, candied citron and Pontefract cakes to all parts of the country. Many of these old-style confections made from original recipes have been preserved as part of the reconstructed street, house and shop displays in the Castle Museum.

Coaching was big business in York until the railway caused inn yards to sprout weeds. The Black Swan in Coney Street which rang to the arrivals and departures of the Leeds Highflyer and the Harrogate Tally-Ho, was just one of the many focal points of the trade. Others included the George Inn, Coney Street, once rich with elaborate plasterwork, and the York Tavern in St Helen's Square. All have now been demolished.

Four days was the time allowed by coach between London and York in 1706. Some 70 years later it had been cut to 36 hours and by 1836 it had dropped to 20 hours. When York's first railway station opened in 1841 coaches were still running and in those days flintlock pistols were fired to warn platelayers of approaching trains.

Much of the raw material of the social history of this period is to be found in the pages of local newspapers. The first copy of the *York Mercury* was printed in Coffee Yard and went on sale on 23 February, 1718–19 (allowing for the old-style calendar). Its mantle has passed, through many changes of site and title, to the present *Yorkshire Evening Press*, first published in 1882.

One of the most protracted north–south battles to be fought in recent years was over the siting of the National Railway Museum. But common sense prevailed and this great museum was placed in the north where railways began in 1825. Nineteenth-century York was otherwise bypassed by the Industrial Revolution, leaving Bradford, Leeds and other smaller West Yorkshire towns to bear its full brunt.

When the pioneer photographer William Henry Fox Talbot set up his camera in the streets on 29 July, 1845, he found the City largely unchanged by the passage of time. Apart from Clifford Street, York's wholly Victorian thoroughfare, examples of Victorian architecture tend to be isolated and do not cluster into what is popularly supposed to be the Victorian urban scene of pubs, chapels, canals and viaducts.

Probably the City's finest building of this period is G T Andrews's Yorkshire Insurance Company office of 1847 which gazes down Coney Street from its St Helen's Square site like a small Italian Renaissance palace.

Since the Baedeker Raid of 1942 which destroyed homes and historic buildings, the City has been transformed, to become vital and confident. One of the strongest stimulants was the establishment of the University in the early 1960s, something the City had desired since 1641.

The creation of the University was officially approved in April 1960 and in time colleges, a central hall and a landscaped lake were established at Heslington on the city boundary. At the heart of the scheme was the restored Elizabethan mansion Heslington Hall, complete with the wildlife of its park.

Viscount Esher's 1968 report on the conservation of York's historic core has led to a number of developments including housing schemes within the City Wall. People are returning, as Lord Esher hoped, to the City's heart, reversing the trend of the last 150 years.

Drawing all the threads of the City's life together is a remarkable development in the castle yard. Well in the forefront of such ideas, York Castle Museum opened on St George's Day 1938 to provide an enchanting interpretation of the concept 'museum' and a lasting monument to the principles laid down by Dr John Kirk, a country physician who collected 'bygones'.

BEFORE THE RAILWAY
Evocative relics of a stage-coaching past – the Black Swan Inn that still stands, a mention of one that has gone and the gravestone of notorious highwayman Dick Turpin

TOOTHSOME TERRY'S
Facsimile of Joseph Terry's original confectionery shop which stood in St Helen's, part of a period-display street in Castle Museum

York Minster

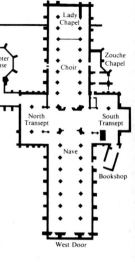

Standing on the foundations of an ancient Roman fort and the remains of Saxon and Norman cathedrals, the Medieval Minster towers over York City with the full weight and authority of its many centuries.

The largest Gothic cathedral in Europe north of the Alps, it is visited by nearly two-and-a-half million people every year. Primarily a church for Christian worship — there are services every day and anyone is welcome to attend — it is the Mother Church of the Northern Province of the Church of England, its official title being 'The Cathedral and Metropolitical Church of St Peter in York'. It is a cathedral because it has the *cathedra* (throne) of the Archbishop of York, a Minster because it was founded in Anglo-Saxon times when a 'mynster' was a mission centre for evangelism.

It is also, however, a magnificent heritage from the past, with a wealth of treasures — Medieval architecture, stone- and wood-carvings and 128 windows whose priceless stained glass spans 800 years of glass-painting.

SOUTH TRANSEPT

The South Transept dates from the 13th century when Early English architecture was the fashion. Mostly, the windows are simple lancets (long, narrow and pointed), the exception being the elaborate carving in the gable which provides a frame for the famous Rose Window whose outer petals are red and white roses, the work of 16th-century Flemish glass-painters. The glass in the centre, however, dates from the 18th century and is in the form of a sunflower from which golden rays radiate beyond a circle of blue. Little yellow suns were added with the letter 'S' when the window was restored in 1970 as a memorial to the late Earl of Scarborough, first High Steward of the Minster and the Provincial Grand Master of the Order of Freemasonry. The Freemasons of England gave a generous donation towards its restoration.

The oldest monument in this transept is the tomb of Archbishop Walter de Grey who was largely responsible for the building of the present south transept. This was begun about the year 1220 as part of a rebuilding plan started under Archbishop Roger with his new choir, 40 years earlier.

De Grey realised that, although he would not live to see it completed (it took 250 years), he had set the scene for a grand cathedral and the builders who came after him would have to continue in the grand style if they were to maintain balanced proportions. A marble effigy of the Archbishop lies beneath the tomb's elaborate canopy, his staff plunged into the mouth of a dragon at his feet, symbolising the conquest of evil.

In 1968, when the canopy was found to be unsafe, the tomb was completely restored, most of the cost being met by the Earl of Stamford, a co-lateral descendant of Walter de Grey, and his personal friend Haile Selassie, late Emperor of Ethiopia. The Queen Mother also sent a donation. When the marble effigy was removed, a painting of the Archbishop was found underneath on the coffin lid and inside, apparently buried with him in 1255, were his silver-gilt chalice and paten, his crozier (pastoral staff) and episcopal ring with a sapphire. These were restored and are now in the Undercroft.

Also in the south transept are two interesting Victorian monuments. Archbishop Thomson has his pet dog, Scamp, at his feet and in front, on the plinth, symbols of the Crucifixion, while Dean Duncombe has three little alabaster choir boys kneeling before him, a reminder of his work for the Minster Song School. Dean Duncombe is also to be thanked for introducing services into the great nave, which formerly was only a place to walk.

Today, services are held there regularly, often with capacity congregations. The City has a close relationship with its cathedral and the Lord Mayor and Corporation are often present at special services. Members of the Royal Family, too, following a tradition of centuries, are frequent visitors. The Duke and Duchess of Kent were married there in 1961, and in 1967 the Duke took part in a service of thanksgiving for the restoration of the Great West Window; the Queen and Prince Philip came in 1971 when York celebrated its 1,900th birthday, and the following year the Queen kept her Maundy in the Minster; the Queen Mother was present when the Friends of the Minster celebrated their Golden Jubilee in 1978 (she is their Patron). In 1984 the Duchess of Kent and the Duke of Gloucester were among the people who came after the fire to see the damage for themselves and offer sympathy and help.

NORTH TRANSEPT

The North Transept is also in the Early English style, the most striking feature being the giant lancets, each 53 feet long and over five feet wide, which frame the Five Sisters Window. This architecture was a source of inspiration to Sir Basil Spence, architect of Coventry Cathedral. On seeing the great lancets for the first time in 1927 when he was still a student, he realised that the sheer beauty of carved stone could have great spiritual significance, and from that time his dearest ambition was to build a cathedral.

The Five Sisters Window is the largest expanse of ancient grisaille glass in existence; its date is 1260. In *Nicholas Nickleby* Dickens told the story of five sisters who worked

---

ORDER OF WORSHIP
Sunday
   Holy Communion
   Holy Communion
   Sung Eucharist
   Choral Matins
   Choral Evensong

Weekdays
   Matins
   Holy Communion
   Choral Evensong

MINSTER FROM THE AIR
Opposite: this 'bird's-eye' view shows how the Minster's Gothic completeness dwarfs and dominates its surroundings

MINSTER CRAFT
The superb Chapter House ceiling with (inset) the famous Rose window, seen being restored by Peter Gibson of the York Glaziers Trust

lengths of tapestry and then had them copied in stained glass; alas, only fiction. But there is a true story which is tantamount to a modern miracle. The 100,000 pieces of glass the window contains were taken out and buried for safety during World War I. At

their replacement in 1925 they were releaded with contemporary lead which had been unearthed by archaeologists at Rievaulx Abbey in North Yorkshire. The cost of releading was met by an Appeal launched by two York women to make the restoration a memorial to the women of the British Empire who had lost their lives during the war.

In the base of the central lancet is one of the Minster's panels of 12th-century glass; it shows Daniel in the lions' den being fed by the Prophet Habbakuk. (Another easily seen panel of glass from the Norman cathedral is above the entrance to the bookshop in the south nave aisle; it is a scene from a miracle performed by St Nicholas.)

The massive Astronomical Clock on the east side of the transept is a memorial to 18,000 Airmen who died in World War II and had been stationed in the north-east. A page of the book in which their names are written is turned regularly, a touching ceremony performed by the RAF. On the clock's reverse side are the chief stars of the northern hemisphere, their positions altering according to the time of year. The theme of the memorial, Flight and Time, is extended to the supporters of the lights around it in the form of wyverns, mythological birds which are supposed to fly straight to the sun.

St Nicholas Chapel has the tomb of 14th-century Archbishop Greenfield with one of the Minster's three Medieval brasses. The others are Elizabeth Eynns (south choir aisle) and James Cotrel (south nave aisle). The kneelers here illustrate the carol *The Twelve Days of Christmas*, and are the work of the Minster Broderers.

THE CRAFTSMEN

Decayed and crumbling stone has to be renewed constantly, including the gargoyles — those figures, often in grotesque shapes, that jut out from a building and were formerly waterspouts.

Woodcarvers and joiners make and look after the furniture. They also shape and carve the ribs and bosses of a vaulted roof. After the 1984 fire almost all the ribs and bosses in the south transept had to be renewed. The theme adopted for the new bosses was *The Benedicite*, 'O All Ye Works of the Lord, Bless Ye the Lord', and the woodcarvers were given a free hand to produce what they fancied. So we have such designs as God the Father holding the world, fowls of the air, whales that move in the water, beasts and cattle, etc. Some of the oak for the roof came from the Royal forests.

In addition, some of the smaller bosses were designed by children. The BBC children's television programme *Blue Peter* held a competition to draw designs that

Flowers of the World embroidered on a kneeler by the Minster Broderers

would remind people of the achievements of the 20th century and there were over 3,000 entries. The three prizewinning designs were: An Astronaut on the Moon, Famine Relief in Africa — a child drinking precious water, and A Diver between Two Whales. Some 60 of the children's runner-up designs are on show.

The Glaziers Trust, with seven glaziers and two apprentices, is responsible for the maintenance of the 128 windows of stained glass. In the 1984 fire the great Rose Window (22 feet across) was badly damaged, but owing to the glaziers' skill and ingenuity not a piece of glass was lost despite the fact that the heat had caused 40,000 cracks in it.

The Broderers (47 women and two men) employ their craft to beautify the building and their exquisite needlework and embroidery may be seen in many parts of the Minster.

CHAPTER HOUSE

The Chapter House, reached from the north-east corner of the transept, was completed about 1286, the vestibule being added later. A large octagonal building, 63 feet across and about the same height up to the dome, it is an architectural wonder in that it has no

central pillar to take the downward thrust of the great domed roof with its forest of timber inside and its outer covering of lead. (There is a model of the dome.) Canopied stalls round the walls are carved with a variety of heads, animals, birds and foliage. These, together with others in the vestibule, are some of the finest Medieval stone-carvings in the world.

NAVE

The Nave, begun in 1291, is in Decorated Gothic, while the Great West Window, completed in 1338, has tracery in the curvilinear style — elaborate stone-carving whose heart-shaped centre is known as the Heart of Yorkshire. Most of the glass in the windows dates from the 14th century.

The twin west towers, built between 1438 and 1472, terminate in pinnacles 30 feet high. The south-west tower houses 14 bells, only 12 of which are rung at any one time. They date, with two exceptions added recently, from the 19th century, though they were recast in 1926. There were bells before that time, but during a fire in 1840 they crashed to the ground. Sufficient money, by way of a public appeal, had been collected for a new peal when Dr Stephen Beckwith died and left £2,000 for new bells, so the money already collected was used to provide an 11-ton bell named Great Peter which was hung in the north-west tower. However, it was so heavy that it could not be swung, but only struck with a hammer, and, due to a fault in the casting, it could not be rung with the peal. So in 1927, when the Beckwith peal had returned after being recast, Great Peter was also recast. When it came back the other bells pealed a welcome as it stood outside the West Front and the Minster Choir, assembled on the steps, sang an anthem to *The Chieftain of the Bells* composed by the then Precentor. His name was Canon Bell!

Great Peter now weighs nearly 20 tons, but being on ball-bearings, it can be swung by one man. It is heard at noon, one of the

deepest-toned bells in Europe.

All round the Great West Door outside the Minster are carvings which few people notice. They tell the story of Adam and Eve, exquisite little figures only nine inches long.

THE FIRST MINSTER

Inside, between the Great West doors, is a charming statue of St Peter holding only one key — unusual since he is normally portrayed with cross keys. In front of him, at floor level, a stone commemorates 1,300 years of worship on this site from AD 627 to AD 1927, the first church having been built for King Edwin of Northumbria.

The story of Edwin's conversion reads like a present-day thriller. He was still pagan when he fell in love with the Princess Ethelburga, daughter of the King of Kent. She was already a Christian but she was allowed to come north to marry him on one condition — that she took her chaplain, Paulinus, with her so that she could still worship as a Christian. The marriage took place in AD 625.

Some time later, the King of the West Saxons (north-west Britain) sent one of his servants to visit Edwin, on the surface as a friendly visit but with instructions to kill him if opportunity offered. Edwin, not suspecting treachery, ordered wine to be served, but as he put his head back to drink, the West Saxon pulled out his dagger and lunged forward to plunge it into the King's heart. Lilla, Edwin's chief theyne (bodyguard) had no time to cry out a warning so he rushed in front of the king and took the thrust.

Edwin, furious, decided to wage war on the West Saxons and this was Ethelburga's and Paulinus's chance; they suggested that he pray to the Christian God for help. This he agreed to do, promising that if he was victorious he would come back and be baptized. So, having gained a great victory, he called his Council together to discuss the matter, for to forsake the old gods was a daring step to take. However, after a long discussion, the decision was taken to embrace Christianity. Edwin was baptized at one of the wells in his capital city, *Eoforwic* (Anglo-Saxon York) and a little wooden church was built for him to worship in. That was the first Minster and Paulinus was its first Bishop.

Edwin did not forget the debt he owed to Lilla who had died for him and he arranged for a stone cross to be set up in his memory on the highest point of the Yorkshire moors. It is still there, above the village of Beckhole.

Today, the Minster's font is in the Crypt — the place where Edwin's baptism is traditionally commemorated. It has a modern cover featuring the King and his Queen, Paulinus, St Hilda (Edwin's great-niece and the most famous Abbess of Whitby) and James the Deacon who came north with Ethelburga so that if the King became a Christian he would be able 'to teach the boys

FIRES

The Minster has suffered three major fires.

THE FIRST FIRE

In 1829 Jonathan Martin, a madman, believed that God wanted him to destroy it. So, on 1 February after evensong, he hid behind a tomb until everyone had left the building. Then, making a pile of hymn- and prayer-books, he started a fire and, leaving it to burn, let himself out of a window by climbing up a movable scaffolding known as the Fleet, using a rope ladder to get down on the outside.

The next morning, choristers who had come to early service were sliding on the ice when one of them fell and, looking up, saw smoke pouring out of the central tower. By that time the east end was a blazing inferno, all the stalls in the choir except two being destroyed and the rest of the east end being badly damaged.

Jonathan Martin ended his life in a mental asylum.

Top: the man who thought God wanted him to burn York Minster down, and (above) a 19th-century souvenir of the fire he managed to set

THE SECOND FIRE

Eleven years after the first there was another major fire, when a careless workman left a candle burning in the south-west tower. The central vault of the nave (being wood) was destroyed, together with most of the carved bosses. Fortunately, a man named John Browne had sketched the eight main ones, and so the Dean and Chapter were able to replace them.

THE THIRD FIRE

The third fire, which took place in July 1984, was probably caused by lightning. It destroyed the central vault of the south transept (again, a timber one) and all but two of its 68 bosses. Firemen worked all night to save the rest of the cathedral, pouring tons of water on to the burning timbers to collapse them, so preventing the fire from creeping towards the central tower.

the Latin so that they could sing the services'.

Edwin's church was rebuilt in stone and later enlarged, but William the Conqueror, unable at first to subdue the northern people, laid waste a large area of land, including in this destruction St Peter's Minster in York. However, having established himself, he sent Thomas of Bayeux to rebuild it, and since that time it has been a Collegiate church, with a Dean and Chapter as its governing body.

CENTRAL TOWER

Standing in front of the Choir Screen, it is easy to look up (about 200 feet) into the central tower which was completed about the year 1480. The central boss, 4ft 6in across, shows St Peter with two keys and St Paul with his symbol, a sword.

EASTERN ARM

The Eastern Arm, the last part to be built except for the towers, is in the Perpendicular style, the third stage of Gothic architecture. It was completed in 1472. Most of the glass dates from the 15th century, including the tall windows in the false transepts.

The Great East Window, jewel of the Lady Chapel, was created between the years 1405 and 1408 by the Coventry glass-painter John Thornton; his initials are way up at the top. It is the size of a tennis court, the largest single area of Medieval glass in the world.

Beyond the tomb of Archbishop Bowet to the south is All Saints', the Chapel of the Duke of Wellington's Regiment. To the north, beyond Archbishop Scrope's tomb, is St Stephen's Chapel. The terracotta reredos (panel behind the Altar) with a scene from the Crucifixion, is so Victorian (its date is 1854) that all the figures on it have flowing moustaches — even Christ.

The kneelers are the work of the Minster Broderers and depict the flowers of all the world, grouped in countries. The stalls, however, bear a carved animal — the famous mouse trademark of the wood-carver Robert Thompson of Kilburn, near York.

THE CHOIR ENTRANCES

At the east end an arch forms the main entrance to the choir. In its vault is a beautiful carving of the Assumption — the Virgin's body being taken up into heaven by angels. The arch is flanked by effigies of the Kings of England from William I to Henry VI, all being the original 15th-century figures, except for that of Henry VI which is a 19th-century replacement. Probably William Hyndley carved the Screen, for under King John there is a hind, his sign and a play on his name. Other carvings of interest are a lion and a lamb (Edward II) and a cat and a mouse (Henry IV). Above the kings, angels play on Medieval instruments to the glory of God the Father who sits over the arch.

NORTH CHOIR AISLE

The only royal tomb is in the north choir aisle. King Edward III and Queen Philippa were married in the Minster in 1328 and when their second son, Prince William of Hatfield, died in York they allowed him to be buried there. His alabaster monument shows a boy about 10 years old with angels (much worn) at his head and a lion at his feet. Although he was not buried in this place originally, the triple canopy in which his effigy lies was probably made for him at a later date, for on the wall behind is the *planta genista* (broom plant), badge of the Plantagenets.

Detail from a Roman painted wall panel in the Minster Undercroft, repository of various other contemporary remains, and open to view

SOUTH CHOIR AISLE

Monuments in the south choir aisle include two modern, painted panels of the 'Architects and Healers of All Time'. They commemorate in particular Sir Frederick Milner, a well-known architect, and Headley Visick, a much-loved York surgeon. Almost opposite is the standing figure of Archbishop Lamplugh — with two right feet.

The High Altar is a memorial to the second Viscount Halifax who died in 1934. On the south side is the throne of the Archbishop of York (there is another on the north side of the nave).

The splendid Altar Cloth was presented to the Minster in 1970 by the Yorkshire Federation of Women's Institutes to mark their golden Jubilee.

POLICE

After the fire of 1829, which was started deliberately, the Minster Police Force came into being. Today there are 11 policemen and the building is guarded day and night both inside and out. The Minster is believed to be the only church outside the Vatican to have its own Police.

CRYPT

The Crypt, reached from the south choir aisle where the font is situated, is the earliest part of the present Minster, its style late Norman, from the time of Archbishops Thomas and Roger. Also Norman is the Doomstone, a tablet on the south wall depicting Hell as a cauldron in which are the Seven Deadly Sins, with devils beneath stoking up. There are several 'entrances', the chief in the form of a face with toads in the nostrils.

There are three Altars on the east wall — to Paulinus, Hilda and Edwin. Their crosses and candlesticks were given by the Worsley family in memory of the Dowager Lady Worsley, mother of the Duchess of Kent. The Duke and Duchess were married in the Minster in 1961. Between the Altars are a 12th-century bass-relief of the Virgin and Child (much damaged) and a Medieval statuette showing St Anne teaching the Child Virgin to read.

The tomb of St William of York is in the western crypt; he was a 12th-century Archbishop at whose shrine (destroyed at the Reformation) miracles of healing are said to have taken place.

Also in the crypt, at Roman level, is the base of a pillar, reminder that the Legions had their military headquarters where the Minster now stands. By the year AD 300 *Eboracum* (Roman York) was an important fortress and colonia (place for civilians) — one of only four in Britain — and in AD 306 Constantine was proclaimed Emperor of Western Rome there. Later, he became Emperor of all Rome, and the first Emperor to become a Christian.

UNDERCROFT

Further Roman remains are in the Undercroft. In 1967, the massive central tower (it weighs over 20,000 tons) was found to be in need of new foundations. It was then floated on a bed of concrete reinforced with steel rods, work being carried out, of course, below the Minster where Roman walls and wall-paintings, Anglo-Saxon and Norman remains were found still intact.

There was also a whole Roman pillar, 30 feet long, lying in sections just as it had collapsed some time after the Romans left Britain about the year 410. This the Dean and Chapter gave to the York Civic Trust who re-erected it outside the Minster (near the Minster Gates) as a tangible memorial to the fact that York was 1,900 years old in 1971.

In order that visitors might actually walk in history and also see the new foundations, the Undercroft was created. There is also a section known as the Treasury where church silver is displayed, together with some of the Minster's most valuable treasures.

ORGANIZATION

The Minster is a vast organization, including, as well as the Dean and Chapter and visiting Chaplains, Cross-bearers and Servers, about 500 paid lay staff and voluntary helpers. There are six vergers, 11 policemen, four Church of England Sisters (who help with visitors and the education of visiting schoolchildren), three marshals (who man the entrance), 'Minutes of History' assistants (the Minster costs £2 a minute to run and visitors like to buy a minute or more in the form of a certificate), bookshop, Undercroft and Chapter House staff, parties desk assistants, librarian (with seven staff and 50 voluntary helpers), archivist and archaeologist, office staff and clock winder (there are nine clocks) — all these under the Chapter Clerk. There are also the Bursar who looks after the finance, the Glaziers Trust who maintain the glass and the Minster Broderers whose embroidery and needlework beautify the Minster.

GLOSSARY OF TERMS

Gothic Architecture

EARLY ENGLISH (*13th century*) – lancet windows

DECORATED (*14th century*) – wider windows in lights (sections) divided by vertical bars (mullions) with carved tracery (above the lights)

PERPENDICULAR (*15th to 16th centuries*) – mainly vertical lines, even in tracery

CURVILINEAR – tracery in curved lines with elaborate pattern

GRISAILLE – a greenish grey glass with conventional foliage delicately outlined. In the Five Sisters Window some colour has been added by a series of geometric patterns.

LANCET – long narrow window with pointed arch.

VAULTED ROOF – arched roof with ribs (lengths of carved and moulded wood or stone) which strengthen the arched roof above. In a criss-cross pattern the ribs carry the weight of the roof down to the pillars. There are usually bosses (carved knobs of wood or stone) where two ribs meet and cross.

My Little
SWEETHEART MIXTURE

NINE
PRIZE
MEDALS

TRADE MARK

JOSEPH TERRY & SONS LTD
YORK

Sweet Taste
of
Success

The confectionery of York has changed with the times.
'Motoring chocolate' has given way to chunks for truck
drivers, and 'Theatre Chocolates' are no longer sought for their
ingenious no-rustle wrappers.

**ROWNTREE'S
COCOA**

BUILDS BONE AND MUSCLE

*Above: it seems that cocoa
could achieve far more in the
past than modern parents
would imagine*

Interdependence of the the chocolate and
railway industries was a significant factor
in the growth of York at the beginning of this
century. The chocolate factories benefited
both from their situation at the hub of a rail
distribution network and from the
availability of the families of the men
working in the railway workshops to staff
their rapidly expanding factories.

Two firms have been producing
chocolates for close on 100 years. Both,
however, developed from retail establishments set up in the 18th century. These
served both the citizens of York and the
nobility and gentry who came to York for the
social round centring on the Assembly Rooms.

Rowntree Mackintosh had a direct
connection with Mary Tuke, a Quaker and
Freeman of the City, who set up her own
grocery business in an unfashionable part
of York when she was 30. She survived a
seven-year commercial struggle with the
powerful Merchant Adventurers' Company
which controlled local traders dealing with
imported and exported goods. Her business
expanded into tea-dealing and was inherited
in 1752 by her nephew William Tuke, also
a Quaker and active in social reform.

Terry's stemmed from a retail
confectionery business which moved in 1824
to a site near the Mansion House where the
Lord Mayor of York resides during his year
of office. About this time Joseph Terry, an
apothecary, joined the business which had
been operating elsewhere in York since 1767.

Mary Tuke's successors operated a small
plant for grinding cocoa and chicory and also
produced a rudimentary form of chocolate.
This manufactory was hived off from the
retail tea business and sold to Isaac Rowntree,
the son of another York grocer. The output
of cocoa at this time was 12 cwts per week.
The business passed to Joseph Rowntree
who purchased Dutch machinery in 1889
to produce an improved cocoa product and
enable him to expand the manufacture of
much-improved chocolate goods. Local
deliveries were made by donkey cart —
perhaps pulled by the first mint-fed donkey.
The 1,000 employees in 1897 had doubled
by 1902, and again in the next five years.

Terry's had diversified some years earlier
from retailing into the manufacture of cakes
and comfits, sugar sweets, candied peel,
marmalade, mushroom ketchup and
medicated lozenges. By 1840 the company
was sending its products all over England,
and employing about 100 people in the 1850s
compared with 12 at Rowntree's. Terry's
began the manufacture of chocolate products
in 1886 and introduced the first boxed
assortment early in the new century.

By 1939 the confectionery industry in York
employed over 12,000 people including some

seasonal workers. There was a shortage of labour in York in the 1950s and Rowntree's expanded elsewhere. The total labour force in the local confectionery industry has declined in recent years partly as a result of increased mechanisation. No longer do teams of girls sit shoulder to shoulder marking every sweet by hand — though deft cake decorators still abound in York. Rowntree Mackintosh has extended its interests abroad and moved into the so-called fast food industry; Terry's is now a part of a major food group.

The two leading manufacturers moved out of the centre of York as their businesses prospered. Terry's factory occupies an elevated position beside the Racecourse and Rowntree Mackintosh is based on a site containing several miles of private railway sidings which lies between one of York's ancient Strays and the River Foss. These dispersed locations are responsible for another characteristic feature of York — legions of cyclists.

Earlier job titles in the industry such as 'cherry dipper' and 'mogul operator' have now been replaced by 'process workers'. In the past, chocolate packers sat beside long conveyors which brought to them supplies of sweets, cartons and labels. Mugs of tea were sent down the same conveyors prior to morning and afternoon breaks. The conveyors were speeded up to ensure that the last girl did not get cold tea.

York has its share of heat waves which, before the widespread introduction of air-conditioning in food factories, affected the handling of chocolate goods. On hot days female packers were sent home and traditionally seized the opportunity to complete their spring cleaning and wash and air their blankets.

The 1939 Rowntree Christmas catalogue is almost a collectors' item and contains over 200 lines including Riviera, Emperor and Gipsy assortments. Biscuit barrels, 'Triple cheese dishes' and chromium teapots were filled with assortments. Theatre chocolates

with rustleproof packaging were no longer on offer. Terry's original shop is reproduced realistically, complete with authentic aroma, in a street in the Castle Museum in York. Brightly coloured marzipan sweets are on display alongside jujubes, pomfrit cakes and sugar mice.

Conversation lozenges helped the tongue-tied with such pre-printed opening gambits as 'Can you polka?', 'I want a wife' and 'Do you love me?'

A third York confectionery manufacturer, Craven's, has its origins in two shops inherited in 1862 by Mary Ann Craven when she was widowed at the age of 33. For 54 years Mary Ann applied her qualities to building up a business which, at its peak in 1908, employed 800 people in the factory and four shops.

She is commemorated by a stained glass window which was erected by her children in All Saints' Church, Pavement, near the site of the original factory.

The business declined after World War I but has been re-vitalised in recent years. Nowadays, the company has in the region of 350 employees.

Joseph Rowntree and his son Seebohm were influential contributors to social reform and between them made comprehensive studies of poverty, housing and working conditions in industry. They pioneered the introduction of many wide-ranging improvements in their factories and in the garden village which Joseph established at New Earswick.

The Terry family has played a prominent part in civic affairs in York in the past. Joseph Terry was four times Lord Mayor of York and was knighted when holding this office in the year of Queen Victoria's Golden Jubilee.

More recently, Noel Terry assembled a remarkable collection of fine Georgian furniture, which is now on public display in the carefully restored Georgian mansion of Fairfax House.

QUALITY WITH QUANTITY
Luxury and quality remained important after boxed chocolates had been invented

Coronation tins for Edward VII were packed by a production line of girls at Rowntree's factory at Haxley Road

A City
and its
Railways

Y ork is well blessed with railway installations, including buildings of such magnificence that at least one Victorian shareholder was moved to make comments about a 'splendid monument of extravagance'.

OFF THE RAIL.

This seems remarkable in a City that has never had much in the way of heavy industry, yet is more easily understandable when the impetus for development is traced back to George Hudson, three times Lord Mayor and known to his contemporaries as 'The Railway King'. His was the often-quoted remark, made to George Stephenson, the pioneering railway engineer, 'Mak all t'railways cum t'York'. From this simple statement of policy came, in due course, not only the City's excellent train services to many parts of the country, but also some of its most impressive secular buildings, such as the station and the Royal York Hotel.

The City's first railway was opened when Hudson was Lord Mayor, and only ran for some 15 miles to York Junction on the Leeds & Selby Railway. Even so, the inaugural day was celebrated in typical Hudson style, beginning with a huge breakfast at the Mansion House. In the early afternoon the invited passengers joined the first train at the temporary station in Thief Lane for the run to York Junction and back. After its return, the official party adjourned to the Guildhall, where they partook of dinner from 4.30 pm to 10 pm. They then returned to the Mansion House, where the Lady Mayoress led off the dance that lasted until 4 am.

It was not until the summer of the following year that the York & North Midland Railway was completed which, by joining the North Midland Railway near Normanton, put York in direct contact with London for the first time. In due course the 1,450 miles of railway that Hudson controlled extended from York to London, Bristol,

Norwich and Berwick, yet the route used by today's 125-mph High Speed Trains between York and King's Cross was built by a rival company. Indeed, at the time the Great Northern was seeking to get the necessary Parliamentary powers for its railway, Hudson boasted that he would be able to leave London by his lines with 20 carriages, and beat them to York.

The Great Northern's route between London and York was, initially, not particularly direct but this was steadily improved, a process that is still continuing.

As recently as the autumn of 1983, 15 miles of new high-speed railway were opened south of York, bypassing the developing Selby Coalfield. By 1991, York will have become the central point of the largest electrification scheme in Britain, when the new traction takes over between London and Edinburgh.

Today's fastest trains between York and London require only two hours for the $188\frac{1}{2}$ miles but in September 1985 a special train run to launch the new 'Tees-Tyne Pullman', the crack morning southbound service from the city, averaged just over 119 mph from York to King's Cross.

George Hudson's career rose to its zenith during the 1840s, but his financial jugglings between the various different companies he controlled finally caught up with him, and he was forced to resign all his railway connections. For over a century his name was shunned in York, but in recent years he has been rehabilitated, with the new railway offices in the city being named 'Hudson House' in 1968 and the nearby 'Railway Street' becoming 'George Hudson Street'.

A large, full-length portrait of him in the Lord Mayor's robes dominates the staircase of the Mansion House, while a reproduction of another portrait has been hung in the Board Room of the headquarters of the North Eastern Railway, which still houses the General Manager and the staff of British Railways Eastern Region.

The gaze of visitors arriving in York by rail is met by the splendid curve of the station with its triple-arched roof, one of the finest examples in the country of Victorian railway architecture. Referred to by one of the shareholders as 'a very splendid monument of extravagance', it was opened in 1877 and has been extended on a number of occasions. In spite of its being damaged during the air raids of World War II, it is now a listed building. A refurbishment scheme for the entrance area costing £900,000 was completed in 1984. This provided the new Travel Centre, entered off a completely rebuilt outer concourse, a striking feature of which is an old North Eastern Railway semaphore signal.

Adjoining the station is the hotel, built by the railway and opened in 1878. A wing was added in 1896, known as 'The Klondyke' because of the gold rush which took place that year. The hotel, like all those owned by the railways, was sold in 1983, and the new owners, Sea Containers, the firm that operates the 'Venice–Simplon Orient Express', renamed it the Royal York Hotel. Long-term refurbishing plans include the embellishment of the magnificent staircase with Venetian glass chandeliers, while visitors in the new executive suites can admire the incomparable view of the Minster on the skyline, even when sitting in their baths!

Not far from the present station and hotel lies York's first station. This was a terminus, reached through an arch in the City Walls,

and is now used as railway offices. This fine building was designed by a local architect G T Andrews, and the original colonnaded entrance can still be admired from Tanner Row. The North Eastern Railway built a magnificent new headquarters in 1906 on the opposite side of the road. The fine lines of this 'Huge Palace of Business' were enhanced by the major restoration and cleaning programme completed in 1979. Even the locomotive weather-vane was re-gilded.

In 1927 the first museum in Britain devoted to the railways was opened in York by the London & North Eastern Railway, and became very popular in spite of its somewhat cramped buildings. After nationalisation of the railways, the Museum of British Transport was opened at Clapham, in south London, and took over the responsibility for the older museum at York.

When British Railways wanted to be relieved of their museum responsibilities, plans were made to build a new National Railway Museum which would be handed over to the London-based Science Museum. After considerable lobbying, a derelict steam depot in Leeman Road was chosen, and the new museum opened in September 1975.

It immediately became the most popular museum in the north of England, and in its first 11 years attracted 14 million visitors. Its arrays of beautifully-restored locomotives and carriages appeal to wives, mothers and daughters as well as to 'boys of all ages', while the restaurant and shop provide opportunities for visitors to refresh themselves physically and mentally.

York's century and a half of its special relationship with the railways has provided the visitor with not only good train services to the City but also with the heritage of many of its magnificent buildings.

VICTORIAN EXTRAVAGANCE
British Rail staff and management still occupy the magnificent old North Eastern Railway headquarters, perhaps the best building of its type in the British Isles

SPEED-RECORD BREAKER
York Railway Museum's famous exhibit, Mallard, on one of its rare outings at York Station. It set an unbeaten 126 mph world steam record in 1938

York's Rivers & Bridges

I**n many ways York is the product of its rivers, the stately Ouse and smaller Foss — important to Viking traders. Their bridges and boats add a magical dimension to the old City.**

From Ouseburn, the River Ouse flows south-east towards York, being swelled by the River Kyle above Newton-on-Ouse and by the River Nidd near Beningborough Hall. On the opposite bank of the river is Nun Monkton, site of a Benedictine nunnery, and a little farther down Overton where once the Lord Abbot of St Mary's had a country house. He travelled up the river from York in his state barge, accompanied by a grand and numerous retinue.

Past Nether Poppleton the Ouse is crossed by the British Rail East Coast main line before reaching Clifton Ings. Records tell us that in 1730 the racecourse here was flooded.

The modern six-span concrete road bridge at Clifton is currently the first road crossing below Aldwark Toll Bridge. Discussions about building a bridge here went on for 50 years before it was finally opened in 1963, the first new Ouse bridge since 1881.

However, about a mile upstream, another bridge carrying an outer bypass has been designed to enable traffic from the north to travel eastwards or westwards without having to enter the city to cross the river.

The railway crosses the river again on a cast-iron structure built in 1844–5 to take the York–Scarborough line. It has been supplemented by a footway for pedestrians.

Adjacent is Marygate Landing. A row

between the Mayor and the Bursar of St Mary's Abbey in 1377 resulted in a ditch being dug across Marygate to prevent traffic passing and a ship's rudder was seized by the bursar to assert his claim that the landing was private property.

In 1840 the creation of York's first railway station in Toft Green made it necessary to provide a river crossing for the increased traffic being generated. The site of an existing ferry at Lendal was the obvious choice for a bridge. After years of disputes about the site, the design and who should pay for it, work started in 1860 but after a year the whole lot collapsed into the river killing five men. The present ornate structure by Thomas Page, engineer of Westminster Bridge, was opened in 1863.

Immediately north-west of Lendal Bridge are two stone towers, one each side of the river, each at the end of a section of city wall. The larger tower, Lendal, provided a home in 1682 for York's first waterworks — one of the oldest in the country. The other is Barker Tower, around which a leather manufacturing industry once prospered.

Immediately below the bridge on the east bank — where visitors queue to board river cruises — is the back of Guildhall.

Ouse Bridge is the oldest in the city and the present structure is the third on this site. William the Conqueror found a narrow bridge here and when William, Archbishop of York, returned to the city in 1154 the crowd that welcomed him was so great that the timbers collapsed and many people fell into the river. The present bridge of five Gothic arches, completed in 1820, was the first place to have a continuous flagged footway and was also one of the first three locations to be lit up at night with an oil lamp.

In Medieval times traffic and trade were

FROM THE RIVER OUSE

This antique view of York from the banks of the City's premier waterway, the Ouse, has an almost Mediterranean atmosphere

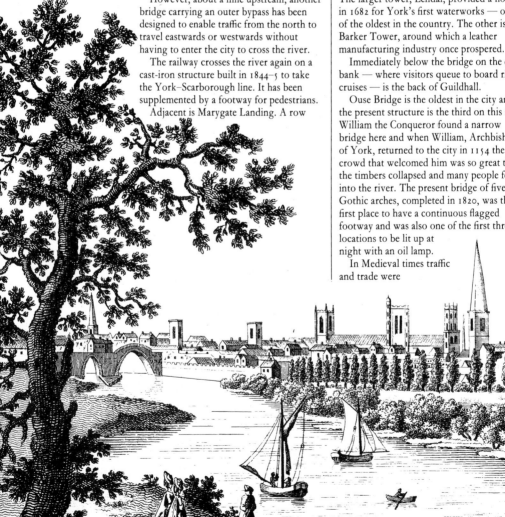
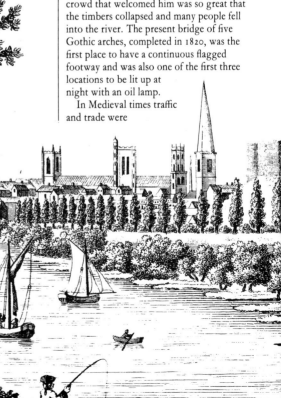

hampered by the bridge toll system. Its abolition in 1829 brought 'bridge fever' to the City. Amidst 'great bustle and excitement', at the stroke of noon a carrier crossed Ouse Bridge with a load of timbers destined for repairs to the Minster, followed by a brewer's dray and two mail-coaches. Blunderbusses and cannon were fired into the air, a band played, and everyone celebrated by dressing up in colourful costumes.

Yet this celebration pales into insignificance against that for the Prince of Wales's visit to the City in 1866. In the centre of the bridge a 28-foot high and 24-foot wide arch was erected, crowned with a massive dome topped by a gas star some 64 feet above the pavement and adorned with wreaths, medallions, statuary, floral messages, flags and a frieze.

Immediately below Ouse Bridge the river passes between two staiths. King's Staith is now lost in summer beneath a sea of tourists and moored pleasure cruisers and in winter is inundated by the swollen Ouse.

Queen's Staith, on the opposite bank, built in 1660, is site of several warehouses. When a butter factory was built on adjacent land, it became known as Butter Staith and for about a century great quantities of butter were landed here, weighed and shipped to London and other places. In the 19th century it served as the centre of the river coal-trade, becoming known as 'Coal Staith'. Coal-keels would lie head on to the quay along its length, moored as closely as possible and alive with coal-wagons, hawkers, heavers and merchants. Barges still moor here with the occasional cargo of nuts and beans.

In Skeldergate two bonded warehouses opened for business in the 1870s. Here, at the heart of York's thriving river-borne commerce, were handled wine, spices, grain, salt, wax, steel, iron, linens, lead, sea-coal, wood and madder.

Skeldergate Bridge opened for public use in 1881. The little castellated toll-house remains to remind motorists that, until 1914, it cost a halfpenny to cross.

In St George's Field opposite, the ducking stool was operated, at first for females who used false measures or brewed bad beer, but later also for 'flyters or scolds'.

Here too is the confluence with the River

Foss. It has its source about 24 miles away at Pond Head near Oulston. Some people contend that in Viking times the River Foss was the principal route for commerce. A wooden drawbridge which had its structures painted blue as far back as 1736 gave its name to Blue Bridge here.

Near by is Foss Bridge, built in 1812, but first mentioned in the early 12th century and the site of the sea-fish market in 1253.

About 1,200 acres of arable land here were flooded in 1068 when the Foss was dammed to provide water for the castle moat and the resultant lake became known as the King's Fish Pond, extending as far as the present Foss Islands area.

Continuing down from Blue Bridge, the River Ouse comes to Middlethorne Ings where a white headless lady is reputed to haunt the towpath. Many years ago she is said to have been murdered and decapitated when out for an evening stroll. Ever since she has haunted the bank looking for her murderers.

Lifting the Leeds/Scarborough A64 road over the river here is a five-span concrete bridge which forms part of the nine-mile, £9,000,000 bypass opened in 1976 to relieve York's traffic congestion.

Passing Bishopthorpe Palace the Ouse then flows beneath the 280-foot wide twin-span Naburn Bridge. Opened in 1871 to carry the North Eastern Railway, it is now part of a cycle-way. The river here is especially popular with boating enthusiasts.

FLOOD AND TOLLS
Tolls were once charged to travellers who crossed Skeldergate Bridge

Toll of a different kind has been taken by the river, as these old flood levels show

Dukes & Duchesses of York

Regardless of the mocking nursery rhyme, the Grand Old Duke of York was popular with his men and a fine administrator. But others of the 14 title holders behaved badly, constantly courting scandal.

Prince Andrew became the most recent in a long and illustrious line of Dukes of York on the morning of his marriage to Miss Sarah Ferguson, in July 1986

Richard Plantagenet, perhaps the first to use the famous white-rose emblem, was killed in battle against the House of Lancaster while fighting for his claim to England's crown

Edward IV fared better than his father Richard, the 3rd Duke, and was crowned King of England after winning the Battle of St Albans against feeble-minded King Henry VI

During the last six centuries, the ancient City of York has given its name to a series of 14 Dukes, all members of the reigning Royal Family, and since the late 15th century invariably younger sons or younger brothers of the monarch.

At the time of their creation, indeed, none of the Dukes was next in line to the throne, yet six Dukes of York have in the event been crowned King. Two of this varied and notable group of men have been killed in battle, one murdered and one executed, six have served as soldiers and five as sailors, and nearly all have married, four of them more than once; while four — the 4th, 6th, 8th and 10th Dukes — have been noted for their amorous exploits.

The most recent Dukes, moreover, have enjoyed close links with the city that gave them their title — though they do not own any specific estates there, or indeed any hereditary lands. The title has long been purely an honorary one, annexed to the crown since the 4th Duke of York became King Edward IV in 1461.

Since then it has been 10 times in abeyance, being conferred only when a suitable candidate was available. Thus nearly 50 years elapsed between the temporary extinguishment of the title in December 1936 (when the 13th Duke became King George VI) and the great day in July 1986 when the citizens of York rejoiced to hear that Prince Andrew had been named their 14th Duke.

His earliest predecessor, first Duke of York in 1385, was Edmund of Langley (1341–1402), fourth son of King Edward III. A brave but somewhat unsuccessful commander in the wars with France, he was at home a respected conciliator in the disputes between Richard II and his rebellious subjects. His son Edward 'Aumerle' (1373–1415), the 2nd Duke, was a far more dubious character, who betrayed his cousin Richard II to Henry IV and was then twice implicated in conspiracies against Henry. Notable as the author of 'The Master of Game', (the first hunting manual in English and the only book written by a Medieval Royal) he is best known for his part in the Agincourt campaign, when he probably invented the sharpened stakes used by English archers for defence.

During the battle the overweight Duke commanded the English right wing, but apparently collapsed and suffocated inside his heavy armour: his skeleton, boiled to remove the flesh, was carried home for burial in Fotheringhay church.

There too lies his nephew Richard (1411–60), the 3rd Duke, who headed the 'Yorkist' party during the early part of the Wars of the Roses and who was perhaps the first to use the famous White Rose badge.

The richest and most powerful landowner in England, he claimed through his mother a better right to the crown than his feeble-minded cousin Henry VI; but in December 1460 he was defeated and slain at Wakefield, his head being set on York's Micklegate Bar and ironically crowned with paper.

Richard's son Edward (1442–83), the 4th Duke, was more successful, holding the title for only two months before being crowned King Edward IV. Exceptionally tall by Medieval standards — he was six foot three and strikingly handsome — he proved a popular monarch and a triumphant

His Royal Highness the DUKE of YORK.

commander, though an inveterate womaniser and glutton.

His debaucheries are said to have hastened his premature death at the age of 40, leaving as his heirs two young sons. The younger of these 'Princes in the Tower', Richard (1473–c1483), was the 5th and most tragic of the Dukes of York, for he and his brother were secretly murdered, most probably at the instigation of their uncle Richard III.

Henry VIII was the only Tudor Duke of York

The 6th (and only Tudor) Duke of York was Henry (1491–1546), the second son of Henry VII. On the death of his elder brother Arthur he became Prince of Wales, and later succeeded as Henry VIII, perhaps the most notorious of English monarchs. Thereafter, more than a century passed before the creation of a 7th Duke, Charles (1600–49), who was likewise a younger son, of James I; but his brother Henry died prematurely, and the Duke became King Charles I. It was he for whom the city of York was held during the Civil War. He was the only holder of the title to suffer execution.

James (1633–1701), his second son, was the 8th and probably the least popular of the Dukes, principally because of his Roman Catholic sympathies. An able general and admiral, he was equally renowned for the number (though not the good looks) of his mistresses — his brother Charles II jocularly suggested that they were inflicted on him as a penance, while Nell Gwynn nicknamed him 'Dismal Jimmie'. His relations with the city of York were particularly unhappy, and on his accession as James II he sacked the corporation; the citizens were thus quick to support his deposition by William III in 1688.

The 9th Duke, Ernest Augustus (1674–1728), was little known in England, for this youngest brother of George I spent most of his life in his native Hanover, while the rival Jacobite 'Shadow Duke' — Henry (1725–1807), brother of the exiled Bonnie Prince Charlie — never set foot on British soil, where his title was not recognised.

Prince Frederick, 11th title holder and second son of George III, was the Grand Old Duke of nursery rhyme fame. The song mocks his lack of military skill against the French

The official 10th Duke was therefore Edward Augustus (1739–67), younger brother of George III. 'Remarkably plain, with strange loose eyes', Edward was nevertheless notorious for his many affairs, and was packed off into the navy to avoid scandal, but he found time to receive the Freedom of York in 1761, before dying of a fever contracted while galloping to a mistress after an all-night ball.

Frederick (1763–1827), the 11th title-holder and second son of George III, is famous as 'the Grand Old Duke of York' who endlessly marched his soldiers up and down a hill — a nursery rhyme which mocked his largely ineffective handling of campaigns against the French in Holland. Though his period as army Commander-in-Chief was also bedevilled by scandals involving the sale of commissions by his mistress, this bluff and corpulent Duke was popular for his humane treatment of his troops, and highly praised by Wellington for his administrative efficiency.

The 12th Duke, George (1865–1935), grandson of the reigning Queen Victoria and son of Prince Edward (later Edward VII), was likewise exceedingly popular in York — which he visited in 1893, following his creation as Duke and marriage to Princess Mary of Teck. The pale Princess was immediately christened 'The White Rose of York', and on receiving the Freedom of the City the Duke delighted its inhabitants by declaring himself 'a citizen of no mean city'.

He succeeded as George V in 1910, and 10 years later his second son George (1895–1952) became the 13th Duke, receiving the Freedom of York soon afterwards. He revisited the city in 1925 with his Duchess, Elizabeth (now the Queen Mother and always a favourite royal visitor).

Heroically overcoming his shyness and stammer, the Duke stepped into the breach as George VI in 1936, on the abdication of his brother Edward VIII. His grandson Prince Andrew — already glimpsed informally in York during flying training at a nearby base — was created the 14th Duke of York on 23 July 1986, the morning of his marriage to Miss Sarah Ferguson.

The 10th Duke, Edward Augustus was the younger brother of George III, and an unashamed womaniser. Sent to the navy to avoid scandal, he eventually died of fever caught while visiting a mistress

George V, 12th Duke of York and father of two kings, Edward VIII, and his brother, George VI

Traditions & Ceremonies

I n keeping with its history — centuries of community development and a mixing of cultures from as far apart as Italy and Norway — York has a fine and colourful tradition of civic and social ceremony.

Wherever you look in York — on public buildings, lamp-posts and bridges, on buses and litter-bins and car-park signboards — you will find emblazoned the distinctive arms of the City: the shield with its red cross and five golden lions, backed by a crossed sword and mace topped by a scarlet and ermine 'cap of maintenance'.

These devices, like the real sword and mace borne at the head of many annual civic processions, are the proud symbols of York's most ancient and colourful traditions, those surrounding its Lord Mayor and Sheriff.

York, indeed, was one of the first towns in England to elect a mayor, in token of the much-valued privilege of self-government which its citizens purchased from a needy King John in 1212, paying in return the then immense sum of £200 and adding a trio of horses for good measure.

The chief citizen of York, moreover, is not merely 'the mayor': he or she is 'the Right Honourable the Lord Mayor of York', with official precedence immediately after the Lord Mayor of London and, apart from him, the only Lord Mayor in England entitled to be addressed as 'Right Honourable'.

This pre-eminence dates from the later 14th century, when York (apart from London) was the largest and most prosperous town in Medieval England. King Richard II even seems to have contemplated making York his capital, and in 1396, he promoted the City to the status of County in its own right. To emphasise this great and unusual honour, its mayor was granted the right to have carried before him both a mace (the symbol of his authority in the city) and also a mighty sword, the badge of his office as the monarch's direct representative in the county.

Subsequently, York's chief citizen became so important a figure that he was known as 'my lord the mayor' — hence 'Lord Mayor' — and since 1396 he has been seconded by York's own county Sheriff.

The sword and mace always depicted with the City Arms, therefore, are a reminder of York's special position among the ancient towns of Britain, and though it officially ceased to be a 'City and County' in 1974, · Queen Elizabeth II specifically decreed that its privilege of bearing these symbols before the Lord Mayor should continue.

The silver mace carried by the cocked-hatted macebearer was made in 1647, but York's great sword of state is older still: over five feet long, it dates from about 1416, and once belonged to the German Emperor Sigismund, the Holy Roman Emperor.

Its bearer traditionally wears the third of York's status symbols, the red velvet 'cap of maintenance' with its ermine brim. The

One of the most impressive pieces of Regalia kept at Mansion House is the great silver Mace of 1647

present cap dates from 1915, and was given by George V, but the original example is said to have been presented by Richard II as a mark of exceptional royal favour.

The Elizabethan silver chains worn by both swordbearer and macebearer are likewise part of York's history: they were made for the City's Waits, a band of musical watchmen who patrolled the streets by night as well as performing at civic ceremonies. Their descendants, the revived York Waits, clad in scarlet livery gowns over Elizabethan costumes and with Renaissance instruments, can again be seen and heard.

When not in use, the sword and mace may be viewed (on written application to the Lord Mayor's Secretary) at the Mansion House, along with York's fabulous collection of civic regalia. Valued at over half a million pounds, this includes treasures like the Lady Mayoress's Staff of Honour — which was jocularly lent to the wives of new Sheriffs, to keep their spouses in order.

Lady Mayoresses of York also once enjoyed the unique distinction of retaining their titles for life, though their husbands relinquished theirs on leaving office: thus

He is a Lord for a year and a day
But she is a Lady for ever and aye.

Surely the most unusual item of regalia, however, is York's famous silver chamber-pot, presented in 1672: it incorporates a whistle, blown to summon a servant to empty it, and rumour relates that at least one Lord Mayor has used it for its proper purpose within living memory.

The Mansion House itself, a stately red-

CHAMBER MUSIC
*Unusual item – a silver
chamber pot, with whistle*

painted Georgian building in the City centre, is yet another expression of York's civic pride, as well as of its long tradition of hearty hospitality.

Begun in 1726, it remains the actual residence of the Lord Mayor and Lady Mayoress during their year of office, and comes equipped with butler, under-butler, chauffeur and cook-housekeeper. It continues to be the hub of civic hospitality, though Lord Mayors are no longer required to 'keep up the Grandeur and Dignity of the City' by holding 'two Publick Dining Days in every week at least'.

Georgian York, indeed, was renowned for its gargantuan meals, and a contemporary physician lamented that, 'Feasting to excess with one another is very strongly in use . . .'

Some of the most stupendous of York's banquets — including the one given for Prince Albert when the centrepiece was a dish including nearly 500 game birds — took place in the adjacent Guildhall, where mayoral elections and other ceremonies have been held since the mid 15th century. Beneath it runs the underground passage called Common Hall Lane, which leads directly to a riverside quay. Several of the ancient York guilds (originally a blend of trades union and friendly society) still survive, notably the Merchant Adventurers and Merchant Taylors, both with their own fine Medieval halls. About a dozen times a year, they process in their colourful robes to their Guild Church of All Saints', Pavement, where their coats of arms are permanently displayed.

Outside this church stood the pillory for punishing minor criminals — except during the Christmas season, when one of York's strangest customs allowed them free rein for their dubious activities.

The amnesty began on St Thomas's Day (21 December), when the Sheriffs blew a horn called 'the Yule-girthol' at the pillory, announcing that 'all manner of whores, thieves, dice-players and other unthrifty folk be welcome to the town, at the reverence of the high feast of Yule, till the 12 days be past'. They then repeated the proclamation at each City Gate — a tradition recently revived, though the police emphasise that Yuletide lawlessness is no longer tolerated!

Another ancient and unique York Christmas custom is the decoration of the Minster high altar with mistletoe. This magical plant, with its pagan associations, is rarely allowed into Christian churches. How the practice became established in York is wrapped in obscurity.

So too are the origins of the local 'Yorkshire Longsword' dances, performed by teams of six or eight men each bearing a three-foot sword. Grasping the hilt of their own weapon and the point of their neighbour's, the dancers form a ring which turns itself inside-out and right-way-about as they trace many complicated figures.

Eventually they plait their swords into a star-shaped lock, which they place round the neck of a 'victim', then the weapons are suddenly drawn, and the victim falls as if dead.

Quite unlike the more familiar Morris-style dancing, these very distinctive and exciting dances were once performed by farm labourers from the surrounding villages of York, and a display often takes place in St Sampson's Square on the traditional date of 'Plough Monday' (the Monday after 6 January).

**THE FREEMEN
OF YORK**
*Until the early 19th
century, only those who
possessed the 'Freedom
of York' were permitted
to carry on a trade there,
to practise as master
craftsmen, or to vote
in Parliamentary elections.
Citizens could become
'Freemen' either by
being born the child of
a Freeman, by serving
a long apprenticeship
to a Freeman, or by
purchase — which could
be expensive, especially
for 'strangers' not born
in York.
After 1835 the Freemen
lost most of their privileges,
and the buying of Freedom
was prohibited. However,
anyone who can prove
him- or herself the child,
grandchild or great-
grandchild of a Freeman
can still claim to be enrolled
in the city's Guild of
Freemen, and though
the practical advantages
are now few and nebulous
(they include the nominal
right to graze animals
on the 'Strays' or pastures
surrounding the city),
many are still proud
to boast themselves
Freemen of York.
The honorary Freedom
of the City also continues
to be offered to monarchs
and other eminent visitors.*

**LONGSWORD
DANCERS**
*Snow is no obstacle to
York's intrepid sword
dancers, who brave cold steel
in an old and obscure
ceremony*

A Treasury
of
Culture

Culture has a high profile in York, birthplace of writers and artists, and itself a treasury of the architect's art. Here, where the ancient Mystery Plays of the City Guilds survive, music and theatre flourish and the street-corner buskers entertain passers-by with the classics.

OF BOOKS AND BRUSHES
Both York's Roman history and its academic tradition are represented by this statue of the Goddess Minerva, with her books, looking regally down over the Minster Gates

Painter and academic William Etty was an active champion of York's architectural heritage, and a noted artist of the early 19th century

In a City full of museums and architectural riches, it is fitting that York's cultural heritage goes back over 1,000 years.

As early as the 7th century, European noblemen were sending their sons to be instructed by St Wilfrid at his school in York and by the 8th century Alcuin, a former pupil, had made the school famous throughout Christendom.

Distinguished by his scholarship, innovative teaching and fine library, Alcuin of York, as he was known, was persuaded at the age of 50 to become tutor and adviser to the great Charlemagne in Aachen. He left England to become one of the most influential men in Europe, encouraging learning throughout the Church as well as at court. The foundation of the ancient universities, it is recognised, owes much to his achievements.

His great library at York was destroyed by the Vikings and no further books survived from the next two centuries. Alcuin's school had a direct successor in St Peter's School, controlled by the Minster until 1898.

His library was re-established in Medieval times to become, even today, one of the most significant of the cathedral libraries, but it was not until the 1960s that the University was established here to enrich still further the cultural life of the City.

Printing and bookselling have been major industries in York since the earliest printers in the 15th century. The Stonegate/Petergate areas still retain their bookselling traditions — Minerva with her pile of books can be seen looking down on the Minster Gates and the 'Sign of the Bible' at 35 Stonegate marks a shop doorway where, for almost two centuries, from 1682 to 1837, there was one of the most fashionable and important bookshops and publishing houses in the north of England. The first 'modern' novel, Laurence Sterne's *Tristram Shandy* was published from here in 1760 and sold 200 copies in the first two days.

Craftsmanship and the decorative arts are well represented in the City with collections of York silver in the Mansion House, the Minster Treasury in the Undercroft and the superbly preserved interiors of such places as Fairfax House, built in York's Georgian heyday of social life. The architect of Fairfax House, John Carr, was one of the most noted of architects in 18th-century England, designing many stately homes (including Harewood House), bridges and civic buildings. He was twice Lord Mayor of York.

That York's buildings and artefacts have survived so well is often attributed to the city fathers' resistance to change, as much as to their far-sightedness. Credit must also be given to the citizens of York who have rallied in defence of conservation, now with the Civic Trust but in the early 19th century with the 'York Footpath Association' which was formed to save the derelict City Walls and Bars from destruction. Among its members was the painter and Academician, William Etty (1787–1849), most noted in his day for his large exhibition pictures and nudes.

Someone who shared his feelings was fellow 'antiquarian' and York painter Mary Ellen Best (1809–1891). As a woman she was unable to attend art school like Etty, so was

Mary Ellen Best, whose self portrait (right) hangs in the York City Art Gallery, is known for her faithful observations of domestic surroundings during the 19th century

THE YORK PAGEANT

JULY
26ᵀᴴ TO 31ˢᵀ
1909

largely self-taught, but much in demand as a portrait painter. Her studies of still life and of domestic interiors were only 'discovered' in the 1980s and are as complete a picture of early 19th-century life as we have anywhere.

She was also unable to join the Yorkshire Philosophical Society, founded in 1823 to promote 'the diffusion of scientific knowledge generally and more particularly the elucidation of the Geology, Natural History and Antiquities of Yorkshire'. It became an influential body in Yorkshire and the focus of cultural life. Still existing today, we owe to it the preservation of St Mary's Abbey, the creation of the Museum Gardens and the Yorkshire Museum.

The Quakers' influence in the City has been strong, not only in the present day confectionery and printing industries, but also in the founding of famous schools – The Mount for girls and Bootham for boys. Their enlightened views also created The Retreat, a hospital of great repute which opened in 1796 and was the first in England to regard 'mental disorders as illnesses requiring sympathy and scientific treatment'.

York has been well known for its festivals since 1791. The Early Music Festival is held every year and has achieved international standing, while the four-yearly York Festival and Mystery Plays has become, after Edinburgh, the largest festival in the country.

The Minster, the churches, halls and open spaces provide inspiring settings for all kinds of performances. Between Festivals, local orchestras, choirs and the Music Department of York University, not a month goes by without a performance of high standing.

The Theatre Royal has maintained a strong tradition of live theatre since the 18th century and still supports its own repertory company, while the Arts Centre was created in a converted church in North Street for smaller-scale 'alternative' productions. Half-a-dozen well-established amateur groups provide many of the cast for the Mystery Plays and maintain regular programmes of plays and musicals every year.

MASTERY OF MYSTERIES

Festivals and pageants of various descriptions have long been a well-known aspect of York life, but the most famous are the Mystery Plays, once enacted by the City Guilds. In recent times, the plays have made several acting reputations. Mystery is a derivation meaning 'mastery', and the plays are biblical.

Spider's Web
of
Alleyways

L inking street and yard, alley and square in the tangled throughways and thoroughfares that make up central York are the 'snickelways' — strange, twisty little passages leading to secluded city secrets.

York is not the easiest City to look down on from above. The Vale of York, in which it lies, is too flat and too expansive to provide a birds's eye view. But if one could rise over the Minster — in a hot-air balloon, let us say — there would unfold below an intricate hologram. In one light, one would see the great Medieval buildings and walls; in another, the rivers, roads and railways. Tilting one's gaze yet another way, the view would open on a sea of crowded, terracotta rooftops and chimney-pots, with the Minster seeming to sail across them like a great, white ship.

What would not be discernable below the surface of the rooftops, however, would be the hidden pattern of the hologram: the fascinating network of York's little streets and alleyways.

So let us come down to earth and find it. This spider's web is unique to York. Its foundation strands were spun 2,000 years ago by the Romans when they built the streets of their fortress which survive to this day as Petergate, Stonegate and Chapter House Street. Superimposed were the streets of Viking and Medieval times, like Coppergate (the street of the coopers) and the Shambles (fleshammels, or butchers). Intertwined among them all are the narrow footpaths — the alleyways, ginnels and snickets or 'snickelways'.

Most of these snickelways originated centuries ago as shortcuts to market, business or pleasure; they have survived as public rights of way, despite being built over, above and around.

So what does this mean to the people of York, where a Gate is a street, a Bar is a gate, a Yard is an alley, and a Court is a yard? It means that they can accomplish a remarkable feat. Starting and finishing at Bootham Bar (which was one of the main Roman gateways) they can, without retracing their steps or recrossing their paths, walk for three-and-a-half almost traffic-free miles through these narrow places — and all within a quarter of a mile of the Shambles!

It's an infinitely varied tapestry. Sometimes following in the footsteps of the Romans along Chapter House Street, as they marched to face the perils of the Forest of Galtres. At other times taking a route along Medieval lanes between towering cliffs of Victorian brickwork, with names like Pope's Head Alley and Little Thief Lane. Suddenly on the way, there may be havens of rest and seclusion, like the leafy churchyard of the 11th-century Holy Trinity church, insulated from bustling Goodramgate by Lady Row cottages, the oldest surviving houses in York,

dating back to the early 14th century. Only too often, the route leads down the paths of Medieval (and subsequent) shame and iniquity — Penny Lane, Straker's Passage and Mucky Peg Lane.

Very few of the snickelways would make any claim to fame. Apart from the odd famous name like Shambles or Stonegate, most are modest and unsung. They are merely routes that people use to get from one place to another (a requirement of a snickelway is that it must lead from somewhere to somewhere else). But in following them, an intriguing and vivid mixture of past and present opens up from time to time, more evocative than any historic tour.

Take the peaceful Precentor's Court, for instance, separated from the noisy High Petergate by the Hole-in-the-Wall passageway. The Precentor was an officer of the Minster, in charge of the choir. One Precentor, according to the account, clapped his choirboys into jail for singing rude words to the anthem. The jail, conveniently enough, was tacked on to the Minster itself.

The snickelways, indeed, keep leading to a variety of former jails. There is another, tucked away beside the market, in a building where Wesley used to preach and which subsequently became a slaughterhouse.

Ouse Bridge, near Fish Landing passage, had its own jail (not to mention a chapel and a hospital) to accommodate travellers converging on what was then the first and last bridge over the Ouse before the North Sea. And inevitably one comes to that imposing and handsome concentration of former places of punishment around York Castle: prisons for debtors, females and felons respectively.

It was there that, in the 1830s, they hanged one Alice Smith, for the offence of insanity. She gave her name to Mad Alice Lane, a narrow snickelway linking Swinegate and Low Petergate, which emerges through what can only be described as a sort of cupboard, open at both ends. But Mad Alice Lane is not the narrowest snickelway. Pride of place goes to Pope's Head Alley, 31 inches wide and a 100 or more feet deep, it seems, as one squeezes through from Peter Lane to High Ousegate. Its other name was Introduction Lane, where if one wanted to be introduced, one simply timed the encounter to meet the lady half-way!

But for the most of everything, Coffee Yard links upmarket Stonegate with the less exalted Grape Lane, the repute of which was distinctly downmarket. At the entrance to Coffee Yard is a red devil, symbolic of the printing industry, which had its York origins

NARROW WAYS
This thin passage between looming Victorian brick is Pope's Head Alley

SECRETS OF 'SNICKELWAYS'
Two pleasant surprises.to cheer the wandering visitor are Lady Peckett's Yard (opposite) and the handsome, red printers' devil at the entrance to Coffee Yard. The former offers picturesque, paved and half-timbered seclusion, while the latter is a reminder of York's early association with the printing industry

Spider's Web
of Alleyways

YARDS OF ALLEY
This secret 'garden' at the end of Powell's Yard is a typical snickelway surprise

Part of the charm of York's alleyways and yards is fine and unexpected embellishment, like this ornate street lamp

Coffee Yard, with its good paving and relatively wide passage, is one of York's longer snickelways. It is of Medieval origin, and finishes close to the Minster

right there. On and on, as the footsteps echo along this Medieval common lane — through three tunnels, two ginnels and a dog-leg until one emerges, close to (exactly where cannot be revealed!) an old barnyard, hidden from, and unknown to the population of York, but within a stone's throw of the Minster.

In contrast to the lengthy Coffee Yard, there is a host of brief snickelways beside the market. The connoisseur can use them to evade — and bemuse — the crowds in the Shambles by shuttling in and out along them, to emerge down Whip-Dog Lane into York's shortest street, Whip-ma-whop-ma-gate. Although this name conjures up pictures of chauvinistic punishment, and its generally accepted meaning is of a whipping post and pillory, it is also known as a Medieval term of scorn: 'What-sort-of-a-street-do-you-call-*that*?', or words to that effect.

Maybe similar scorn might be poured upon a favourite snickelway, which leads from Stonebow down towards a secret little vista of York's unsung River Foss. At first sight, this Black Horse Passage is no more than an unkempt tangle of vegetation, beaten earth and broken glass. It saw slightly better days in Victorian times, as a furtive route for gentlemen of pleasure. But it goes back far

further than that, and deserves the same treatment as the others, if only for its advanced years.

The wall on the right is the remains of a Carmelite friary. The missing bricks — 20,000 of them — were sold second-hand 650 years ago to the Merchant Adventurers for the sum of £6! The Adventurers duly built their Hall with them in 1358, and the perfect match with the humble Black Horse Passage is there for all to see.

And so one can keep on strolling round the snickelways, wandering from one distraction to another: from the tree-shaded peace of Dean's Park behind the Minster to the animated and friendly market stalls; and from the half-timbered seclusion of Lady Peckett's Yard to the crowded Minster Gates, where a girl playing the harp is accompanied by the Minster bells and the hum of 100 conversations of passers-by. The way will have led, not around the celebrated tourist attractions, but among the sights and sounds of York as it has been lived in by ordinary — and extraordinary — people down the ages.

Mark Jones is the author of the book *A Walk around the Snickelways of York*, which features all 51 snickelways, with notes, maps and pen-and-ink sketches.

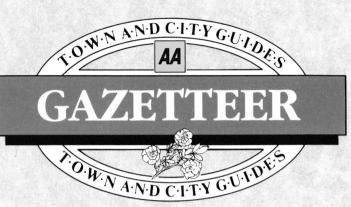

GAZETTEER

Places of Interest in York

Toothsome display in the Terry's sweetshop at Castle Museum, part of a facsimile period street. Contemporary vehicles and other memorabilia are also featured

One of two famous windows at All Saints', North Street

Curious 'mouth-of-hell' door knocker at All Saints', Pavement

ALL SAINTS' CHURCH

North Street

The 120-foot slender spire of this church is a landmark on the west bank of the River Ouse. The church itself is largely late Norman, but the aisles are older. The interior has a fine hammerbeam roof with good bosses and angels, and a 20th-century wooden screen by Ridsdale Tate.

The church is also famous for its stained glass, with two 13th-century windows dipicting the Last Fifteen Days of the World and the Six Corporal Acts of Mercy. Its pulpit dates from 1673, and it also contains 18th-century Mayoral and Benefaction boards. In 1977 the building was restored by the York Civic Trust. The entrance is along a passageway on the right-hand side.

ALL SAINTS' CHURCH, PAVEMENT

High Ousegate

One of the most interesting churches in York, All Saints' (Pavement) is hemmed in between Coppergate and High Ousegate. Its famous lantern tower is a landmark on the York skyline. Tradition recalls that in Medieval times the light guided travellers to the city through the Forest of Galtres. The lantern tower is a 19th-century reproduction of an original tower. The light that shines today in the tower after dusk is a memorial to the citizens of York who died in the two World Wars.

The present building is mostly 14th and 15th century and was built on the site of an earlier church. The *Domesday* book in 1087 records a church here known as All Hallows, and in the churchyard Saxon and Danish burial stones have been found, which suggest an early Christian site.

In 1782 the chancel was demolished to provide more room for the grain market, and over the years the churchyard has gradually disappeared as a result of road widening. However, the small garden to the west of the church has been given in compensation for the losses.

During the last century the church was restored, and in 1887 the eastern end was remodelled. In 1898 an organ chamber was built on the southern side of the church. However, modern traffic problems in Coppergate became so bad that in 1963 this extension had to be demolished and the organ rebuilt.

The interior of the church has much to offer. In the north aisle there is a memorial to the 17th-century theatre manager Tate Wilkinson, whose work in York's Theatre Royal upgraded it to one of the foremost provincial theatres in the country. Much of the stained glass in the church is by Charles E Kempe – look for his trade mark, a wheatsheaf.

In the Great East Window many saints are depicted. The Great West Window, dating from the 14th century, is by Richard Caldbeck and shows scenes from the Passion of Our Lord. This window was formerly located in St Saviour's, and was removed when that church became redundant. A window in the south wall shows three northern saints, Aidan, Paulinus and Cuthbert. The lectern is of note. Originally it stood in St Crux Church and dates from the 15th century. It has some fine carving and once held a chained book, which is now in the vestry. The pulpit is dated 1634 and is by Nicholas Hall. Records show that it was seven years before he was paid for it.

All Saints' Church has strong connections with the city's Guilds, some of which have been in continuous existence since Medieval times. On the south wall hang many of the Guilds' shields. Also on the south wall are two lenses from the ancient tower light. The Lord Mayors' board records that 46 Lord Mayors have been buried here. The charity Boards in the church provide some interesting reading. On the north door of the church is a rare knocker which dates from the 12th century and represents the Mouth of Hell.

Outside the church, on the Pavement, Thomas Percy – the 7th Earl of Northumberland – was executed in 1572 on a scaffold especially set up for the purpose. His body was buried in an unmarked grave in the churchyard, whilst his head was displayed on Micklegate Bar.

ANGLIAN TOWER

Museum Gardens

Tucked away behind the Central Library, this tower was built between AD 600 and 700 in a breach in the 4th-century Roman fortress. It is constructed of limestone from the nearby Howardian Hills. Later ramparts buried the tower, until 1839 when a tunnel being dug into the bank came against it. In 1969 it was excavated by archaeologist Jeffrey Radley who was tragically killed in 1970 by an earth fall near by. Adjacent to the tower are four banks showing the height of the ground in Roman times, the Dark Ages, the Norman and the Medieval periods.

ARMY MUSEUM

The Regimental Museum of the 4/7th Royal Dragoon Guards and the Prince of Wales's Own Regiment of Yorkshire

Tower Street
This modern museum traces the history of these two famous regiments from when King James II in 1685 first raised the Regiments to assist him in crushing the Duke of Monmouth's rebellion. Yorkshire is the recruiting ground for both and the Battle Honours emblazoned on their Guidons and Colours embody the history of the British Army over 300 years.

The museum has displays of the Old Regimental Colours, Guidons, weapons, medals and uniforms. Showcases contain models of the many battles in which the two Regiments have fought in India, the North-West Frontier, Egypt, Sudan, Canada, America and Europe. Further displays show the Regiments' action during both World Wars.

The Regimental March of The Prince of Wales's own Regiment of Yorkshire is unique as the only March in the British Army to have its origins in the field. The 4/7th Royal Dragoon Guards was the first Regiment to see action in the 1914–18 war, in a minor skirmish near Mons in Belgium.

ART GALLERY

Exhibition Square
Overlooking Exhibition Square, the building has a five-arch portico containing four roundels of some notable York artists, Camidge (musician), Carr (architect), Flaxman (sculptor) and Etty (painter). The gallery has many old masters and includes the Lycett Green collection given in 1955. Another collection of English paintings is dominated by William Etty (1787–1849), who was born in York. His statue stands in Exhibition Square. Also on display is a selection of Victorian and 20th-century paintings. There is a regular programme of temporary exhibitions.

ARTS CENTRE

St John's Church, Micklegate
The Arts Centre which is housed in St John's Church is a centre for theatre, films, live music and exhibitions. Part of the building is used as a café. St John's Church became redundant in 1934. The building dates from the late 12th century, with much of it being built in the 13th and 14th centuries. The old tower was blown down in a gale in 1552 and the half-timbered belfry that replaced it is a rare example of church building under the Parliamentarians. In 1850 the east wall was rebuilt when North Street was widened. The church contains four Medieval walls and two 17th-century ones.

ASSEMBLY ROOMS

Blake Street
Designed and built by Richard Boyle, the 3rd Earl of Burlington in 1730, the cost of the Assembly Rooms was raised by public subscription. It is one of the earliest neo-classical buildings in Europe. The main hall is in Egyptian style surrounded by 48 Corinthian columns with a clerestory above. At one end of the hall are the Royal Arms of Queen Victoria. In 1951 the Assembly Rooms were restored by York City Council.

Superb centrepiece depicting the Black Prince in battle, one of many fascinating exhibits in Tower Street's regimental museum

ASSIZE COURTS

Tower Street
Designed by John Carr, the Assize Courts were built between 1773 and 1777. The building which faces the Castle Museum across the green, known as 'The Eye of York', has a grand Ionic elevation and recessed portico. There are two fine courtrooms, still regularly used, which in the past have seen some notable trials – including those of Dick Turpin (1739), Eugene Aram (1759), the Luddites (1812), and the Peterloo rioters (1820). During court sittings the public is admitted to the Public Gallery.

ASTRONOMICAL OBSERVATORY

Museum Gardens
Located in the Museum Gardens, the Observatory was built by the Yorkshire Philosophical Society following the inaugural meeting of the British Association for the Advancement of Science in 1831. John Smeaton, who designed the famous Eddystone Lighthouse near Plymouth, designed the Observatory's rotating roof (which has since been replaced). The Observatory housed for many years the largest refracting telescope in the world, designed and built by Thomas Cook of York. His firm also built the Greenwich transit instrument. In 1981, to mark its 150th anniversary, the Observatory was restored, refitted and re-opened by HRH the Duke of Kent.

BAILE HILL

Bishopsgate Street
Situated at the junction of Bishopsgate Street and Skeldergate, Baile Hill is one of two man-made mounds standing on either side of the River Ouse. Baile Hill is on the west bank and the castle known as Clifford's Tower stands opposite on the east bank. On these mounds William the Conqueror built two castles during his campaign to quell resistance from the Saxons. In 1068 he built a castle where Clifford's Tower now stands and in the following year, 1069, he built another on Baile Hill. Like the earlier castle, this was constructed of wood and surrounded by a moat.

The motte and bailey covered an area of three acres and during

Medieval times was used for the grazing of cattle, archery practice and for various sports. In 1722 Baile Hill was planted with trees, and between 1802 and 1807 a prison known as the City and Ainsty Gaol was built here. Prisoners were later transferred to the new prison near Clifford's Tower, and the City and Ainsty Gaol was demolished in 1880. Undamaged building stone was used to provide the foundations of the new Skeldergate Bridge. By 1882 the bailey was levelled for housing development.

BARKER TOWER

Lendal Bridge
Standing in the shadow of Lendal Bridge, Barker Tower is also known as North Street Postern Tower. The name derives from the barkers who prepared oak bark for the nearby tanners' yard. In the 14th century the building consisted of a single storey and flat roof. An upper floor and conical roof were added in the 17th century. The tower has had many uses and was once a watch tower. A chain was hung between Barker and Lendal Towers across the river to prevent traders with goods entering the city without paying the tolls. For several centuries until Lendal Bridge was

A chain hung across the Ouse between the Barker (front) and Lendal Towers barred the progress of ships trying to avoid paying tolls

built in 1863, ferrymen leased the building and operated a ferry to the opposite bank. During the latter half of the 19th century the building was used as a mortuary for bodies pulled out of the river. More recently it was used by the Parks Department as a store. In 1970 the building was restored, and it is now a craft centre.

BISHOPTHORPE PALACE

Bishopthorpe
In 1230 Archbishop Walter de Grey bought the manor in the village of Thorpe St Andrew, now named Bishopthorpe, about three miles south of York. He demolished the manor house and used some of the stone to start a new one in 1241. The house was completed about 1250 and consisted of a great hall, a chapel and the Archbishop's rooms. Grey decided that when each Prelate ended his term of office the house should revert to the Dean and Chapter of York.

In 1364–5 private rooms were added by Archbishop Thoresby, and in 1483 a further extension doubled the residential part and improved the kitchens.

In 1647, during the Commonwealth, Bishopthorpe Palace was sold to Colonel White, who added north and south extensions. At the Restoration, Bishopthorpe reverted to the Church and the great hall was rebuilt in unusual brickwork by Archbishop Accepted Frewen. Quadrangular stables were added by Peter Atkinson in 1761–3. Between 1766 and 1769 an extension to the west of the house was added by Archbishop Drummond, which provided a new entrance hall and drawing room.

Bishopthorpe Palace today is not only the home of the Archbishop, but is used to entertain dignitaries and provide working accommodation for the chaplains and secretariat.

The building history of Bishopsthorpe Palace spans some seven centuries, from 1241. Its site is older.

BLACK SWAN INN

Peasholme Green

Situated in Peasholme Green, this Medieval timber-framed building has not always served as an inn. It was once the home of William Bowes, a wealthy merchant who in 1402 was elected Sheriff of York and in 1417 and 1428 Lord Mayor. During the reign of King Henry V he represented York in four Parliaments. In the 16th century Sir Martin Bowes was twice elected to the office of Lord Mayor of London, and was the goldsmith to Queen Elizabeth I.

The parents of the famous military leader General Wolfe lived at the Inn between 1724 and 1726. The Black Swan has also served as an important coaching inn. On the first floor there is a fine Delft tile fireplace. Another room on the first floor was used for cock-fighting; this was illegal, and a grill was built into the wall overlooking the stairs for the convenience of a guard.

A striking architectural contrast at ancient Bootham Bar

BOOTHAM BAR (AM)

High Petergate

The only gate to stand on the site of the *Roman Porta Principalis Dextra*, Bootham Bar protected the road entering York from the north west. The archway dates from the 11th century and is the oldest of York's gates. Much of the building, however, dates from Medieval times. A barbican, said to be the first in York, was added later but was demolished in 1831. The Bar contains its original portcullis, which is now fixed in a raised position. In 1719 the interior of the Bar was remodelled. During the 19th century the artist William Etty, who led a party of conservationists, saved the Bar from being demolished altogether.

During Medieval times armed guards were posted on the Bar to guide visitors entering the city from the nearby Forest of Galtres, the main purpose being to protect them from packs of wolves. Heads of traitors have been exposed on the Bar, including Thomas Mowbray, the Earl Marshal in 1405, and three rebels who in 1663 were accused of attacking the restored monarchy. In 1894 three new statues were erected on top of the Bar to replace the decaying Medieval ones. They depict three 14th-century figures, Nicholas Langton Lord Mayor, a builder and a knight.

Leading away to the north-west is Bootham, which is derived from an old West Scandinavian word *Butham* meaning an area of temporary dwellings. During Medieval times the area was disputed between the City and St Mary's Abbey.

BORTHWICK INSTITUTE OF HISTORICAL RESEARCH

Peasholme Green
St Anthony's Hall, in which the Institute is housed, was built in the second half of the 15th century for the religious and social Guild and Fraternity of St Anthony. On the ground floor two sides are stone, two brick. The upper floor was originally of timber-framed structure. The roof has some fine timberwork, with interesting bosses. In 1627 the Guild was dissolved and St Anthony's Hall became an arsenal, then a workhouse, and later a prison. Between 1705 and 1946 it housed York's Bluecoat School. It is now the Borthwick Institute of Historical Research and belongs to the University. It has a collection of ecclesiastical archives and an exhibition of documents.

Victorian York Station, with its great, curving roof, is considered one of the finest of its type in the country. The site on which it stands is Roman

BRITISH RAIL EASTERN REGION HEADQUARTERS

Station Road
This large brick building is the Headquarters of British Rail Eastern Region, and was designed in 1906 by William Bell and Horace Field. The building exhibits many different styles of architecture, with Dutch gables and balconies. Its bricks were hand-made at Sudbury in Suffolk and its stone dressings are of Portland Stone. The large badges on the building are of the York and North Midland Railway, the Leeds Northern Railway and the York, Newcastle and Berwick Railway.

York Station, which is situated just outside the City Walls, is considered to be one of the great buildings of Victorian England. On the site of a Roman cemetery, the station was constructed between 1873 and 1877 when it was said to be the largest in the world. The building was designed by Thomas Prosser. The main platforms are covered by a sweeping, curved roof about 48 feet high, of which the uppermost part is of glass. The station opened on 25 June 1877, replacing the old station which was just inside the City Walls.

CASTLE MUSEUM, THE

Tower Street
Housed in the city's prisons, which were built within the Castle walls, conveniently next to the Assize Courts in the 18th century, the Museum contains perhaps the most comprehensive and imaginatively displayed collection of domestic 'bygones' in the world.

'Bygones' was the name that John Lamplugh Kirk, a young country doctor at the beginning of this century at Pickering on the edge of the North York Moors, gave to everyday objects used by country people and which were fast disappearing. What other people threw out, he collected and as his collection grew, patients sometimes gave him things in return for treatment – everything from furniture, farm implements, fireplaces and shop fittings, down to policemen's truncheons and Valentine cards.

His vision was that, properly cared for and displayed, his collection would depict a way of life that would soon be gone forever. He approached several towns and cities in Yorkshire, but none accepted his offer until York, on the instigation of Alderman J B Morrell, agreed to convert the old Female Prison to house the 'Kirk Museum'. Most of the displays and reconstructed rooms and streets owe their inspiration to Dr Kirk's designs and advice. His was one of the first of the folk museums where visitors were invited to walk right into the past and where every detail was authentic.

The Museum was an immediate success when it opened in 1938, and Dr Kirk lived another two years to enjoy it.

The highlights of the Museum are the period rooms and two reconstructed indoor streets. The Victorian cobbled street is built in what was once the prison's open-roofed exercise yard. Complete with hansom cab (Joseph Hansom was born in York), pawnbrokers, tallow-candle factory, post office, police station, haberdashers, toyshop and – exuding the aroma of sugar-mice and humbugs – the original sweet shop of Joseph Terry.

An Edwardian courtyard contains an ironmongers' shop stacked to the ceiling with every conceivable item, its 'Strong errand boy wanted' notice still unanswered. The King William Hotel advertises 'Good Beds for Cyclists' and in the bar a penny-in-the-slot Polyphone grinds out a tune to order. The garage houses Dr Kirk's veteran cars – look for his doctor's bag left on the seat and his motoring trophies in the glass case.

In the original 18th-century cells are the workshops of craftsmen, the brush-maker, the comb-maker, the printer, the pipemaker, and the clogger – to name a few. Starkly empty, however, is the condemned cell where that most infamous of criminals, Dick Turpin the highwayman, was imprisoned before being hanged in 1739.

There are four centuries of everyday life depicted at the Castle Museum, with extensive galleries – from Dr Kirk's collection of fire-insurance marks, to musical instruments, toys and costumes.

Befitting York's standing as a great military centre for over 2,000 years, the city's collection of militaria is reputedly one of the finest in the country. The Anglo-Saxon helmet found in Coppergate in 1982 is here. Dating from the 8th century, it is made of iron with brass fittings and is richly decorated. Only the third ever found, it is the most complete, with even the chain-mail still in place. Coming through the centuries, the visitor sees a re-created First World War trench with sound effects and the contrasting Officers' Mess next door.

Among several major attractions at the Castle Museum are two reproduction 'period' streets, complete with shop fronts, fixtures, cobbles, and various appropriate vehicles

CLIFFORD'S TOWER (AM)

Tower Street

In 1068 William the Conqueror journeyed to York to quell Saxon resistance. He built a wooden castle on top of a large mound which is now known as Clifford's Tower. Across the River Ouse from Clifford's Tower is Baile Hill, where William built a second castle the following year.

Henry II carried out further work on the castle. In March 1190 it was burnt down by a mob which had driven the Jews of York to seek refuge there. It was rebuilt, again in timber. During the reign of King John it was rebuilt in stone. During the 13th century Henry III spent a small fortune on building work. By 1312 it was complete.

The castle mound was surrounded by a moat fed by the River Foss. From the onset there were problems with subsidence and flooding, and in 1360 the tower cracked from top to bottom in two places.

Since 1596 York castle has been known as Clifford's Tower, possibly because the body of Roger de Clifford was hung in chains from the tower in 1322 after the Royal forces had defeated a band of rebels at Boroughbridge.

The powerful bulk of Clifford's Tower is a reminder of William I's strongarm tactics at York during the mid-11th century

During the 14th century the castle buildings served as the administrative centre for Yorkshire and also the county gaol. By the 15th century Clifford's Tower had been abandoned for a while and was

Sumptuous decor and fine furnishings are the norm at 18th-century Fairfax House, a showpiece of style

falling into disrepair. By the 16th century a gaoler named Robert Redhead decided to demolish the tower, but the citizens of York and the Corporation soon stopped him as they considered Clifford's Tower to be a treasure of beauty second only to the Minster.

The Royalists garrisoned Clifford's Tower during the Civil War, but they surrendered to the Parliamentarians after the Battle of Marston Moor in 1644. In 1684 a fire gutted the interior. By 1825 Clifford's Tower was bought and included in the grounds of the new prison then under construction. For the next 110 years there was no public access, and a high wall surrounded the area. By 1935 parts of the prison had been demolished.

Clifford's Tower is an ancient monument in the care of the Historic Buildings and Monuments Commission for England, popularly known as English Heritage.

DE GREY ROOMS

St Leonard's Place

Now the Tourist Information Office, De Grey Rooms were built by G T Andrews in 1841–2 and have been little altered. There are round-headed windows with pediments. The building served as an officers' mess for the Yorkshire Hussars. It has also been used for concerts, public meetings and entertainments.

FAIRFAX HOUSE

Castlegate

Fairfax is an elegant 18th-century house with a richly-decorated interior. It contains the Terry Collection which was given by the great grandson of the founder of the Terry confectionery business, Mr Noel Terry, who died in 1980 and who was the Honorary Treasurer of the York Civic Trust for 25 years. The collection contains fine Georgian furniture, porcelain, paintings and clocks. In the past the house has had various uses, including a cinema and dance hall. In 1983 the house was acquired by the York Civic Trust and restored.

FISHERGATE BAR

George Street

One of six lesser gateways to the city, Fishergate was built in the 15th century and has also been known as St George's Bar. The

*Detail of the fine wood carving
preserved at Herbert House*

central arch was made wide with
round grooves to enable the
portcullis to be raised and lowered
easily. Heavy taxation in 1489
resulted in the peasants hereabouts
rioting and setting fire to the gate,
and as a result it was bricked up.
The scorch marks can still be seen
beneath the central arch. In 1827
the gate was re-opened, providing
access to the nearby cattle market.
Access through the Bar is now
restricted to pedestrians and
bicycles.

FISHERGATE POSTERN TOWER

Piccadilly
Of York's six original postern
towers, the one at Fishergate is the
only one to remain unaltered. On
the side of the tower is an arched
gateway; this is called the postern.
The gateway once had a portcullis
and the groove is still visible,
together with the crook hinges of
the wooden door. The base of the
tower once overlooked King's
Pool, which separated it from
York Castle. A projecting lavatory
on the first floor once discharged
into the lake.

FRIARGATE WAX MUSEUM

Lower Friargate
Housed in Friargate, the Museum
exhibits 60 of the world's best-
known characters, re-created in
wax in realistic surroundings,
including sound effects. The
collection includes members of the
Royal family, Margaret Thatcher,
Ronald Reagan, Winston
Churchill, Adolf Hitler, Ghandi
and many more. Recent
acquisitions include the Duke and
Duchess of York.

GUILDHALL (AM)

Lendal
There has been a guildhall on this
site since 1378, but the present
building dates from 1446. The hall
was first used for festivities and
for Pageants and Mystery Plays.
The west window contains stained
glass which dates from 1682, by
Henry Giles, a York glass painter.
Many of the windows in the
Guildhall were unglazed until the
middle of the 18th century.
On 29 April 1942 an air raid
virtually destroyed the building,
leaving only a shell. Subsequently,
the Guildhall was painstakingly
restored as an exact replica. In

1960 it was re-opened by Queen
Elizabeth the Queen Mother. The
building now contains an arch-
braced roof decorated with
colourful bosses and supported by
12 solid-oak pillars. A fine
modern stained-glass window by
Harry Harvey depicts the story of
York, including its architecture,
local military history, the city
arms and civic processions, fairs
and markets, and education and
social life. Adjoining the Guildhall
is the Inner Chamber, which is
now used as a committee room.
This part of the Guildhall escaped
destruction in 1942. It was in this
room that the £200,000 reward
was counted before being paid to
the Scots for helping Cromwell in
the Civil War. The room has also
two secret doors. A passageway
runs beneath the Guildhall to the
river.

*Appropriately, York's fine and
beautifully-restored 15th-century
Guildhall includes a modern stained-
glass window depicting the city's long
and colourful history*

HERBERT HOUSE

Pavement
One of the finest timbered houses
in York and dating from 1620,
Herbert House is known for its
richly-carved woodwork.
Christopher Herbert, a wealthly
merchant and Lord Mayor of
London, bought a house on this
site in 1557. His great grandson
Sir Thomas Herbert was born in
the house in 1606, and was
Gentlemen of the Bedchamber to
Charles I. Alongside Herbert
House is Lady Peckitt's Yard,
a Medieval alleyway with
overhanging houses. The yard is
named after the wife of Lord
Mayor Peckitt (1702–3).

HOLY TRINITY CHURCH

Goodramgate
Holy Trinity is one of York's most fascinating old churches, tucked away behind shops. It was constructed between 1250 and 1500 on the site of an earlier church. The tower has a rare saddle-back pitched roof. The interior comprises a nave with north and south aisles and a chapel on the southern side. This was at one time blocked off and used only by lepers. A squint (or hagioscope), a hole in the wall which can still be seen today, enabled the lepers to see the high altar. The church also contains many Jacobean box pews which sit unevenly on the undulating floor; the altar rail is also Jacobean. The double-decker pulpit dates from 1785. The eastern window contains some ancient glass. Holy Trinity was untouched by the Victorians and remains a good example of how a church was arranged after the Reformation. It is maintained by The Friends of Holy Trinity.

This hole, or 'squint', allowed lepers to join in the worship at Holy Trinity Church, in Micklegate

HOLY TRINITY CHURCH

Micklegate
This church originally formed part of a Benedictine priory founded in 1089 by Ralph Pagnell and attached to the Abbey of Marmoutier, near Tours. In 1137 the church was badly damaged by fire and was rebuilt between the late 12th and mid-13th century. In 1397 Richard II attended the church. The priory was dissolved in 1538 and the church became parochial. In 1552 the tower collapsed, bringing down the chancel. A new tower was built; 19th-century restoration work included the building of a new chancel and the addition of a south aisle. The west front and porch were rebuilt between 1902 and 1905. The 16th-century roof retains some earlier timberwork, and portions of the west pillars are Norman. A memorial to Dr John Burton, historian and prototype of Dr Slop in Laurence Sterne's *Tristram Shandy,* is on the south wall of the chancel. The church has three Kempe windows. Medieval Mystery Plays were first performed outside the gateway of Holy Trinity Priory. The Priory was demolished in 1856 and moved to other parts of the city. The churchyard retains some ancient stocks.

HOSPITIUM

Museum Gardens, Museum Street
Situated in the Museum Gardens and not far from the River Ouse, this building once served as the guest house for St Mary's Abbey. The ground floor was built about 1310, whilst the timber-framed first floor dates from 1420. The building has been much restored over the years and a new roof was added in 1930. It is currently closed to the public.

ICE HOUSE, THE

South-East of Monk Bar
Some 50 yards south-east of Monk Bar is an ice house which stands on the rampart outside the City Wall. Ice houses were used to store ice which was collected in winter (for domestic use in summer), and packed between layers of straw.
    They incorporated deep, brick-lined pits which had a domed roof above ground, surrounded by soil, and were reached by an enclosed access passage. This particular ice house was constructed in 1800.

IMPRESSIONS GALLERY OF PHOTOGRAPHY

Colliergate
Two galleries located above this shop display many historic photographs of York, from the last century until the present day. They include some interesting photographs of the Minster. There is a further gallery on the ground floor.

Detail from the rare, canopied wooden porch of Jacob's Well

JACOB'S WELL

Trinity Lane
Situated in a less-visited part of York, Jacob's Well is a fine, small, timbered house in Trinity Lane. It has a unique 15th-century canopied wooden porch, a type that was once common in York. The porch was transported here from a house in Davygate and is York's only surviving example.

Period tableau of a Viking household, part of the extensive Jorvik Centre museum and displays

JORVIK VIKING CENTRE

Coppergate

In the 9th century, the Vikings set about the conquest of England. York was rich and the home of kings, and the invading armies from Scandinavia were quick to attack and conquer it. The new Viking rulers swiftly rebuilt *Jorvik,* and soon streets of houses and workshops began to thrive. One of the main streets in the town was called Coppergate, and the Vikings who lived there were craftsmen. It was here, between 1976 and 1981, that the York Archaeologists Trust made astounding discoveries in a series of excavations.

The head-high remains of houses and workshops, plus tools, clothing and shoes were uncovered – in fact, the minute details of everyday life a thousand years ago. The dig shed a totally new light on the northern Viking kingdom based on York. Its trade with the rest of the world, the crafts that took place here, even the health and living conditions of its inhabitants, were revealed by a pioneering study of tiny plant and animal remains in the soil.

The Jorvik Viking Centre is built above the Coppergate dig and opened in 1984. It involves an imaginative presentation of the actual archaeological remains, the manificent timber buildings, leather, textile and metal objects, together with a detailed and vivid reconstruction of the street.

The 'journey' around the Centre is made in a number of distinct stages. Firstly, in the orientation hall, clear and concise displays explain who the Vikings were, dispelling some of the common myths and misconceptions. The journey back in time begins as visitors step into the four-seater 'time-cars' which are electronically guided along a track laid in the concrete floor. The passage through the time tunnel starts with a procession of figures representing the different eras from World War II back to Norman times.

Having been given a perspective of the time span they are passing through, visitors find themselves in a full-scale reconstruction of 10th-century Coppergate. The street scene includes a bustling market, craftsmen working in antler and wood, a family gathered around the hearth, and a river wharf where a rowing boat and a fully-rigged sailing ship are moored. The scene is given added authenticity with recordings of voices speaking in Old Norse. The atmosphere is completed by the sophisticated lighting system, and by bringing to life the smells which would have permeated such a street – from the scent of fresh fruit (in the market) and a tasty stew for the evening meal, to the less appetising aroma of pigsties and backyards.

The second sequence of the 13-minute journey passes through a reconstruction of Coppergate as it was when the dig of the 1970s was in progress. Displayed here are the original timbers, located where they were found.

The tour of Jorvik ends in the Skipper Gallery, which has a rich display of 500 of the 15,000 small and delicate objects rescued from the excavation.

JUDGES' LODGINGS

Lendal
These were built about 1720 on the site of St Wilfred's Church by William Kent for Dr Clifton Wintringham (1689–1748), a well-known physician. He was father of Sir Clifton Wintringham, physician to George III. The building served as lodgings for HM Judges of Assize between 1806 and 1979, then the building was converted into an hotel. Over the main door is the carved head of Aesculapius, the Greek god of healing.

KING'S MANOR

Exhibition Square
Built about 1280 as a residence for the Abbot of St Mary's Abbey and enlarged at the end of the 15th century by Abbot Sever, this building became the Headquarters of the Council of the North after the Dissolution of the Monasteries, and here resided the Lord President. Despite being owned by the King, the building never became a Royal residence. However, Henry VIII is recorded as staying there with Anne Boleyn and again with Catherine Howard. Charles I and Charles II also stayed there. The Royal coat of arms of Charles I can be seen above the main door. James VI of Scotland also stayed at the King's Manor en route from Scotland to London before becoming James I of England, and his monogram appears on another doorway. Charles I moved his court to York and stayed at the King's Manor on several occasions. Between 1628 and 1640 it was also occupied by the Earl of Stratford. The Council of the North was disbanded in 1641 and the King's Manor was converted into private dwelling houses. It later became a girls' school and from 1835 was the home of the Yorkshire School for the Blind. It was at this time that the headmaster's house was built near by – a good example of 19th-century work.

Today the building belongs to the University of York. Parts are open to the public, including the splendid Huntingdon Room in the north wing. This was built by Henry Hastings, the Earl of Huntingdon, Lord President 1572–95. Of note is a fine plaster frieze incorporating a Tudor badge, and an unusual chimney-piece.

LADY ROW

Goodramgate
This group of buildings in Goodramgate is the oldest row of cottages surviving in York. They were built in the year 1316 in the churchyard of Holy Trinity to endow a chantry of the Blessed Virgin Mary. The buildings are the earliest example in England of an upper floor projecting beyond the lower. The name Goodramgate derives from the 12th-century Scandinavian word *Gutherungate*.

LEETHAM'S MILL

Navigation Road
A towering building dominating the skyline north of Walmgate, this Mill is surrounded on three sides by the River Foss and Wormald's Cut. The building was erected in 1895–6 to designs of W G Penty. Its main tower has cylindrical turrets and battlements. The building is best viewed from behind the Telephone Exchange.

LENDAL TOWER

Lendal Bridge
On the opposite bank of the Ouse to Barker Tower, Lendal was once linked to it by a chain that prevented boats entering the city without paying taxes. Lendal Tower has been much altered, and in 1677 was made taller using stone from the ruins of St Mary's Abbey. There was an attempt in 1616 to supply the city with piped water from this point, using a waterwheel and hollowed-out tree trunks. The scheme proved generally unsuccessfull.

Lendal Tower, which guards the River Ouse from a bankside position directly opposite Barker Tower

MANSION HOUSE

Coney Street
This building is the official residence of the Lord Mayor during his term of office. Built between 1725 and 1730, the house was designed by Richard Boyle, Earl of Burlington. In the pediment is the city coat of arms – five golden lions superimposed on a red cross surrounded by four Ionic pilasters. The interior of the Mansion House is richly furnished. There is a valuable collection of antique silver plate, including Sigismund's Sword (1416), the Great Mace (1647), a Cap of Maintenance (1580) and a gold cup by Marmaduke Best of York (1671). The Mansion House is not normally open to the public, but may be visited by prior application at the discretion of the Lord Mayor. Near by is the site of Praetorian Gate, once principal entrance to the Roman city.

MARGARET CLITHEROW'S SHRINE

Shambles

Margaret Clitherow was born in the Shambles in 1556. At the age of 15 she married a butcher who had his business at No. 10 Shambles. An upstairs room in the house was kept to hide Catholic priests from persecution, and under darkness Margaret Clitherow would smuggle them in and out of York. In 1586 she was caught and tried at the Assizes and was sentenced to death by being pressed under a heavy wooden door on which rocks were placed. At this time, when Queen Elizabeth I was on the throne, the Catholic faith was renounced. On 25 October 1970 Margaret Clitherow was made a saint, and a house in the Shambles has been set aside as a shrine to her.

MARYGATE TOWER

Bootham

This small round building at the junction of Bootham and Marygate formed part of the fortifications of St Mary's Abbey. The building dates mostly from the late 14th century. After the Dissolution of the Monasteries the building became the repository for the records of the Yorkshire monasteries. On 16 June 1644 Parliamentarian besiegers successfully mined the tower, blowing it up and destroying the records. Through the breach they spread into the Abbey Grounds to attack the King's Manor. The Royalists, seeing this attack, marched up Marygate and in the following battle the Parliamentarians were caught in a trap. Those who were not killed surrendered.

The tower was later rebuilt on a smaller scale, together with the adjoining wall which too had been destroyed during the siege. Today, sections of the Abbey Wall can be seen running south-west alongside Marygate and south-east alongside Bootham.

MERCHANT ADVENTURERS' HALL

Fossgate

Reached through an alleyway from Fossgate, over which is the coat of arms of the Merchant Adventurers' Company, the hall was founded in 1357 as a religious institution, the Guild of Our Lord and the Blessed Virgin. The building subsequently became the home of the Merchant

Fine timbering and aristocratic banners bring history closer at the Merchant Adventurers' Hall

Adventurers' Company of the City of York, and Edward III granted the company a licence. The building comprises an Undercroft, Chapel and Great Hall.

The Undercroft is the oldest part of the building. The chapel was rebuilt in 1411 and retains part of the original 15th-century oak screen and a 17th-century pulpit. The Great Hall is the largest timber-framed building in York and contains several portraits of past Governors and benefactors. There are many colourful banners of York's Medieval Guilds in the hall.

In its time the Merchant Adventurers' Company was one of the most powerful in York, dealing with foreign trade and bringing trade into York and the surrounding area.

Heraldic glass (top) in the Merchant Taylors' Hall, and (inset) Micklegate Bar – the city's most important entrance

MICKLEGATE BAR (AM)

Micklegate
The most important gate to the city, being the main entrance from London, this Bar was erected between 1196 and 1230 – although the foundations are older. The Bar originally had a barbican, but this was demolished in 1826. On the face of the Bar are the arms of the city of York and the arms of Edward III. Above the King's arms is his crested helmet. Nearly every sovereign in England from William the Conqueror to Edward VII has entered York through this gateway. Micklegate Bar was made famous as it was regularly used to expose the heads of traitors, among them the heads of Lord Scrope of Mastan (1415), Richard, Duke of York after the Battle of Wakefield in 1460, The Earl of Devon after the Battle of Towton (1461) and The Earl of Northumberland in 1572. The last heads to be exposed on the Bar were those of the Jacobites William Conolly and James Mayne in 1746, after the Battle of Culloden. The Bar was extensively and sympathetically restored in 1952.

MINSTER LIBRARY

Deanery Gardens
Located in Deanery Gardens to the north of the Minster, the main part of the Library was built about 1230 by Archbishop Walter Gray as a private chapel for his York Palace. On 8 September 1483 King Richard III invested his son as Prince of Wales here. By the 16th century the chapel had become derelict, but between 1806 and 1813 it was restored to accommodate the Minster Library, which with 6,000 volumes had become too large to be stored in the Minster. The building has been extended in recent years, with a wing added for the archives and local history section in 1959–60 and a reading room in 1962–3.

The original Minster Library was begun in AD 750 under the impetus of successive archbishops, notably Egbert, Albert and Alcuin; the latter was directly in charge of the Library between 778 and 781. Unfortunately, the Viking raids of the 860s destroyed all the early material and in 1069 the collection was destroyed by William the Conqueror.

During the Middle Ages there

MERCHANT TAYLORS' HALL

Aldwalk
The Company of the Merchant Taylors has been known by that name since its members received a Royal Charter of Incorporation from King Charles II in 1662, which allowed three distinct Medieval York guilds, – the tailors', drapers' and hosiers' – to be amalgamated into one large company. Its primary function was the economic regulation of the clothing trades, but in 1835 the removal of all guild restrictions on industry jeopardised its survival. However, the company owed much of its cohesion and vitality to the ownership and maintenance of its late 14th-century Great Hall, now the only example of a craft guild hall in the city.

Within the brick exteriors of 1672 and 1715 the original internal fabric of both the Great Hall and the Little Hall survives intact. The older Great Hall, 60 feet long and 30 feet high, still preserves its 14th-century arch-braced roof and the main outer doorway. The large fireplace, originally of 1730 and rebuilt last century, is of interest. The Little Hall is probably of Tudor origin, its most striking features being two heraldic windows. Near by are the Almshouses built in 1729–30, which are still inhabited.

Since the Middle Ages Merchant Taylors' Hall has been used for a wide variety of social, ceremonial and other functions, including judicial courtroom, theatre and schoolroom.

was no Cathedral library as the Minster Clergy had its own private collection of books. The present collection was begun in 1414 when John Newton, the Canon Treasurer, bequeathed 40 books to start a library. The library soon grew and in 1628 Archbishop Tobie Mattrew donated his collection of 3,000 books. Today the Minster Library contains some 90,000 volumes, of which 20,000 are early books, and is the largest Cathedral library in the country. The Library covers a wide range of subjects from theology and church history to art and architecture. Also included in the library are maps, prints and Medieval illuminated manuscripts. Visitors are able to see the showcases on the first floor, which include the parish register of the Church of St Michael-le-Belfry, showing the baptism of Guy Fawke (Guy Fawkes) on 16 April 1570. There is a signature of Anne Boleyn, one of the six wives of Henry VIII, and an example of the first edition of King James I's authorised version of the Bible of 1611, complete with chain. The first printed map of Yorkshire, dated 1577 by Christopher Saxton, is also on show.

MONK BAR (AM)

Goodramgate
Built to replace an earlier gateway a short distance to the north-west, Monk Bar was originally known as Monkgate Bar and is most probably named after the monks of a nearby monastery. The Bar stands on the line of the Roman wall and is the tallest of York's Bars at 63 feet. During the 14th century the Bar was built as a three-storey structure with an additional storey being added in the 15th century. The Bar had the strongest defences on the City Walls, being a self-contained fortress with each floor defensible even if the others had been captured. The rooms, which in their time have been used as a Freeman's Prison, have fine stone-vaulted ceilings and bartizans – small circular rooms.

In 1825 the barbican was removed. The portcullis, however, has been restored and is in working order. On the outer side of the Bar is the coat of arms of the Plantagents. During 1953 the Bar was extensively restored and in 1979 it was strengthened. The Bar today is open to the public and serves as a small art gallery.

MULTANGULAR TOWER

Museum Gardens
The best-preserved Roman remains in York, the Multangular Tower formed the south-western corner of the Legionary Fortress of *Eboracum*. The tower can be viewed from either the Museum Gardens or from the green alongside the Central Library. The lower 19 feet are Roman and date from about AD 300. The remainder of the tower was added in the 13th century. In 1831 the interior was cleared out, revealing Roman walling and chisel marks made by Roman masons. Several stone Roman coffins, found in various parts of York, are laid out inside the tower. Features close by include the Yorkshire Museum, set in 10-acre gardens.

Authentic Roman building that formed part of the original fort, the Multangular Tower is an appropriate feature in the attractive and historic Museum Gardens

MUSEUM GARDENS

Museum Street
These gardens came into being in 1827 when the newly-formed Yorkshire Philosophical Society purchased three acres of land around the ruins of St Mary's Abbey, which included the Yorkshire Museum and the recently-restored observatory. The gardens were extended to five and a half acres in 1836 to take in the Hospitium and St Mary's Lodge, which was formerly the Abbey Gatehouse. By 1843 the gardens were extended yet again and soon afterwards a plan was prepared by Sir John Naysmyth for the enlarged gardens.

In 1961 the Yorkshire Philosophical Society transferred maintenance of the gardens to the York City Council. Then in 1974 the gardens became the responsibility of North Yorkshire County Council. Since 1978 the gardens have been managed by the Askham Bryan College.

Gleaming, gargantuan machinery has its place at the National Railway Museum – but not at the expense of small items like the luncheon basket and badge shown inset

NATIONAL RAILWAY MUSEUM

Leeman Road
The National Railway Museum in York has welcomed well over a million visitors every year since it opened in 1975. The steam railway was invented in Britain, and the collection chronicles the whole spectrum of British railway heritage from the earliest horse-drawn vehicles.

The Museum building was once part of the motive-power depot in York, and the Main Hall retains the atmosphere of the old steam-engine shed. The exhibits are arranged around two turntables; locomotives around one and carriages around the other. Motive power in the collection ranges from the ungainly *Agenoria*, built in 1829 by George Stephenson, to the prototype of British Rail's Experimental Advanced Passenger Train.

Among the more recent additions to the collection is the massive 190-ton steam locomotive that was built in Lancashire in 1935 for China, and presented back to the Museum 40 years later by their Minister of Railways. To the technically-minded, the Ellerman Lines *Pacific* locomotive is of particular interest. It was rescued from Barry scrapyard in 1973 and it has been 'sectioned' by removing 11 tons of metal from the right hand side, enabling visitors to see its interior construction. The most famous of all the locomotives in the National Collection is *Mallard*, which on 3 July 1938 reached 126mph (203km/h) and thus broke the world speed record for steam locomotives. The easy interchange of rolling stock by rail is facilitated by the Museum's direct rail connection with the British Rail system. This also enables the museum to operate some of its historic rolling stock and carriages.

The carriage collection includes magnificent Royal saloons complete with the opulent furnishings of a bygone age. Of all the Museum's Royal vehicles, it is probably Queen Victoria's saloon which attracts most interest. The carriage, constructed in 1869 and lavishly upholstered, is a superb example of Victorian design and workmanship. It was her favourite railway vehicle and the one in which she made her long journeys from the South of England to Balmoral. The collection also includes the more modern Royal vehicles of 1941 which were used by the present Royal Family until 1977. The ordinary passenger vehicles in the Museum range from the Bodmin and Wadsbridge carriages (parts dating from 1830s), to the British Railway Mk1 open saloon of the 1950s.

While it is undoubtedly the magnificent display of locomotives and carriages which first catches the visitor's eye upon entering the main hall, the Museum houses exhibitions covering the many facets of more than 150 years of railways in Britain.

On the balcony of the main hall, a wide range of historical material including timetables, model trains and railway equipment, tells the story of the social and economic developments of British railways. An audio-visual presentation illustrating the varied aspects of railway operations by means of colour slides and commentary has been prepared by museum staff, and is shown in a theatre. The Museum also has a fine collection of paintings, photographs, glass and chinaware which exemplifies the use made by the railways of art and design in their business.

OLD STARRE INN

Stonegate
Located in an alleyway off Stonegate, the Old Starre Inn is the oldest public house in York, dating from the middle of the 17th century. The building, however, has been much altered. The pub displays a rare beam sign across Stonegate.

RAIL RIDERS' WORLD

Railway Station, Tearoom Square
Hemmed in between the station and the Royal York Hotel, this museum has two very fine-detailed railway layouts. The larger of the two has as many as 20 trains running at any one time. There are hundreds of buildings, about 5,500 miniature trees, over 2,000 lights and around 2,500 people and animals. The second, much smaller layout shows a typical German town at night and is lit by hundreds of tiny lights. A third display is a static model of a typical coal-burning power station. York is well known among railway enthusiasts, having been the home of Hudson 'the Railway King'.

RED HOUSE

Duncombe Place
This fine Georgian house stands in Duncombe Place and was built for Sir William Robinson, Lord Mayor of York in 1700 and Member of Parliament for York 1697–1722. In 1725 the city council asked Sir William Robinson if he would give them the house for the use of the city; he declined, so the council went ahead to build the Mansion House. Over the main doorway is the city coat of arms and to the right is a torch snuffer.

RED TOWER

Foss Islands Road
Built in 1490 at the edge of the large lake known as King's Pool, which stretched northwards to the Layerthorpe Postern (now demolished), this tower is unique in the City Walls, being made of brick whereas the rest of the walls are constructed of magnesian limestone brought from nearby Tadcaster. The tower derives its name from the colour of its bricks. During 1644 the tower was severely damaged in a Civil War siege, but has since been restored. On its northern wall there is a projecting lavatory. The tower has had many uses, including the manufacture of gunpowder. It was also a stable.

ROMAN BATH INN

St Sampson Square
Large glass panels in the floor of this modern pub reveal remains of a Roman bath excavated in 1930–1. Visible is a corner of the *frigidarium* (cold bath), part of the *caldarium* (hot bath) and *hypocaust* pillars for heating.

ROMAN COLUMN

Minster Yard
Originally this Roman column, which stands 30 feet high, stood within the Great Hall of the Headquarters building of the Fortress of the Sixth Legion in about the 4th century AD. It was found during excavations within the Minster in 1969, lying where it had fallen. In 1971 the Dean and Chapter gave the pillar to the York Civic Trust, who erected it in Minster Yard to mark the 1,900th Anniversary of the arrival of the Romans in AD 71.

ST CRUX PARISH ROOM

Pavement
One of the finest Medieval churches in York stood on this site until its demolition in 1887. The church was dedicated to St Crux, an unknown Saint. However the church is mentioned in the *Domesday* book. A parish room is now on the site of the old church, and the building incorporates part of a Medieval wall and several post-Medieval brasses.

To the east of the parish room is a street with a curious name – Whip-ma-whop-ma-gate – York's longest name for its shortest street.

ST CUTHBERT'S CHURCH

Peasholme Green
After the Minster this is the second earliest known church in York. Roman stone is incorporated in the building. The church is largely 15th century, with earlier foundations. In 1547 it was threatened with demolition but the intervention of Sir Martin Bowes, who was a Lord Mayor of London, saved the building. Between 1724 and 1726 the parents of General Wolfe worshipped in the church when they lived at the nearby Black Swan Inn.

Today the church serves as an administrative centre for the parish of St Michael le Belfry. The interior has been largely spoilt by recent building.

ST DENY'S CHURCH

St Deny's Road
The church was once double its present size but in 1798 the nave and spire were demolished. During the 19th century there was further reconstruction of the tower. Most of the surviving building dates from around the mid-14th century. Features of note include a fine Norman doorway and the north aisle windows, which are examples of early 14th-century carved tracery. The church also contains some of the oldest glass in York, dating from the 12th century.

ST GEORGE'S CHURCHYARD

George Street
This small, quiet churchyard ringed by trees is the resting place of the notorious highwayman Dick Turpin. His grave can be easily identified as it is the only one in the churchyard that is upright.

Dick Turpin was born at Hempstead in Essex in 1706 and was the son of an innkeeper. He was apprenticed to a butcher but was caught stealing cattle, and as a result joined a gang of smugglers and deer stealers. Later he teamed up with highwayman Tom King, but accidently shot his partner dead. Dick Turpin escaped to Yorkshire, where he became a horse trader, but in 1739 he was caught horse stealing, was found guilty and condemned to death. On 7 April 1739 he was hanged at York Tyburn by the racecourse. The legend of Dick Turpin's ride from London to York on Black Bess as told in Harrison Ainsworth's romance *Rockwood* is fictitious.

ST HELEN'S CHURCH

Stonegate
St Helen's was built in the 14th century. During the 16th century it was partially demolished, but was saved by parishioners who obtained a private Act from Queen Mary to re-erect it. The font has a 12th-century bowl with a base from the 13th century. St Helen's was formally the Guild Church of the Medieval glass painters and in the south-west window is their coat of arms. Since the destruction of St Martin-le-Grand during the Second World War, St Helen's is now the Civic church when the Lord Mayor and Corporation attend Harvest Thanksgiving in state every year. St Helen's Square was originally the churchyard of St Helen's Church.

ST LAWRENCE'S CHURCH

Lawrence Street
A dominant building with a tall spire, this church lies a short distance outside the City Walls, south-east of Walmgate Bar. The original church of St Lawrence was largely destroyed during the Civil War in 1644, and the churchyard was the scene of some of the bitterest fighting. The church lay in ruins until 1669, when it was gradually restored. However, now only the tower remains. The parish registers date from 1606 and include the marriage of Sir John Vanbrugh, the architect of Blenheim and Castle Howard, to Henrietta Mana Yarburgh on 14 January 1719.

The new church dates from 1883 and is the largest parish church in York. It was built following an appeal by the vicar of St Lawrence, the Reverend George Frederick Wade. Due to its size the church has often been referred to as 'The Minster without the Walls'. Of note are three interesting stained-glass windows. The 14th-century font was transferred to the new church (usually locked).

Ancient St Leonard's Hospital – ruined but distinctively Norman

ST LEONARD'S HOSPITAL

Museum Street
A ruinous building on the western side of Museum Street, this one-time hospital comprises a vaulted undercroft with a chapel above, and was the largest in the north of England. It was founded soon after the Norman Conquest, attached to the Minster and first called St Peter's. When the building was destroyed by fire in 1137, it was rebuilt and enlarged by King Stephen and refounded as St Leonard's. It was dissolved in 1540 by Henry VIII. Between 1546 and 1697 part of the building was used as a Royal mint.

ST MARGARET'S CHURCH

Walmgate
Largely rebuilt in 1852 and now redundant, St Margaret's is of little historical interest except for its fine Norman porch and doorway. It is picturesquely set among trees.

ST MARTIN-CUM-GREGORY

Micklegate

Surrounded by trees and set back from Micklegate, this church is no longer used for services but is the premises of the Diocesan Youth Office. The building has much of interest to offer the visitor. The church dates from the 12th century. John Troushall, Rector in 1230, built additional aisles and much of the remainder of the church was constructed between the 13th and 15th centuries. The tower plinth is of Roman masonry from the Temple of Mithras, which stood opposite the gate. Several windows contain Medieval glass and the pulpit is Jacobean. The parish registers date from 1538 and include records of the Great Plague. William Peckitt (1731–95) is buried in the chancel and Henry Gyles (1645–1709) is buried in the churchyard; both were noted York glass painters. Until the 19th century a Butter Market was located outside the church and butter from surrounding areas was brought here to be viewed, searched, weighed and sealed.

ST MARTIN-LE-GRAND

Coney Street

The church, mainly 15th century on older foundations, was gutted by fire during an air raid in 1942 but has since been cleverly restored. It now consists of the 15th-century tower and 14th-century south aisle. The remainder of the building has been converted into a paved garden in

Finely-crafted Norman stonework on the porch at St Margaret's

Two notable features of St Martin-le-Grand are its fine clock and the Great West Window, only a detail of which is shown in this picture

remembrance of the fallen of the City of York in the two World Wars. The Great West Window, considered to be one of the finest 15th-century windows in the country, was removed for safety before World War II. It has since been replaced in the new north wall and depicts the life of St Martin of Tours in 13 scenes. Robert Semer, who gave the window in 1437 when he was vicar, is seen kneeling at the base.

Another feature outside the church is the distinctive clock which overlooks Coney Street. It was first erected on this site in 1668 and in 1754 was overhauled and renovated. In 1778 it was given a new dial. At the same time the little admiral was placed on it with his sextant which, until World War II, rotated. During an air raid of 1942 it was extensively damaged, but has since been restored, and was returned to its original position in 1966.

ST MARY'S

Bishophill Junior

Situated within the City Walls but in a relatively quiet area south-west of Ouse Bridge this church has a tower that retains some typical Saxon windows and herringbone work. Inside are remains of a Saxon cross. The aisles were built between the 12th and 14th centuries. The chancel was rebuilt in the 13th century and restored in 1860.

Features of two St Mary's – Saxon windows in the Bishophill Junior church (top) and remains of the Abbey in Museum Gardens (right)

ST MARY'S ABBEY (AM)

Museum Gardens
There are various stories of how St Mary's Abbey was founded, one of which begins with a soldier serving under William the Conqueror being saddened to see the damage the Danes had done to Whitby Abbey 200 years previously. The soldier decided to seek a monastic life and entered the Benedictine abbey at Evesham to train as a monk. Eventually he travelled north, along with two other monks, and was granted Whitby Abbey and surrounding lands by William de Percy. Stephen, another monk, joined them but quarrels developed between the monks and William de Percy which resulted in the monks fleeing to Lastingham, a small village north-west of Pickering. After further quarrels between the monks, Stephen departed for York and there he was given the minster church of St Olaf's (St Olave's) by Alan, Earl of Richmond.

When William II visited York in 1088 he found that Alan's provision of land for Stephen and his monks was inadequate, and a further 12 acres were added. In the following year a start was made on the abbey church.

The Abbey quickly became rich, and with Royal favours the strict monastic life for which the monastery had been set up became so relaxed that in 1132 the prior and 12 monks left to seek a stricter life. In doing so they eventually set up Fountains Abbey and were received into the Cistercian Order. Meanwhile, at St Mary's, monks were sent out to set up nine daughter houses in the north of England, the most important being at Wetherall and at St Bees.

St Mary's Abbey continued to become wealthier and the abbot very powerful. In the North of England only the abbots at Durham and York had the privilege of wearing a mitre and having a seat in Parliament. The Abbey had control of the area around Bootham and the abbot administered justice and collected taxes. This was unpopular with the local people, who from time to time rose in revolt. In 1262 when violence flared up the abbot was forced to flee. In 1266 a wall was begun to protect the Abbey, and in 1318 the wall was given towers and battlements.

In the early 14th century, during the war with Scotland, Edward II moved his government north to York from London and the Abbey accommodated the King's Chancery. During the 14th century a monk called John Gaytrick translated the Catechism into English verse.

The Abbey was dissolved in 1539 and pensions were found for the abbot and 49 monks. The Abbey was then partially pulled down and the stone used for local buildings. However, much remained standing well into the 17th century.

During the siege of York in 1644 the area saw some fierce fighting with many casualties around the Abbey. By the 18th century the Abbey was again reduced when it became a main source of building stone for many local buildings, including St Olave's Church and the County Gaol. Some stone from St Mary's Abbey even went to repair Beverley Minster.

When the Abbey grounds were acquired by the Yorkshire Philosophical Society a large-scale excavation was carried out to trace the flow plan of the Abbey. The Yorkshire Museum now covers part of the site and contains considerable collections of archaeological finds. The Abbey ruins, in fine botanical gardens, are used as the setting for the York Mystery Plays.

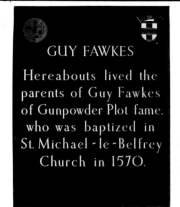

GUY FAWKES

Hereabouts lived the parents of Guy Fawkes of Gunpowder Plot fame, who was baptized in St. Michael - le - Belfrey Church in 1570.

A cautionary plaque

ST MICHAEL-LE-BELFRY

Minster Yard
The church is so named because of its closeness to the bell tower of the Minster. The present church was almost entirely rebuilt by the Minster's master mason John Forman between 1525 and 1536. An earlier church on the site was first recorded in 1294. The interior of the church has an interesting example of early Tudor ecclesiastical architecture. The western end of the church was rebuilt in the latter part of the 19th century. Much of the glass in the church is 16th century, which is unusual as this was a time when glass was scarce in York. The east window contains glass from about 1330, saved from the previous church. The panels in the centre row depict, from the left, St Peter and St Paul, the Annunciation, the Nativity, the Resurrection, and the Coronation of the Virgin. The reredos and rails are particularly fine, dating from 1712. Guy Fawkes was baptised in the church on 16 April 1570.

ST MICHAEL'S CHURCH

Spurriergate
St Michael's Church has been reduced in size by the widening of Spurriergate. The outer walls were rebuilt in 1821, which gives the church a drab appearance from the outside. The interior is far more interesting, with some fine late Norman arcades. The church also contains a fine 18th-century reredos and a rare 15th-century chalice brass. There is some 15th-century stained glass and part of a Jesse window. A daily curfew at 8 pm used to be tolled from the tower.

ST OLAVE'S CHURCH

Marygate
St Olave's Church was founded by Srivard, Earl of Northumbria in about 1050. The church, which at first was known as St Olaf's, (a Norwegian saint), passed to Alan, Earl of Brittany, after the Norman Conquest. He in turn gave it to Stephen, a monk from Whitby, to be the nucleus of a new monastery. Stephen was given four acres of ground when William Rufus visited the city in 1088 and as this was found to be inadequate a further 12 acres were given in the following year, when a start was made on St Mary's Abbey.

At the beginning of the 14th century a chapel was added to the western end of St Olave's church. However, the church gradually became neglected as it was thought unnecessary to retain two places of worship so close together. In 1395 the parishioners asked Archbishop Arundel to restore the church, but nothing was done until Archbishop Neville, in 1466, ordered the monks to assist in restoration. A tower was added in 1500.

Great damage was done in 1644 when Parliamentarian soldiers used the tower as a gun platform. The damage was not put right until 1721, when much of the church was restored and permission to use stone from the ruinous St Mary's Abbey was granted. In 1879 the chancel was extended at the eastern end, and the roof was restored in 1889. The east window contains some Medieval glass. In the churchyard is buried Sir William Etty, the famous York artist.

THE YORK MYSTERY PLAYS

Performed in the open-air setting of the ruins of St Mary's Abbey in the Museum Gardens, these Medieval plays form the nucleus of the four-yearly York Festival. They depict the whole sweep of the Bible, from Creation to the Day of Judgement, condensed into three or four hours and performed by a large cast of mainly local amateurs. The liveliness of the language, the special effects and the impressive setting draws audiences from all over the world.

From the early 14th century to the late 16th century they were performed every year, on the Feast of Corpus Christi in June (when the hours of daylight were longest), on pageant wagons trundled around the streets to traditional stopping places. The audience would watch from dawn to dusk, either at one station, where all 48 plays could be seen one after the other, or moving about the city to watch their favourites.

It was a matter of civic pride to

put on the best show possible every year, and any actor forgetting his lines, or any play failing to arrive on time, was subject to a heavy fine. The word *mystery* derives from the Medieval word meaning mastery or skill, and each play was the responsibility of one of the guilds. Thus, the Bakers performed the Last Supper, and the Pynners nailed Jesus to the Cross.

Although each city had its own

plays, those of York have survived most intact. The full script is today in the British Museum. One battered prompter's copy survives in York Archives.

The revival, in 1951, was York's contribution to the Festival of Britain. Many amateurs have established their own family traditions of taking part, and some (the most notable being Judi Dench), have gone on to successful professional careers.

Wood carver Robert Thompson's Mouse 'signature' (top) on a door at St William's College, the fine, timbered building pictured underneath

ST OSWALD'S HALL

St Oswald's Road, Fulford
Situated about one mile south of the city centre, St Oswald's Hall is a converted 800-year-old Norman chapel. The hall contains some early oak furniture, Medieval woodcarving, illuminated manuscripts, icons, metalwork and embroidery. The small surrounding gardens contain species of plants recorded as having been grown in the Medieval period. The site has been excavated revealing prehistoric, Roman and Saxon material. In 1349 victims of the Black Death were buried here.

ST PETER'S SCHOOL

Clifton
On the A19 about a mile north-west of the city centre, it is claimed that this school was founded by James the Deacon in 627 – but there is no definite evidence. Alain, who became an archbishop, was the school's most famous pupil and also master. In 1069 the library was destroyed by fire, and by the 13th century the school had moved to new premises, when the Minster nave was built. The school had a close connection with St Mary's Abbey, and at the Dissolution of the Monasteries was forced to close. Archbishop Holgate founded his Grammar School in 1546, and in 1557 the Dean and Chapter refounded their school under Royal Licence. At first it was situated in the Hospital of St Mary, Horsefair, then after 1644 in the Bedern and from 1833 in a new building in the close which is now the Choir School. In 1838 the Proprietary School in Clifton opened, but by 1844 it ran out of funds. The Minster School, however, had funds and no pupils. So an agreement was reached and the Clifton buildings were handed over to the Dean and Chapter. The present buildings date from the 19th century and consist largely of mock Gothic architecture.

ST SAMPSON'S CHURCH

Church Street
This 12th-century church was damaged by cannon fire in 1644. In 1848 the church was largely rebuilt, but in recent years became redundant until the York Civic Trust took it over in 1974 for

restoration. With a grant from the Hayward Foundation it has been convered into an Old Peoples' Day Centre.

ST SAVIOURGATE UNITARIAN CHAPEL

St Saviourgate
Set in a quieter part of York, the chapel, built in 1692–3, is the earliest surviving Nonconfirmist Church in York. The building was first used as a Presbyterian Chapel, but later became Unitarian. Between 1800 and 1858, Charles Wellbeloved, an eminent scholar and historian, ministered here. He is also buried here.

ST SAVIOUR'S CHURCH

St Saviourgate
This now redundant church dates from 1090 but was almost wholly rebuilt in Perpendicular style by R H Sharp in 1844–5. Its large 15th-century stained-glass window is now removed and forms the east window of All Saints' Church, Pavement.

In 1976–7 the York Civic Trust took over the church and it is now used as a store for artefacts of architectural, historical and archaeological interest by the York Archaeologist Trust.

ST WILLIAM'S COLLEGE

College Street
The finest building standing in College Street is half-timbered St William's College, which was built between 1465 and 1467. The building is dedicated to William Fitzherbert, great grandson of William the Conqueror, who became Archbishop of York in 1153. At first the building was used as a home for the Minster chantry priests. For a while after the Reformation Sir Henry Jenkins owned the building, until Charles I moved his court to York, when the building was used to house the royal printing press. Since then the building has had a variety of uses, and as a result became very dilapidated and was nearly pulled down. The building has some notable features, including oriel windows. The main wooden doors are by the famous wood-carver Robert Thompson whose trademark, a carved mouse, can be seen on the right-hand door. Above the main door is the stone figure of St William. Inside is a courtyard.

Today the building is used as a restaurant, exhibition centre and brass-rubbing centre. The brass-rubbing centre contains a wide selection of replica brasses from many English churches, and especially those in Yorkshire.

SHAMBLES

Colliergate to Coppergate
The Shambles is the most famous of York's Medieval streets. Its name derives from *Fleshammels*, the street of butchers and slaughter houses. The houses on either side were built so as to keep the street out of direct sunlight. Meat carcasses were hung from hooks outside the houses and displayed on shelves. Many hooks and shelves can still be seen today.

In Medieval times the street was strewn with offal and garbage and during warm weather the stench was unbearable. With overcrowding, bad water and poor sanitation, this area was ofen a source of plague, which ravaged York frequently between the 12th and 17th centuries. As late as 1830 there were still 25 butchers located in the Shambles.

A 'butchers' row' no longer, York's Shambles is a fine example of street architecture that has grown to suit the needs of centuries

STONEGATE

Blake Street to Lower Petergate
This ancient paved street was once used as the main route for carrying stone from barges moored near the Guildhall to the Minster. The street, which is Roman in origin, contains a number of historic buildings including St Helen's Church, Mulberry Hall, The Old Starre Inn and the Twelfth Century House. The rare beam sign of The Old Starre Inn dominates the street. Several alleyways lead from Stonegate. A printer's devil can be seen at the entrance to Coffee Yard, which signifies a printing industry that flourished in the City from early in the industry's history.

The rare beam sign of the Olde Starre Inne (top) in Stonegate is a commonplace sight for one aged inhabitant (left) – a printers' devil

THEATRE ROYAL

St Leonard's Place
The Theatre Royal's own repertory company alternates with touring productions, opera and ballet, and occasional amateur shows to create a continuous, all-year-round programme.

Although theatre outside London was still banned in the late 16th and early 17th centuries, the city actively encouraged Thomas Keregan, manager of an itinerant company of actors, to set up a theatre in a disused tennis court, in what is now Minster Yard, as a means of extending the winter social season. On his death, his widow took over and opened in 1744 the New Theatre in Mint Yard, on the site of the present building. The entrance was built over the vaulted cloisters of St Leonard's Hospital. The remains of the Medieval building can still

be seen backstage, giving credence to the theatre's own ghost, the 'Grey Lady'.

A series of managers had varied personal success in running the theatre. One of the most successful was Tate Wilkinson in the latter part of the 17th century. He bought a Royal Patent for the sum of £500 and brought financial stability and great names – including Mrs Sarah Siddons.

Among the stars in the following years were Edmund Kean in 1819, Sara Bernhardt in 1904 and Mrs Patrick Campbell a year later.

The Georgian theatre was remodelled in the 19th century, bringing the interior into a semi-circle and later adding the dress and upper circles. By 1888 it had assumed the characteristics of a typical Victorian theatre and a new façade and entrance were created on St Leonard's Place.

After resisting pressure to convert to music hall and later to a cinema in the 1920s, the non-

profit-making York Citizens' Theatre Ltd (later Trust) was formed. In 1935 it formed a weekly repertory company, building up a loyal local following and over the years providing opportunities for young actors and actresses and a varied diet of live theatre for York.

A new glass and concrete foyer and restaurant were added in 1967 and the auditorium was redecorated in its traditional Victorian style in the 1970s. In 1984 the Theatre Royal celebrated 250 years of permanent theatre in York.

TREASURER'S HOUSE (NT)

Minster Yard
The first Treasurer's House to stand on this site was built in about 1100. The first treasurer, Radulphus, was appointed by Thomas, Archbishop of York. The treasurer's duty was to look after the Minster's affairs. Treasurers were appointed right through the Middle Ages up until the Dissolution of the Monasteries, when the Minster was stripped of its treasures and

the office therefore abolished.

Treasurer's House then became a private house. Between 1628 and 1648 Thomas Young was its owner and he largely rebuilt it, remodelling the centre range which is now the hall. Further improvements to the house were made about 1700, when a fine staircase was built in the north-west wing and a remarkable plaster ceiling was added in the dining room.

By the 19th century the Treasurer's House was much in decline and had been divided into three dwelling houses. (Gray's Court, which adjoins, originally formed part of a single building with the Treasurer's House.) In 1897 Frank Green, a Yorkshire industrialist, rescued the house and in the following years carefully restored it. He built up a remarkable collection of early English china and pottery, 17th- and 18th-century glass, early oak furniture and many examples of French craftsmanship. Frank Green died in 1930 and left the house, together with its fine furniture, to the National Trust.

In the basement there are remains of the Roman building that once stood on this site.

An exhibition in the basement tells the story of the House since Roman times. There is a small walled garden.

Cool elegance in the Drawing Room of the Treasurer's House

TWELFTH CENTURY HOUSE

Stonegate
This ruined building is reached through an alleyway leading to Stonegate Gallery at No. 52A. Surrounding the paved courtyard on two sides are remains of a two-storey building of good Norman freestone. Evidence suggests that the building once had an undercroft which supported the first floor. One of the windows in the hall on the first floor remains, and has a shaft with a waterleaf capital between two lights. The windows were never glazed but had provision for wooden shutters. A house on the site was once used by Minster clergy until the 19th century. The few decorative details and the masonry that does survive fix the date of the building at around 1180, making it the oldest dwelling house of any substantial remains within York.

UNIVERSITY OF YORK

University Road, Heslington
The University of York has only been in existence since 1963 and now has almost 3,000 students. The University campus, some 190 acres, is set in the landscaped grounds of Heslington Hall. The six colleges, which provide both residential and teaching accommodation, are Alcuin, Derwent, Goodricke, Langwith, Vanbrugh and Wentworth.

The University is set around a large artificial lake, amongst mature trees, and each college is linked by bridges and covered walkways. The administration centre for the University is Heslington Hall, an Elizabethan mansion originally built for Thomas Eynns, Secretary of the Council of the North in 1568. The hall was bought by the Hesketh family in 1601, and despite the siege of 1644 the building survived. In 1708 the building passed to the Yarburgh family. Between 1852 and 1855 the hall was extensively rebuilt. It can best be seen from the southern end of University Road. The most outstanding building of the modern University is the Central Hall, which overlooks the lake in the middle of the campus. Other buildings of note are the Lyons Concert Hall, the J B Morrell Library, the Language Centre and the Physics, Chemistry and Biology laboratories. Two unusual structures on the campus are worth mentioning, both local landmarks – the conical water tower and the boiler-house chimney. The University also occupies some historic buildings in York, including St Anthony's Hall, King's Manor and Micklegate House.

The University gardens and walkways are open to the public, but not the building.

VICTORIA BAR

Victoria Street
This archway was constructed in
1837, the year of Queen Victoria's
accession. It was built to give
access between Bishophill, an area
inside the City Wall, and Nunnery
Lane. When the gateway was
being constructed a blocked
ancient gate known as 'Lounlith'
was found.

WALMGATE BAR (AM)

Walmgate
Probably built during the reign of
Edward I, the Bar is unique in
being the only one in England to
retain its barbican. The barbican
was added during the reign of
Edward III. The Bar guards the
approach to York from the south-
east. It retains a portcullis, 12th-
century archway and 15th-century
oak doors with a small wicket
gate for pedestrians.

The area around Walmgate Bar
took the brunt of the fighting in
the Civil War during 1644. The
Bar was extensively damaged, and
in 1648 stone from St Nicholas
Church (which was destroyed
during the siege) was used to
restore it. Bullet marks on the
face of the barbican gate and the
north turret resulting from the
siege can be still seen today. A
wood and plaster house perched
on the inner side of the Bar was
built in the latter part of the 16th
century and was originally
occupied by the gatekeeper. It is
now a bookshop. In 1959 the Bar
was completely renovated.

YORKSHIRE MUSEUM

Museum Street
The County Museum of North
Yorkshire houses the region's
most important archaeological,
geological and natural history
finds as well as mounting a
regular programme of major
exhibitions. It is set in 10 acres of
botanical gardens which contain
not only sweeping lawns with
strutting peacocks and friendly
squirrels, rare shrubs and well-
established trees, but also the only
remaining corner tower of the
Roman military fortress, known as
the Multangular Tower, plus
substantial remains of the
Medieval St Mary's Abbey – once
the most important Benedictine
monastery in the north of
England – and a restored 19th-
century observatory containing a

Ancient scaffolding that could raise a Minster, and the predatory ships that might have razed such a structure to the ground – all parts of York's story (overleaf), depicted at St Mary's Church by various displays

small exhibition of historical optical instruments.

Inside the neo-classical building, designed by the architect who was later responsible for the National Gallery, William Wilkins, are galleries of Roman, Anglo-Saxon and Viking life containing items of unique importance. In the newly-designed Roman Gallery is the splendid marble head of Constantine the Great, the first Christian Emperor, who lived and died in York. Look for the statue of Mars; the tombstone inscriptions that tell about prominent Roman citizens; a Roman lady's auburn hairpiece; the hoard of coins found in a jar; cooking utensils in the re-created kitchen, as well as pottery, glass and intricate jewellery.

In the Anglo-Saxon section note the delicate silver-gilt Ormside bowl, which dates from the 8th century and is one of the finest piece of metal works of this period to survive in Britain. It is adorned with coloured glass, animal and bird designs and plant scrolls, and was probably hidden by its owner to save it from the plundering Vikings. The Gilling sword, with its silver bands on the grip, was the wondrous find of a small boy gathering tadpoles in a North Yorkshire stream and was featured on BBC TV's *Blue Peter* programme.

The Vikings are represented by items of domestic life and craftsmen's tools found in York, including leather workings, shoes and boots and a fragile silk cap.

Downstairs an important collection of Medieval sculpture includes parts of the shrine of St William of York, originally in the Minster, and life-size figures of the prophets from St Mary's Abbey. The remains of the Abbey, which covered the whole area of the Museum Gardens, can still be seen in the basement, including the great fireplace of the Warming Room.

The Museum has over 100,000 specimens of minerals, rocks and fossils, not all on show. It was in order to house a collection of Ice Age bones of various prehistoric animals that the Museum was originally built in 1823 by the Yorkshire Philosophical Society.

Passing huge Roman mosaics on the staircase walls, the visitor enters the upstairs galleries which house pottery and porcelain from English Delft of 1600 to the present day. Here is one of the finest collections of Rockingham porcelain in the country, and many examples of oddities – such as the fuddling cup, which has six bowls in a circle and one spout.

Wildlife conservation has always been an important theme at the Museum, and Disappearing Wildlife, in association with David Bellamy, was one of several major exhibitions held there. Here the visitor is taken (with sound effects) through the woodlands and forests of the world, complete with live specimens of forest creatures.

The Tempest Anderson Hall, named after a noted York doctor and expert on volcanoes early this century, adjoins the Museum and can be hired for meetings, lectures, film shows and like functions.

YORKSHIRE MUSEUM OF FARMING

Murton

Set in eight acres of country park, three miles from the centre of York, the Museum, created in 1982, won the Unilever Award three years later for the Best Museum of Social and Industrial History in the Museum of the Year awards.

By means of live animals, displays and reconstructions, the Museum sets out to tell the history of the English countryside in the context of farming throughout the ages. Frequent craft demonstrations show that the old skills are still alive; they draw new enthusiasts for such things as spinning, weaving, corn-dolly making, butter making and stone walling.

The main sections to the Museum include the visitor centre with a shop selling gifts ranging from honey to homespun woollens; the Farmhouse Kitchen for traditional, home-baked refreshments; the lecture hall and library; the Four Seasons Building where, in an extensive display area life on the land is related to the season's tasks; the Livestock Building containing live farm animals and the tools of husbandry and the Outdoor Paddocks and demonstration area.

A range of tractors, from early models to present day products, stationary engines, giant threshing machines and hundreds of tools and utensils are popular with the more mechanically minded, while the homely reconstructions of a weaver's cottage, shepherd's hut and turn-of-the-century ironmonger's shop bring the domestic past to life.

In the spring, the Museum has an orphan lamb unit where children can help feed the lambs when they are small. In May, June and early July, the resident flocks of Wensleydales and Swaledales are shorn of their heavy fleeces. As with any farm, the blacksmith calls to see to the horses, although his methods have changed substantially since the days of the old forge, in the Lifestock Building.

The vet, too, may have to call from time to time. He now has more medicines at his disposal than James Herriot, Yorkshire's most famous vet, had in the 1930's when he set up in practice. His reconstructed surgery from that time is here, with many of the instruments actually used.

Outside, as well as the paddocks, there are a duck pond, bee garden and dovecote. An observation bee hive is a popular feature and on occasions a member of the local Beekeepers' Association is available to explain how honey is made.

In the Crop Show a selection of main crops can be seen in eight plots with graphic displays tracing their development from earliest times. Visitors are told that peas were a French fad of the 18th century, that beans were thought poisonous by the ancient Greeks, and that the humble potato has played its part in the history of the Western World.

An independent registered charity, the Museum was created by an alliance of the Yorkshire Farm Machinery Preservation Society, the Yorkshire Folk Park Trust and the York Livestock Centre.

YORK STORY

St Mary's, Castlegate
St Mary's Church, in which this permanent exhibition is housed, dates from the 11th century – but much of the building was constructed in the 15th century, when it was remodelled and extended. During excavations within the church between 1968

and 1970 an early 11th-century foundation stone was discovered with an inscription to the effect that the church was once a *Mynster*. However, this link has never been proved. The church has the tallest spire in York, which rises 152 feet.

In 1958 the church became redundant and stood empty until 1972, when the City Council bought it for five pence. With the aid of the York Civic Trust a heritage centre was planned.

Designed by James Gardner, The York Story Heritage Centre opened in 1975 during European Architectural Heritage Year. The centre traces the history and development of York over the last 1,000 years. There are audio-visual displays and a large three-dimensional model of York, plus a model of Medieval scaffolding.

YORK TYBURN

Tadcaster Road
Situated on the A1036 about a mile south-west of Micklegate and overlooking the racecourse is York Tyburn, the place of public execution. The most famous person to hang here was John Palmer, alias Dick Turpin, in 1739. The site is marked by a paved area with seats.

Skills and impedimentia of rural life as it was can be seen in the Yorkshire Museum of Farming

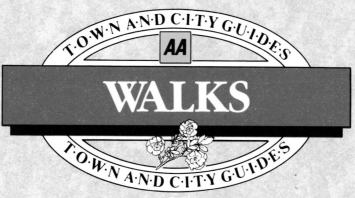

WALKS

TOWN AND CITY GUIDES

Family Walks in York

*The ancient City Walls provide an excellent route for
a walk which encircles the oldest parts of York – though
care should be taken, particularly with young children*

Around the City Wall

*T*here are several places to join this walk along the Medieval wall, but
a good place to start is at Bootham Bar, not far from the Minster and
York's shops. The walls are closed to the public between dusk and dawn.

*Fine stretch of the old walls,
arrowing towards York Minster*

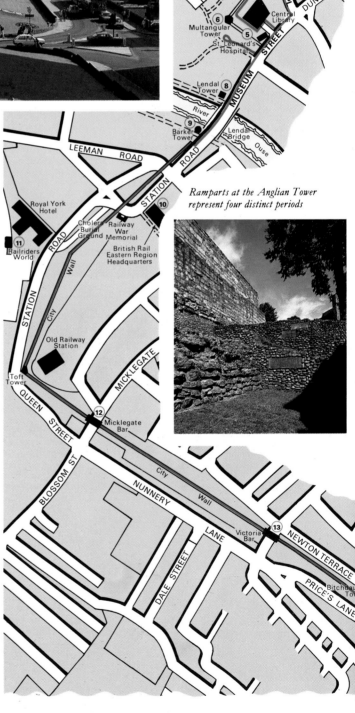

*Ramparts at the Anglian Tower
represent four distinct periods*

---

*Places in bold type are fully described
in alphabetical order (by name) in the
first gazetteer section – page 37. These
and other notable features are keyed to
the accompanying maps by number.*

From **Bootham Bar** ① cross St
Leonard's Place towards the **Art
Gallery** ②. To the left is the **King's
Manor** ③. The wall dates from
the 13th century, but south-west
of Bootham Bar is no longer there.
A 350-foot section of it was
demolished in 1834 to make way
for St Leonard's Place.

From King's Manor turn right
along St Leonard's Place, passing
on the opposite side of the road,
the **Theatre Royal** ④. On your
right are some remains of the
Roman wall, which was built
around AD 300. Next on your right
is a fine curved row of Regency
buildings now occupied by York
City Council.

On reaching the traffic signals
turn right into Museum Street.
In 50 yards a detour can be made
by turning right into a cul-de-sac.
On your left are the ruins of **St
Leonard's Hospital** ⑤. Ahead
is the Central Library. A path to
the left of this building leads to the
Multangular Tower ⑥, and by
walking to your right behind the
Central Library, a further portion
of the wall can be seen, including
the **Anglian Tower** ⑦ and the
four banks showing the different
rampart levels in Roman, Dark
Age, Norman and Medieval times.

Retrace your steps to Museum
Street and turn right. After passing
the entrance of Museum Gardens

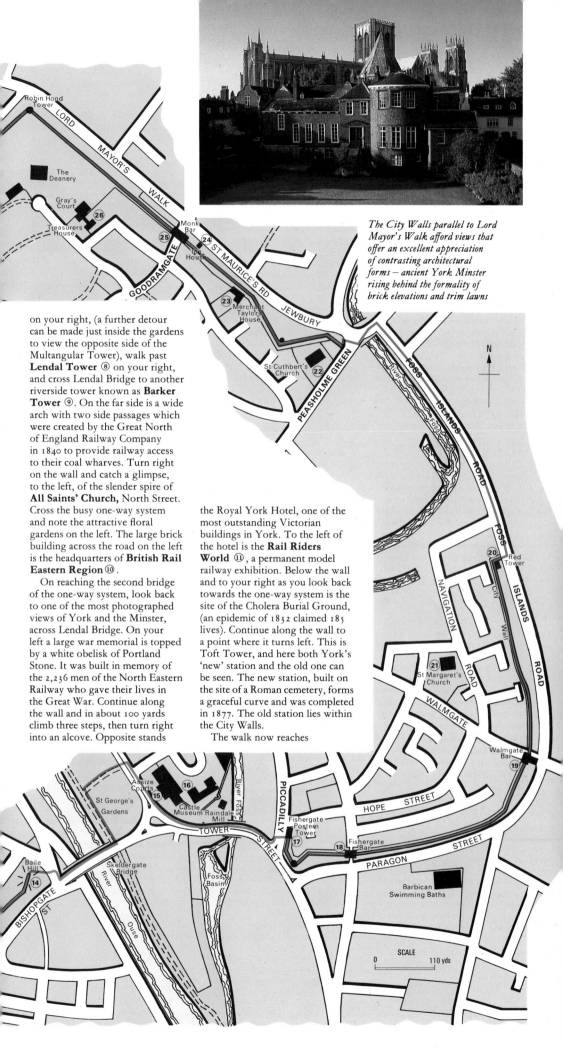

on your right, (a further detour
can be made just inside the gardens
to view the opposite side of the
Multangular Tower), walk past
Lendal Tower ⑧ on your right,
and cross Lendal Bridge to another
riverside tower known as **Barker
Tower** ⑨. On the far side is a wide
arch with two side passages which
were created by the Great North
of England Railway Company
in 1840 to provide railway access
to their coal wharves. Turn right
on the wall and catch a glimpse,
to the left, of the slender spire of
All Saints' Church, North Street.
Cross the busy one-way system
and note the attractive floral
gardens on the left. The large brick
building across the road on the left
is the headquarters of **British Rail
Eastern Region** ⑩.

On reaching the second bridge
of the one-way system, look back
to one of the most photographed
views of York and the Minster,
across Lendal Bridge. On your
left a large war memorial is topped
by a white obelisk of Portland
Stone. It was built in memory of
the 2,236 men of the North Eastern
Railway who gave their lives in
the Great War. Continue along
the wall and in about 100 yards
climb three steps, then turn right
into an alcove. Opposite stands

the Royal York Hotel, one of the
most outstanding Victorian
buildings in York. To the left of
the hotel is the **Rail Riders
World** ⑪, a permanent model
railway exhibition. Below the wall
and to your right as you look back
towards the one-way system is the
site of the Cholera Burial Ground,
(an epidemic of 1832 claimed 185
lives). Continue along the wall to
a point where it turns left. This is
Toft Tower, and here both York's
'new' station and the old one can
be seen. The new station, built on
the site of a Roman cemetery, forms
a graceful curve and was completed
in 1877. The old station lies within
the City Walls.

The walk now reaches

Micklegate Bar ⑫ — there is access here to Micklegate. Further along the wall, there is a glimpse on the left through the trees of **St Mary's Church,** Bishophill Junior. A little farther on, Terry's Chocolate factory and clock tower can be seen about a mile away to the right. Before reaching **Victoria Bar** ⑬ there are some typical back-to-back Victorian houses complete with their corner shops, and beyond, the Minster is dominant above the array of chimneypots. Walk across Victoria Bar — there is access on the far side to street level — and continue to Bitchdaughter Tower, where the wall swings left to reach the tree-clad mound of **Baile Hill** ⑭. Descend the flight of steps, then cross the road to gain access to Skeldergate Bridge, where there are fine views upstream to the Ouse Bridge.

On the far side of Skeldergate Bridge, turn left down a flight of steps, then follow the river bank towards Ouse Bridge, with St George's Gardens on your right. In about 70 yards turn right . . . now the wall is on your left. On leaving the park note the plaque on your left marking various flood levels in the past, the highest of which was in 1625. Cross the zebra crossing, keeping **Clifford's Tower** on your left.

Turn right along Tower Street, with the **Assize Courts** ⑮ now on your left. Part of the city and castle wall can be seen on your left, forming the base of the Debtor's Prison, which is now part of the **Castle Museum** ⑯. Below the Museum is the small Raindale Mill, which was transported brick by brick from Raindale in North Yorkshire. The mill is in working order and its flour can be bought from the Castle Museum.

Cross York's second river, the Foss. With the **Fishergate Postern Tower** ⑰ now ahead, cross the end of Piccadilly to reach it, and pass through the archway to the right of the tower before climbing the steps on to the wall again. Where the wall swings left to reach **Fishergate Bar** ⑱ descend to street level, then climb back on to the wall. In 100 yards the grey pyramid roof of the modern Barbican Swimming Baths can be seen. Ahead rises the tall sandstone spire of **St Lawrence's Church.**

The next gate in the wall is **Walmgate Bar** ⑲. Descend and cross the street (beware of traffic), then climb on to the wall again. About halfway to the **Red Tower** ⑳, before descending six steps, look left to **St Margaret's Church** ㉑, which is surrounded by trees on three sides. The wall continues to Red Tower.

Continue next along Foss Islands Road, which forms the least interesting part of the walk. The

River Foss, choked by vegetation, emerges on your left. During Medieval times this area formed a large lake, so there was no need for defences. The lake, known as King's Pool, was dammed up near York Castle, and provided a stock of freshwater fish. By the 17th century the lake had begun to silt up, and in 1792 the Foss Navigation Company channelled the river. Later, the Foss Islands Road was constructed.

At the end of this road turn left, crossing the River Foss, then right across the end of Peasholme Green. Keep right and in 20 yards, turn left up a flight of steps to regain the wall. The base of the steps marks the site of Layerthorpe Postern Tower, which was a large embattled, portcullised tower demolished in 1829. On your left now is **St Cuthbert's Church** ㉒. Continue climbing the steps to get a sudden and rewarding view ahead to the Minster. As the wall veers right, the Minster dominates above the modern red pantile roofs. The rear of the **Merchant Taylors' Hall** ㉓ is next passed on the left. Beyond it and below the wall on the left are fragments of a Roman corner tower which formed the

Massive stonework at Walmgate

Medieval structures such as this kept winter ice frozen for use later in the hot summer months

eastern corner of the Roman Fortress of *Eboracum*. The wall next passes a Roman interval tower, also on your left. On nearing Monk Bar look over the wall on your right to view the **Ice House** ㉔. This interesting building can so easily be missed.

Continue to **Monk Bar** ㉓. Descend the wall and cross Goodramgate (watch for traffic). To climb back on to the wall, you must find the hidden staircase on the inward side of Monk Bar. Along the next section of wall there are fine views to the north side of the Minster and its Chapter House, the largest in England. Below there are some neatly laid-out private gardens belonging to Gray's Court. On the outer part of the wall there are two depressions marking the site of a ruined tower dating from the 12th century.

The wall follows the line of the Roman wall back to Bootham Bar, but on the way there are several interesting buildings to note. Between the wall and the Minster are Gray's Court, the Deanery and the **Treasurer's House** ㉖. At Robin Hood Tower, the wall turns left, but pause here and look north-east towards the Howardian Hills and York's other chocolate factory, Rowntree Mackintosh. The next section of the wall is surrounded by trees, but there are glimpses of the Minster here and there. This part of the wall can be slippery when wet, as the over-hanging trees prevent the paving stones from drying quickly, and in autumn may be carpeted with leaves.

The wall descends to reach Bootham Bar, and the walk enters the first floor room, in which you can see the original portcullis.

On the opposite side there is a bird's eye view along High Petergate. Descend the steps to complete the City Wall walk.

East of the Ouse

*T*his walk covers the most visited and popular parts of York and takes the visitor past many places of interest. On most days, however, sections of the walk will be rather crowded – notably Stonegate, Shambles, Coppergate and Coney Street.

Places in bold type are fully described in alphabetical order (by name) in the first gazetteer section – page 37. These and other notable features are keyed to the accompanying maps by number.

From the West Front of York Minster cross Minster Yard and branch left into High Petergate. On your left is **St Michael-le-Belfry** ①, and on your right is **Young's Hotel** ②, the birthplace of Guy Fawkes in 1570.

Take the next turning right into Stonegate, which was the road used to transport the stone from the barges moored on the River Ouse to the Minster. **Stonegate** has many interesting buildings, notably the **12th Century House** ③, which lies down a narrow passageway to your right. Farther along Stonegate is the rare beam sign of the **Old Starre Inn** ④, which is in an alleyway on your right and can be visited only during licensing

The Shambles – once a street of butchers and source of diseases, now a survivor unique in Europe

hours. Coffee Yard, a Medieval alleyway, leads away to the left.

Beyond ancient Mulberry Hall, turn left into Little Stonegate and continue into Back Swinegate. In another 30 yards turn right through a doorway leading to St Sampson Square. Entering the square, on your left is the **Roman Bath Inn** ⑤. Keep along the left-hand side of the square, then turn left into Church Street. The church on the right is **St Sampson's Church** ⑥. At the end of Church Street turn right into King's Square. The square marks the site of the *Porta Principalis Sinistra*, or the South East Gate of the Roman Legionary Fortress, which was built by the Ninth legion in the Principate of Trajan. Near by a painting on a shop wall shows a Roman Commemorative Tablet of magnesian limestone found in 1884 between 26–28ft down. Keep along the right hand edge of King's Square, then turn right, then left into the **Shambles** ⑦, York's best-known street and one of the finest Medieval streets preserved in Europe. On the way through the Shambles pass the house on the right dedicated to **Margaret Clitherow's Shrine** ⑧. She was killed in 1586 because she harboured Catholic priests. At

Longest name – shortest street

the end of the Shambles turn left, passing on your left **St Crux Parish Room** ⑨. On its eastern wall is the sign of Whip-ma-whop-ma-gate, York's shortest street which has the longest name, probably derived from the whipping of petty criminals. The walk now crosses the Fossgate, but it is probably best to cross at the end of Colliergate, then at the Stonebow by way of the traffic island.

About 120 yards along Fossgate turn right down a covered passageway displaying a colourful coat of arms. This passageway leads to the **Merchant Adventurers' Hall** ⑩. Leave along the path on the right-hand side of the building, and on the far side climb the steps to Piccadilly. Turn right along this road to reach the traffic signals, then left, crossing the road into Coppergate.

On your right is **All Saints' Church,** Pavement ⑪. Continue along Coppergate, then turn left into Coppergate shopping mall and shortly pass on the right the **Jorvik Viking Centre** ⑫, which is one of York's most popular museums.

The next building on the right is St Mary's, Castlegate, which houses the **York Story** ⑬. Bear right and climb to Castlegate, then turn left. **Fairfax House** ⑭ is passed on your left, while on the right is Castlegate House, which was designed by architect John

Carr and built in 1763. At the end of Castlegate keep ahead along the right-hand side of the car park to reach the **Castle Museum** ⑮.

Bear right, passing the former Debtors' Prison, and then the **Assize Courts** ⑯. The green on your right is called the 'Eye of York'. Cross the road to the base of the steps ascending to **Clifford's Tower** ⑰. Continue down to cross Tower Street at the zebra crossing, then enter St George's Gardens. Note the plaque on the right, just inside the gardens, for monitoring the flood levels. Continue ahead down to the riverside, then turn right along the riverside path leading to King's Staith. Pass on the right Cumberland House, which was built during the early 18th century by Alderman William Cornwell, one-time Sheriff and twice Lord Mayor of York. The house appears to have been named after the Duke of Cumberland, second son of King George II, who was given the freedom of the city on his return from the Battle of Culloden in 1746.

Next, pass the attractive riverside King's Arms public house, with its inn sign of Richard III, then ascend the steps to Low Ousegate. Turn right for a few yards and cross Low Ousegate, then take the alleyway along the left-hand side of **St Michael's Church,** Spurriergate ⑱. From the alleyway keep around to the right, shortly reaching Coney Street, the main shopping street of York. Coney Street was first known as *Cuningestrete* or King Street from the Danish *Kunung*. A street has been here since Roman times.

Turn left and in about 200 yards

This small, Medieval tower at Marygate was once part of the defences around St Mary's Abbey

pass on the left **St Martin-le-Grand** ⑲. Continue to St Helen's Square, which was once the churchyard of **St Helen's Church** ⑳. St Helen's Square stands on the site of the Roman Praetorian Gate, which was the principal entrance to the Roman City around 300 AD. On your left is the **Mansion House** ㉑. An entranceway on the right-hand side of the building leads to the **Guildhall** ㉒. Keep forward into Lendal, soon passing a large house (now an hotel), on the right, set back from the road. This is **Judges'**

The Judges' Lodgings served their named function from 1806 until 1979, but date from 1720

Lodgings ㉓. Proceed to the end of Lendal and cross Museum Street into the **Museum Gardens** ㉔. Keep on the right-hand path, and soon the **Multangular Tower** ㉕ is seen on the right. Keep forward a short distance to the front entrance to the **Yorkshire Museum** ㉖. Continue ahead taking the curved path to the left. Ahead and to your right are the ruins of **St Mary's Abbey** ㉗. The walk passes through the south-western end of the ruins, then beyond the rockery turns right to leave the park via the Abbey gateway. Turn right along Marygate, passing **St Olave's Church** ㉘. Continue along Marygate with the Abbey Wall on your right, and note in this wall the reproduction of the type of wooden shutter which was used in Medieval times to guard bowmen against the return of arrows. The bowman would open the shutter and fire a quick succession of arrows, then close the shutter to protect himself. The Abbey Wall dates from the 13th century, and the only other place in England where shutter grooves survive is Alnwick, Northumberland.

At the end of Marygate turn right into Bootham, passing **Marygate Tower** ㉙. Continue to Bootham Bar, crossing St Leonard's Place, and climb the steps to the right of Bootham Bar. Inside the Bar the original portcullis can be seen.

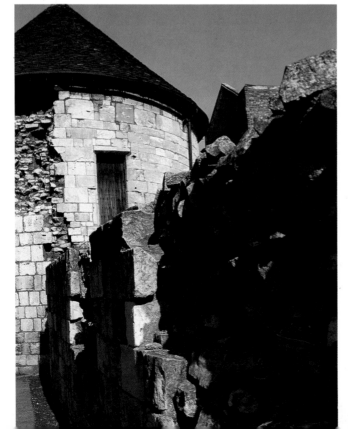

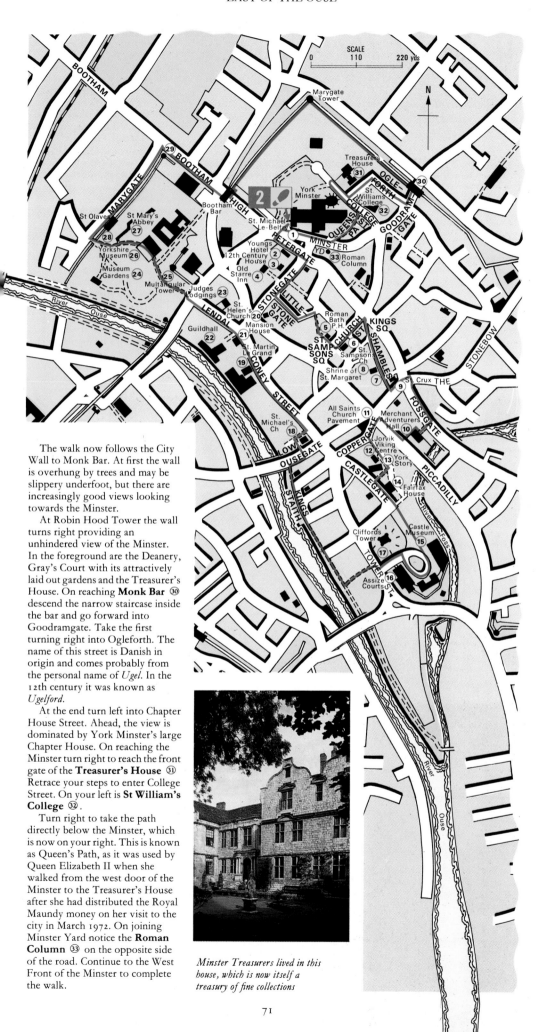

The walk now follows the City Wall to Monk Bar. At first the wall is overhung by trees and may be slippery underfoot, but there are increasingly good views looking towards the Minster.

At Robin Hood Tower the wall turns right providing an unhindered view of the Minster. In the foreground are the Deanery, Gray's Court with its attractively laid out gardens and the Treasurer's House. On reaching **Monk Bar** ㉚ descend the narrow staircase inside the bar and go forward into Goodramgate. Take the first turning right into Ogleforth. The name of this street is Danish in origin and comes probably from the personal name of *Ugel*. In the 12th century it was known as *Ugelford*.

At the end turn left into Chapter House Street. Ahead, the view is dominated by York Minster's large Chapter House. On reaching the Minster turn right to reach the front gate of the **Treasurer's House** ㉛ Retrace your steps to enter College Street. On your left is **St William's College** ㉜.

Turn right to take the path directly below the Minster, which is now on your right. This is known as Queen's Path, as it was used by Queen Elizabeth II when she walked from the west door of the Minster to the Treasurer's House after she had distributed the Royal Maundy money on her visit to the city in March 1972. On joining Minster Yard notice the **Roman Column** ㉝ on the opposite side of the road. Continue to the West Front of the Minster to complete the walk.

Minster Treasurers lived in this house, which is now itself a treasury of fine collections

71

West of the Ouse

T̲his walk visits many interesting and historic places, and — as it covers less visited parts of the city — offers a more peaceful stroll away from the main shopping areas.

Places in bold type are fully described in alphabetical order (by name) in the first gazetteer section – page 37. These and other notable features are keyed to the accompanying maps by number.

The starting point is Ouse Bridge, in the heart of York. From the western side take the riverside path north-westwards, with the River Ouse on your right. Beyond the Viking Hotel the walk enters gardens. Across the river, upstream, is the **Guildhall** ① and opposite, the offices of the *York Evening Press*. Often, barges may be seen off-loading newsprint, demonstrating that there is still trade on the Ouse. Behind, the tower of **St Martin-le-Grand** ② can be glimpsed.

Leaving the gardens, **All Saints' Church,** North Street ③ is an interesting church which should not be missed. Its entrance is along a passageway on the right-hand side of the building. Continue along North Street to pass beneath Lendal Bridge. Immediately beyond the bridge is **Barker Tower** ④. Continue along the tree-lined riverside path as far as the railway bridge, and on the nearside of the bridge turn left along a path to reach Leeman Road.

Here a detour can be made to visit the **National Railway Museum** ⑤, which will add at least two hours to your walk. (The detour turns right and passes through a tunnel to reach the National Railway Museum. To leave the museum and to rejoin the main walk, retrace your steps along Leeman Road and cross the footbridge before the tunnel).

The main walk crosses Leeman Road and turns left. In about 100 yards veer right and ascend Station Rise. Cross the road at the traffic

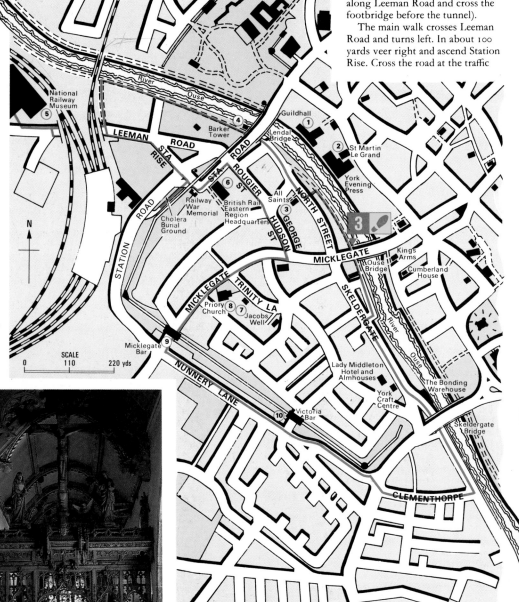

All Saints' Church in North Street is noted for the slender, 120ft spire that has become a well-known west Ouse-bank landmark – but it is also famous for the superb 20th-century screen, executed in wood by Ridsdale Tate, that complements its fine hammerbeam roof inside. Good glass is an additional attraction

George Leeman, three times Lord Mayor of York from 1865–1874

signals, and on the far side note the statue opposite of George Leeman, three times Lord Mayor of York in 1865, 1871 and 1874, and an MP. He was also Chairman of the North Eastern Railway Company. By making a small detour to the right, the tombstones can be seen of the victims of the 1832 cholera epidemic in which 185 people died.

The walk now passes beneath the City Wall; on your right is the Railway War Memorial, erected in remembrance of the 2,236 men of the North Eastern Railway who died in the First World War. Turn left into Station Road (no sign), next passing on your right **British Rail Eastern Region Headquarters** ⑥. Take the next turning right into Rougier Street and continue into George Hudson Street, originally called Hudson Street after George Hudson — MP and three times Mayor of York, who was credited both with being the 'father' of the railways, and a great benefactor of the city. When he fell from grace, the street was renamed Railway Street, but on the 100th anniversary of his death, in 1971, his name was restored to the street.

At the end turn right into Micklegate and cross the road. Meaning 'great street', Micklegate has enjoyed several spellings, going back as far as 1161 when it was spelt *Myglagata*, and in 1189 *Mykelgate*.

On the left is St Martin-cum-Gregory, which is surrounded by trees and easily missed. Further along Micklegate it is worth making a short detour into Trinity Lane on your left to visit **Jacob's Well** ⑦. Continuing along Micklegate, the next church on the left is the priory church of the **Holy Trinity** ⑧. Pass beneath **Micklegate Bar** ⑨, probably the best-known gate in York.

On reaching the traffic signals

Ouse Bridge, the middle of three main crossings into central York

turn left into Nunnery Lane. Soon the City Wall is seen on the left and later **Victoria Bar** ⑩ is also passed. On reaching the one-way system, bear left. At the end cross diagonally to enter Clementhorpe (beware of traffic). Descend along this road to the River Ouse. Turn left to go under Skeldergate Bridge. The next building on your right is The Bonding Warehouse, which dates from 1875, and which has been attractively converted into a riverside bar and restaurant. Keep forward along Skeldergate, next passing on your left the York Craft Centre.

A little farther, an interesting building on the left set back from the road is Dame Middleton's Hospital, which is now an hotel. Built in 1659 and endowed by Dame Anne Middleton, it was originally founded as a hostel for the widows of 20 freemen. In 1829, it was rebuilt and enlarged. Over the entrance is a stone effigy of Dame Anne Middleton. In 80 yards at the Cock and Bottle Inn turn right into Queen's Staith, and shortly reach the quayside, first used for coal and known as Coal Staith.

Turning left, the Ouse Bridge is now ahead. There are many interesting buildings on the opposite bank of the river, including the King's Arms public house and Cumberland House. A flight of steps leads up to Ouse Bridge to reach your starting point.

Once a warehouse, now a stylish restaurant with a difference

Floodlit Walk

Spotlights emphasise the Minster architecture's soaring qualities

*T*here are so many floodlit buildings in York that it is almost impossible to visit all of them in one evening. The following two-hour walk takes in many and the route is designed to be joined at any point. For convenience, the walk has been started at the West Front of the Minster. It cannot be guaranteed, of course, that all buildings indicated will be floodlit at the time of your visit, particularly if the walk is undertaken around dusk.

Places in **bold type** are fully described in alphabetical order (by name) in the first gazetteer section – page 37. These and other notable features are keyed to the accompanying maps by number.

The Minster is by far the largest floodlit building in York, and what better place to start than at the West Front. Walk into Minster Yard on the southern side of the Minster, then keep left into Queen's Path to reach the eastern front. Turn right along College Street, passing St William's College (left).

Towards the end of College Street look back to the stunning view of the floodlit East Front of the Minster. From College Street turn left along Goodramgate and pass through floodlit **Monk Bar** ①. At traffic signals keep ahead into Monkgate (no sign). In about 150 yards cross Monkgate and turn right into Monkgate Cloisters. Ahead now is the floodlit Yorkshire Water Authority, housed in a fine Georgian building. Between 1740 and 1977 it served as the York County Hospital.

Turn right along the path in front of the building to reach St Maurice's Road (no sign). Cross this road and turn left with the City Wall, partly floodlit, on your right. In about 250 yards keep right into Peasholme Green, passing **St Cuthbert's Church** ② on your right. Beyond it is the **Borthwick Institute of Historical Research** ③. Opposite is the **Black Swan Inn** ④.

Branch right into St Saviour's Place, passing Peasholme House, a prominent Georgian building on the left. Built in 1752 this fine building, probably designed by York architect John Carr, was bought by the York Civic Trust in 1975 and completely restored.

Shortly, turn left into St Saviourgate, passing on the right **St Saviourgate Unitarian Chapel** ⑤. Continuing along St Saviourgate, the tower of **St Saviour's Church** ⑥ can be seen floodlit. At the end of this street is the small **St Crux Parish Room** ⑦, lit by streetlight. Turn right into Colliergate, passing on the right the **Impressions Gallery of Photography** ⑧. In about 200 yards turn left along

Georgian home of York's Water Authority – once a hospital

the left-hand side of King's Square, noting floodlit York Minster (right). Keep left into one of the finest preserved Medieval streets in Europe, the **Shambles**. At the end cross and turn right into Pavement. On your left is the fine half-timbered **Herbert House** ⑨. Ahead is All Saints' Church, **Pavement** ⑩, with its unusual lantern tower.

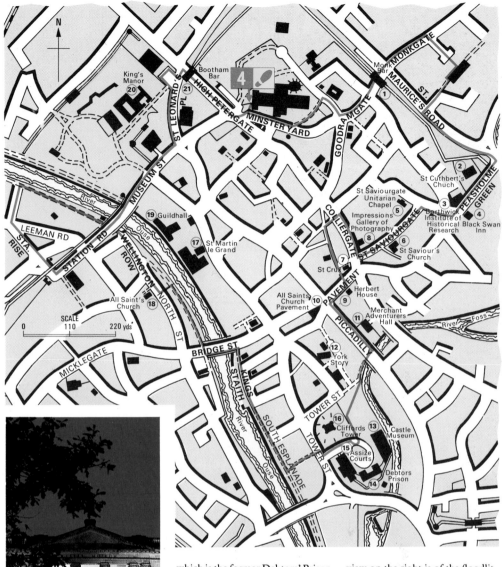

Behind the Castle Museum's classical portico is one of the world's finest folk collections

At the traffic signals turn left into Piccadilly and after about 120 yards pass the **Merchant Adventurers' Hall** ⑪ on the left. On reaching the River Foss cross Piccadilly and walk along the riverside path running parallel with a multi-storey car park. Ahead now is the floodlit view to the Castle Museum, and later Clifford's Tower on the right.

On reaching the car park head towards Clifford's Tower but, before reaching the base of its bank, look right to the floodlit spire of St Mary's, Castlegate, which houses the **York Story** ⑫.

Turn left to cross to the green, surrounded on three sides by floodlit buildings. On the left is the **Castle Museum** ⑬, part of

which is the former Debtors' Prison (ahead), ⑭ and on the right the **Assize Courts** ⑮. Turn right and leave the square with the floodlit **Clifford's Tower** ⑯ on the right.

Cross Tower Street by way of the zebra crossing and enter St George's Gardens. Keep ahead to the River Ouse, then turn right along South Esplanade leading into King's Staith. On the opposite bank Woods Mill, a riverside warehouse (now a restaurant), is floodlit. On your right pass the delightful floodlit King's Arms public house, an ancient riverside inn. Ascend steps to Ouse Bridge.

Turn left, cross the bridge, then immediately turn right along the riverside path. On the opposite bank the tower of **St Martin-le-Grand** ⑰ is floodlit.

Beyond the Viking Hotel bear left through some gardens to North Street. Opposite, the slender spire of **All Saints' Church,** North Street ⑱, is floodlit. Turn right into North Street and note the floodlit **Guildhall** ⑲ on the opposite bank of the River Ouse.

Keep forward into Wellington Row, (no sign) to pass beneath Lendal Bridge. On the far side, the

view on the right is of the floodlit Lendal Bridge and Tower.

In 150 yards, on reaching a car park, turn left up a narrow lane with gardens on your left. At the end, cross Leeman Road, then bear left into Station Rise.

On your right you will note the floodlit Victorian Royal York Hotel. At the traffic signals, cross to the statue of George Leeman (beware of traffic from your right). Keep ahead through the City Wall, then bear left to catch a floodlit view ahead of the Minster. Walk towards Lendal Bridge with the floodlit City Wall on your left and cross Station Avenue.

Cross Lendal Bridge and pass the floodlit Lendal Tower on your left. Walk along Museum Street to reach the traffic signals and turn left into St Leonard's Place. On reaching the Art Gallery turn left to enter the grounds of the floodlit **King's Manor** ⑳.

From the entrance cross St Leonard's Place towards the floodlit **Bootham Bar** ㉑, passing on the way the floodlit fountains outside the Art Gallery.

Pass through Bootham Bar and walk along High Petergate back to the Minster.

Footsteps heard at Raffles are said to be made by the spirit of a tragic little Victorian girl

Ghost Walk

Y ork has the reputation of being the most haunted city in Europe, and within its City Walls there are said to be as many as 140 ghosts lurking. Most evenings during the summer there are guided haunted walks, which are locally advertised. For those visitors who wish to explore the ghostly surroundings of this city alone or with a small group, this walk will give an insight into a selection of 'haunted' buildings.

Ghost No 1. There have been a number of ghostly sightings in York Minster, but one story that has been told many times is about an incident that occurred during the last century. A large party of visitors to the Minster was divided into smaller groups, in one of which was a guide and a father with his two daughters. As the guide and the elder daughter turned away from one of the monuments they had been studying, the guide was surprised to see a naval officer approaching them. Since they were some distance from the sea the guide pointed this out to the girl, who immediately became pale and distressed. The guide called for the other daughter, who was some distance away, to come to her sister's aid. The girls gazed at the officer, who by now was quite close and said in a low voice, 'There is a future state'. Soon afterwards he disappeared. Their father had been some distance off and was unaware of what had happened. The guide searched in vain for this mysterious figure, but the elder daughter begged the guide not to mention the incident to her father; she knew sad news would soon reach the family. It appears that when she and her brother, a naval officer, were children they made a pact that, on the death of either of them, the one who had died would appear to the one still alive. Sure enough, a few days later, news of her brother's death came; he had died the same day and the same hour as she had seen the ghost, in the Minster.

Ghost No 2. King's Manor is reputed to be the most haunted building in York. A figure of a monk is occasionally seen from the days when the building formed part of **St Mary's Abbey**. After an unsuccessful attack by Roundheads on the Manor on Trinity Sunday in 1644, the inner courtyard was used for the dead and dying Roundheads, and their groans are still occasionally heard.

Anne Boleyn walks King's Manor, perhaps seeking a lost lover

A maid several times reported seeing a woman wearing a green dress of the Tudor period and holding a bunch of roses. It has been suggested that this is the ghost of Anne Boleyn, who stayed here and at the time formed a relationship with Henry Percy, while still married to Henry VIII. More recently, a portrait in the Huntingdon Room, of a Stuart nobleman, has come to life and has moved about the room.

The Theatre Royal's ghostly Grey Lady is an omen of stage success

Ghost No 3. The Grey Lady of the **Theatre Royal** makes regular appearances, and there is now a tradition that on each occasion the Grey Lady appears the actors know that their production will be successful. Some people say that the Grey Lady is a Medieval nun who fell in love with a young nobleman, and when discovered was put to death on the site where the theatre now stands.

Ghost No 4. The building which now houses the Raffles Tea Room belonged in the last century to a Victorian doctor, who often entertained friends. His pretty six-year-old daughter, a favourite with the servants and visiting patients, would often be introduced to his friends before being sent to bed. The little girl resented this and preferred to eavesdrop on her father entertaining and holding dinner parties below. She would creep on to the landing and lean over the bannister to listen to the conversation. One night, however, she slipped and fell to her death three floors below. Today, her footsteps can still be heard climbing the stairs, but she has been seen on only one occasion.

Ghost No 5. All Saints' Church, Pavement has a distinctive and unusual tower and is a major landmark within the City Walls. The ghost connected with this church is of a lady dressed in a long, white, flowing dress and with long shining hair. She appears only in the daylight and always ahead of a funeral procession. Once the procession has entered the church

she vanishes as quickly and mysteriously as she appeared, leaving an atmosphere of peaceful calm in her wake. There appears to be no legend connected with her appearance. However, it has been suggested that she is seeking a Christian burial, which she has been denied.

Ghost No 6. There are several ghosts in the Medieval **Black Swan Inn** and most rooms in the building have witnessed a ghost. However, there are two 'regulars'. One is a beautiful young woman with long attractive hair and a long light dress. Each time she has appeared she has been staring into the fireplace or out of the window, and nobody has seen her face. A small, miserable-looking man in an old bowler hat is the other regular. He appears for as long as five minutes, almost as if he is waiting for someone, then gradually fades away again.

Ghost No 7. During Victorian times Bedern was a run-down, dilapidated area of York, with workhouses and orphanages. The York Industrial Ragged School was also sited in the Bedern and one of its masters was a cruel and wicked man. Under his care several children are said to have died. Many of them were not even buried, but were locked away in a large cupboard until there was a suitable time to bury them. In 1855, when the area was being cleared, several bodies of children were reported to have been found. The area around the passageway called Bedern has ever since been haunted by the noises and screams of children late at night, even though there has been a great deal of modern development in the area.

Another story that comes from Bedern is that of an archaeologist who not so long ago was carrying out excavation work on the site. All day he thought he was being watched and kept feeling a small hand pulling at his shoulder. Every time he looked around he saw nothing and, not believing in ghosts, laughingly mentioned it to his wife. The subject was forgotten that evening until he went to bed, when his wife noticed several small scratches and marks on his shoulder, which looked very much as though they had been done by tiny fingers.

Ghost No 8. York's most famous ghost story, and one of the best known in this country, comes from the **Treasurer's House** near York Minster. Several ghosts have been reported in the building, but by far the most famous are the ghosts of the Roman Army. During the 1950s a young apprentice called Harry Martindale was carrying out plumbing work in the cellar of the Treasurer's House. Part of the cellar floor had been dug up,

Part of the walls where the living are not the only walkers

and Harry was working up a small ladder when he heard the sound of a trumpet. The trumpet noise grew louder until out of the wall came a horse with a Roman soldier on it. Harry fell from his ladder in a state of shock — but this was only the beginning. There now followed a procession of Roman soldiers emerging from the cellar wall and marching into the wall opposite. They were visible from the knees upward, except where the cellar floor had been excavated, and at that point Harry could see their feet. Harry watched them, paralysed where he lay, but the soldiers ignored him. He was, however, able to give a very detailed account of the soldiers' clothing and described them as shabby in appearance, with rough handmade clothes, sandals cross-gartered to the knees and green kilted skirts. They carried long spears, short swords and round shields and they had fine helmets. Their trumpet was a long straight instrument, much used and battered. Trembling, Harry climbed out of the cellar, but his story was kept secret between a few friends until 1974, when he was persuaded to make it public. The Roman soldiers were apparently marching on the level of the old Roman road, and the base of the cellar is 18 inches above this. All other sightings have reported seeing the Roman soldiers from the knees upwards.

Ghost No 9. In this small house three centuries ago there was a great tragedy. In recent times the family living there became aware of an air of sadness about the place and a child crying at night in the upper part of the house. The crying was so frequent that the nanny often thought that it came from one of her two charges. As the children grew up they too became aware of the noise, and repeatedly spoke to their nanny of seeing a little girl crying in their room. The children were moved to another room and the nanny slept in their former bedroom. She too witnessed a little girl crying, and it troubled the family so much that a medium was called in to try to discover more

about the child. It was found that the little girl had died from starvation during the 17th century. Her family, like many others near by, had been struck down by plague, and the house and the area around the Minster were sealed off for nearly a year. The little girl had recovered but nobody could hear her cries for help. During this bout of plague several areas of the city were sealed off, and the death toll was 3,512.

A killer and betrayer paces St William's College in the night

Ghost No 10. Four centuries ago two brothers rented a room in **St William's College;** both were jealous and greedy. The elder brother worked out a plan to rob one of the many well-to-do clergymen, and persuaded his brother to assist in the crime. One night they sprang on the cleric between the Minster and St William's College and, in the course of the struggle, killed him. The younger brother had all along been the reluctant partner; at this, he broke down in terror and locked himself in a large oak cabinet with the murdered clergyman's possessions. The other, fearing that his brother would confess all, decided to betray him. The younger man was eventually found and hanged for his crime, while the elder remained free. Haunted by a sense of guilt, he would pace the upstairs corridors of St William's College after the hanging, until he too met an early death. His footsteps can still be heard to the present day.

Ghost No 11. During the 17th century superstition was rife in York, and anyone with a physical defect was treated with suspicion, since this was regarded as a punishment from God or a mark of the devil. A wealthy family owned the house which is now Marmaduke's Restaurant in Goodramgate, and in 1697 a son was born. They called him Marmaduke Buckle, but unfortunately he was born a cripple. Because of their superstitious beliefs people ignored him, and by the age of 17 he was so lonely and depressed he decided to commit suicide by hanging himself. Before doing so he scratched his name,

year of birth and death into the plaster wall of his room. Today his ghost haunts the building; it is only a presence that opens doors and turns on lights, but there is also the feeling that he is watching you.

Ghost No 12. The Anglers' Arms in Goodramgate claims to be the most haunted pub in York and has a ghost on every floor but one. On the top floor a presence has been sensed and sometimes the strong smell of lavender wafts through the rooms. On the middle floor there is a ghost of a Victorian child. She has not been seen for some years, although the pub cat has often been seen playing with this invisible ghost. In the past, she has been seen sitting on the stairs. The story goes that this lively child was tragically killed after running downstairs and out into Goodramgate into the path of a horse-drawn brewer's dray. Finally, the cellar is haunted by a ghost which is unfriendly and evil. The publican's dog and cat will not venture into the cellar.

Thomas Percy seeks his head at Holy Trinity, in Goodramgate

Ghost No 13. Holy Trinity Church, Goodramgate, has all the makings of a haunted church. Set behind other ancient buildings, the church is very old, peaceful, still and dark. Of the ghosts that haunt the church the best known one is of Thomas Percy, the Earl of Northumberland, who lived in the latter half of the 16th century. On the throne at this time was Queen Elizabeth I, a devout Protestant, but Thomas Percy was a Catholic and planned to overthrow the Queen. When his campaign of battles and sieges in the north crumbled, he decided to make for Catholic Scotland, but was captured and returned to York to be executed on a charge of treason. After his execution on 22 August 1572 his body was buried at **St Crux** (now demolished), while his head was displayed on a pole above **Micklegate Bar.** It stayed there for some time before being stolen by friends, who gave it a Christian burial at Holy Trinity. Sometimes, his headless body is seen in the north-west corner of Holy Trinity Church looking for its head.

ROUTE DIRECTIONS

*The walk begins at the west front of the Minster (**See Ghost No** ①). Leave the Minster by High Petergate to pass through the left-hand side of **Bootham Bar.** Cross St Leonard's Place towards the **Art Gallery,** then bear left into the grounds of the **King's Manor** (**See Ghost No** ②). Retrace your steps to Bootham Bar, then turn right along the left-hand side of St Leonard's Place, shortly passing the **Theatre Royal** (**See Ghost No** ③).*

*Continue to traffic signals, keep forward into Blake Street, then after 100 yards turn left into **Stonegate.** Continue along this road, passing beneath **The Old Starre Inn** sign. The inn lies down an alleyway to the left and is reputed to be haunted. Continue a few yards further to Raffles Tea Room on the right (**See Ghost No** ④). Retrace your steps a few yards, but before reaching The Old Starre Inn sign turn left down an alleyway called Coffee Yard.*

*Keep forward into Swinegate, and at far end turn right into Church Street, which soon enters St Sampson Square. Turn left to walk along the left-hand side of Parliament Street to reach **All Saints' Church, Pavement** (**See Ghost No** ⑤) on your right. Turn left into Pavement, then in 50 yards turn left into the **Shambles,** one of the finest Medieval streets in Europe.*

*Continue to the end of the Shambles to enter King's Square and bear right diagonally across it to enter St Andrewgate. Continue along this road for 120 yards to where four bollards block the road, then turn right into Spen Lane and continue to the far end of this road, where the **Black Swan Inn** is directly opposite the end (**See Ghost No** ⑥).*

*Turn sharp left into Aldwark, then in 150 yards turn left into St Andrewgate. In 30 yards turn right into the passageway called Bedern, which lies between modern houses (**See Ghost No** ⑦). Continue to the far end of Bedern, then turn right into Goodramgate. Take the next turning left into Ogleforth and at the far end of this road turn left into Chapter House Street. On reaching the Minster turn right and shortly reach the front entrance of the **Treasurer's House** (**See Ghost No** ⑧). Retrace your steps, then keep forward and shortly pass a small house on your left (No. 5) (**See Ghost No** ⑨). Next door but one is **St William's College** (**See Ghost No** ⑩).*

Continue along College Street, passing beneath the archway at the end, and cross Deangate into Goodramgate. Shortly pass

Ghosts are said to abound at Holy Trinity, in Goodramgate

*Marmaduke's Restaurant on the left (**See Ghost No** ⑪). The next building on the left is the Anglers' Arms (**See Ghost No** ⑫). Continue along Goodramgate for a further 100 yards, passing on the right **Lady Row.** Beyond this rank of ancient buildings turn right through a gateway leading to **Holy Trinity Church,** Goodramgate (**See Ghost No** ⑬). Leave by the gateway in the western side of the church and follow the alleyway to Low Petergate, where the walk turns right. (If the gateway is locked, return to Goodramgate, turn right, then take the next turning right into Low Petergate.) The main walk continues along Low Petergate before turning right into Minster Gate. Cross Minster Yard by way of the zebra crossing, turn left to return to the Minster.*

DIRECTORY

Where to stay and eat in York

SYMBOLS AND ABBREVIATIONS

General

☎	Telephone
Etr	Easter
RS	Restricted service
wk	Week
wknd	weekend
mdnt	midnight
rm	Letting bedrooms in main-building
fb	family bedrooms
✗	Bedrooms or rooms set aside for non-smokers
CTV	Colour television
TV	Monochrome television
✖	No dogs allowed
®	Tea-coffee-making facilities in bedrooms
nc	no children (age limit)
♧	Childrens facilities
P	Car parking on premises
⌂	Garage or covered space
✗	No parking on premises
⇔	No coach parties
⊠	Indoor swimming pool
⊡	Outdoor swimming pool
♣♣	Golf course
✎	Tennis court(s)
✦	Fishing
♿	suitable for disabled
①	Access/Mastercard
②	American Express
③	Barclaycard/Visa
④	Carte Blanche
⑤	Diners

Hotels

★	Hotel classification
▲	Country-house hotel
HBL	Merit award
●	Rosette award
⇌	Private bathroom with own WC
⋔	Private shower with own WC
⊟	Four-poster bed
T	Direct dial telephones in rooms
⊟	Cheap off-season weekends
⏾	Night porter
▦	Air conditioning
❀	Garden over ½ acre
CFA	Conference facilities
V	Type of cooking
♡	Vegetarian meals offered
♥	Afternoon tea
♨	Morning coffee

Guesthouses

hc	Number of bedrooms with hot and cold water
LDO	Time last dinner has to be ordered
Lic	Licensed

·Self catering

C	Cottage
F	Flat
H	House
WHB	Wash hand basin
MWB	Mid-week booking accepted
[ ]	Facility in brackets charged for
◇	Baby sitting/watching/listening service
◆	Cots provided
◆	High chairs provided
◉	Cooking by gas
◉	Cooking by electricity
L	Linen
☎	Public telephone
WM	Washing machine
SD	Spin dryer
TD	Tumble dryer
◉	Electric shaver point provided in each unit
◉	Radio in each unit
◉	Type of electric socket
⌂	Garage and/or lock-up
▥	Milkman calls regularly

HOTELS & GUESTHOUSES

★★★★Viking North St (Queens Moat) ☎(0904) 59822 188rm (176⇌12⋔) (7fb) CTV in all bedrooms ® T ⊟ Lift ⏾ 15P 80⌂ sauna bath solarium gymnasium ✖ English & French V ♡ ♨ Last dinner 10pm Credit cards ①②③⑤

★★★Chase Tadcaster Rd (Consort) ☎(0904) 707171 Closed Xmas 80rm (63⇌17⋔) (2fb) CTV in all bedrooms T ✖ (except guide dogs) Lift ⏾ CTV 100P 12⌂ (charge) CFA❀ putting Live music & dancing Sat (Nov-Etr) ♧ ♿ ♨ English, French & Italian V ♡ ♨ Last dinner 8.45pm Credit cards ①②③⑤

★★★Dean Court Duncombe Pl (Best Western) ☎(0904) 25082 36rm (34⇌2⋔) CTV in all bedrooms T ✖ ⊟ Lift ⏾ 12P ⇔ English & French V ♡ ♨ Last dinner 8.45pm Credit cards ①②③④⑤

★★★BL Fairfield Manor Shipton Rd, Skelton (Consort) ☎(0904) 25621 25rm (20⇌5⋔) (1fb) 2⊟ CTV in all bedrooms ® T ✖ ⊟ 50P ❀ ♣♣ ♎ ♨ English & French V ♡ ♨ Last dinner 9.15pm Credit cards ①②③⑤

★★★Ladbroke Abbey Park The Mount (Ladbroke) ☎(0904) 58301 84⇌ (11fb) ✗ in 5 bedrooms CTV in all bedrooms ® T ⊟ Lift ⏾ 40P CFA V ♡ ♨ Last dinner 9.30pm. Credit cards ①②③⑤

❀★★★★MiddlethorpeHall Bishopthorpe Rd (Prestige) ☎(0904) 641241 31⇌ ⋔ (1fb) 1⊟ CTV in all bedrooms T ✖ Continental breakfast ⊟ Lift ⏾ 70P ❀ croquet nc9yrs V ♡ ♨ Last dinner 9.45pm Credit cards ①②③⑤

★★Post House Tadcaster Rd (Trusthouse Forte) ☎(0904) 707921 147⇌ (30fb) CTV in all bedrooms ® T ⊟ Lift ⏾ 180P CFA ❀ ♨ Last dinner 10pm Credit cards ①②③④⑤

★★Abbot's Mews 6 Marygate Ln, Bootham ☎(0904) 34866 12⇌⋔ Annexe: 30rm (16⇌11⋔) (8fb) CTV in all bedrooms ® T ✖ ⊟ 20P ❀ ♨ International V ♡ ♨ Last dinner 9.30pm Credit cards ①②③⑤

★★Ashcroft 294 Bishopthorpe Rd ☎(0904) 59286 Closed Xmas & New Year 11rm (10⇌1⋔) Annexe: 4rm (3⇌1⋔) (3fb) CTV in all bedrooms ® T ⊟ CTV 40P ❀ V ♡ ♨ Last dinner 8pm Credit cards ①②③

★★Beechwood Close Shipton Rd ☎(0904) 58378 Closed Xmas Day 14rm (8⇌6⋔) (5fb) CTV in all bedrooms ® T ✖ ⊟ CTV 36P ❀ putting ♧ V ♡ ♨ Last dinner 9pm Credit cards ①③

★★Disraeli's 140 Acomb Rd ☎(0904) 781181 Closed 24 Dec–31 Jan 9rm (8⇌⋔) (4fb) CTV in all bedrooms ® T ✖

⊟ CTV 40P ❀ ♧ ♨ Cosmopolitan V ♡ ♨ Last dinner 9.45pm Credit cards ①②③⑤

★★Heworth Court 76–78 Heworth Green ☎(0904) 425156 Closed Xmas Day & Boxing Day 4⋔ Annexe: 9rm (3⇌6⋔) CTV in all bedrooms ® T ✖⊟ CTV 13P 1⌂ ⇔ V ♡ ♨ last dinner 9pm Credit cards ①②③⑤

★★The Hill 60 York Rd, Acomb (Exec Hotel) ☎(0904) 790777 Closed mid Dec–mid Jan 10⇌ (1fb) 2⊟ CTV in all bedrooms ® T ✖⊟ 12P ⇔ ❀ ♧ ♨ ♨ ✗ Last dinner 7.30pm Credit cards ①②③⑤

★★Hudsons 60 Bootham ☎(0904) 21267 Closed 24 & 25 Dec 28rm (25⇌3⋔) (2fb) 1⊟ CTV in all bedrooms ® T ✖ ⊟ Lift 35P V ♡ ♨ Last dinner 9.30pm. Credit cards ①②③⑤

★★Kilima 129 Holgate Rd (Inter Hotel) ☎(0904) 58844 15rm (11⇌4⋔) (1fb) 1⊟ CTV in all bedrooms ® T ✖ ⊟ 20P ⇔ ♧ ♨ English & French V ♡ ♨ Last dinner 9.30pm Credit cards ①②③⑤

★★Railway King George Hudson St ☎(0904) 645161 22rm (6⇌16⋔) (2fb) CTV in all bedrooms ® T ✖ ⏾ 12P ⇔ V ♡ ♨ Last dinner 9.45pm Credit cards ①②③⑤

★★Sheppard 63 Blossom St ☎(0904) 20500 20rm (16⇌) (4fb) 1⊟ CTV in all bedrooms ® T ✖ ⏾ CTV 10P 4⌂ (charge) ✦ ♨ English & Continental V ♡ ♨ ✗ Last dinner 9.30pm Credit cards ①③⑤

★★L Town House 100–104 Holgate Rd ☎(0904) 36171 Closed 24 Dec–31 Dec 23rm (12⇌6⋔) (5fb) CTV in all bedrooms T ✖ 23P ⇔ ♨ European ♡ ♨ Last dinner 9.30pm. Credit cards ①②③⑤

★Fairmount 230 Tadcaster Rd, Mount Vale ☎(0904) 38298 7rm (1⇌4⋔) (4fb) CTV in all bedrooms ® ⊟ 7P 2⌂ (charged) ⇔ ♨ International ♡ ♨ ✗ Last dinner 7.30pm Credit cards ①②③⑤

★Moreland House 106–108 Holgate Rd (Crest) ☎(0904) 35971 13rm (3⇌4⋔) (4fb) CTV in all bedrooms ⊟ 16P ♧ ♨ International V ♡ ♨ Last dinner 9pm. Credit cards ①③

★Newington 147 Mount Vale ☎(0904) 25173 due to change to 625173 27rm (3⇌19⋔) Annexe: 15rm (1⇌14⋔) (2fb) 2⊟ CTV in all bedrooms ® ✖ ⊟ Lift CTV 32P ⊡(heated) sauna bath solarium Disco Sat V ♡ ♨ Last dinner 8.30pm Credit cards ①②③⑤

○**York Crest** Cliffords Tower, Tower St (Crest) ☎(0904) 648111 130⇌ ⋔

GH Aberford Hotel 35–36 East Mount Rd ☎(0904) 22694 13hc (2⋔) (2fb) CTV in all bedrooms ✖ ® LDO2pm Lic ✖ 9P 2⌂ Credit cards ①②③

GH Abingdon 60 Bootham

Cres, Bootham ☎(0904) 21761 Closed Xmas 7hc (4⋔) CTV in 4 bedrooms ✖ ® ✖ CTV ✗

GH Acomb Rd 128 Acomb Rd ☎(0904) 792321 14hc (4fb) CTV in all bedrooms ® LDO7.30pm Lic CTV 20P

GH Adams House Hotel 5 Main St, Fulford ☎(0904) 55413 Closed Xmas 7hc (2⇌4⋔) (2fb) CTV in all bedrooms Lic ✖ CTV 8P

GH Albert Hotel The Mount ☎(0904) 32525 10hc (1⇌6⋔) (3fb) CTV in 9 bedrooms TV in 1 bedroom ✖ ® LDOnoon Lic ✖ CTV 6P Credit cards ①②③⑤

GH Alcuin Lodge 15 Sycamore Pl, Bootham ☎(0904) 32222 Feb–Nov 6hc (2fb) TV in all bedrooms ✖ ® LDO9am Lic ✖ CTV 3P nc3yrs

GH Alhambra Court Hotel 31 St Marys, Bootham ☎(0904) 28474 26hc (24⇌2⋔) (3fb) CTV in all bedrooms ✖ ® LDO10pm Lic lift ✖ CTV 26P Credit cards ①③

GH Amblesyde 62 Bootham Crescent ☎(0904) 37165 2nd wk Jan–end Nov 7hc (1fb) CTV in all bedrooms ® LDOam CTV

GH Arndale Hotel (formerly the Voltgeur Hotel) 290 Tadcaster Rd ☎(0904) 702424 Closed Xmas 10hc (5⇌4⋔) (2fb) CTV in all bedrooms ® LDOnoon Lic ✖ 15P

GH Ascot House 80 East Pde ☎(0904) 426826 9⋔ (2fb) TV in all bedrooms ® LDO6pm ✖ CTV 10P 3⌂ sauna solarium

GH Avenue 6 The Avenue, Clifton ☎(0904) 20575 Feb–Nov 6hc (1fb) TV in all bedrooms ✖ LDOnoon ✖ CTV 6P

GH Beckett 58 Bootham Cres ☎(0904) 644728 7hc (4⋔) (2fb) ✗ in 2 bedrooms TV in 1 bedroom CTV in 2 bedrooms ✖® LDO6pm ✖ CTV ✗

GH Beech Hotel 6–7 Longfield Ter, Bootham ☎(0904) 34581 Closed Xmas & New Year 7hc (3fb) CTV in all bedrooms ✖✖ 5P nc5yrs

GH Bootham Bar Hotel 4 High Petergate ☎(0904) 58516 Closed Xmas Eve–Boxing Day 8⋔ (2fb) CTV in all bedrooms ✖® lift ✖ CTV

GH Brönte House 22 Grosvenor Ter, Bootham ☎(0904) 21066 Closed 5 days Xmas 7hc (4⋔) (1fb) ✖ ® LDO4pm ✖ CTV 3P

GH Cavalier 39 Monkgate ☎(0904) 36615 Closed Xmas & New Year 10hc (2⇌4⋔) (4fb) CTV in 9 bedrooms ® LDO4pm Lic ✖ CTV 4P sauna

GH Clifton Bridge Hotel Water End ☎(0904) 53609 Closed Xmas week 14hc (4⇌2⋔) (2fb) CTV in all bedrooms ® LDO8pm Lic ✖ CTV 9P 4⌂ Credit cards ①③

GH Coach House Hotel Marygate ☎(0904) 52780 13hc (6⇌5⋔) ✖ LDO9.30pm Lic ✖ CTV 13P Credit card ③

GH Coppers Lodge 15 Alma Ter, Fulford Rd ☎(0904) 39871 8hc (4fb) CTV in all bedrooms LDO4pm ♨ CTV P Credit card ③

GH Craig-y-Don 3 Grosvenor Ter, Bootham ☎(0904) 37186 6hc (1⇄) CTV in all bedrooms ® ♨ 4P

GH Crescent 77 Bootham ☎(0904) 23216 9hc (5fb) CTV in all bedrooms ✕® ♨ CTV 3P 1▲

GH Croft Hotel 103 Mount Rd ☎(0904) 22747 10hc (1fb) CTV in all bedrooms ® LDOnoon Lic ♨ CTV 1▲ Credit card ③

GH Dairy 3 Scarcroft Rd ☎(0904) 39367 Feb–Nov 4hc (1⇄) Annexe: 2hc (1⇄1▥) (2fb) TV in all bedrooms ® ♨ CTV ♩ ♨

GH Field House Hotel 2 St George's Pl ☎(0904) 39572 17hc (1⇄10▥) CTV in all bedrooms ® LDO7pm Lic ♨ 20P Credit cards ①②③

GH Gables 50 Bootham Cres ☎(0904) 24381 6hc (2fb) CTV in all bedrooms ✕® ♨ CTV

GH Georgian 35 Bootham 12hc (2⇄1▥) (1fb) CTV in 3 bedrooms ® CTV 16P ☎(0904) 22874 Closed Xmas

GH Grasmead House Hotel 1 Scarcroft Hill, The Mount ☎(0904) 29996 6⇄ (2fb) ✗ in 1 bedroom CTV in all bedrooms ✕® Lic ♨ CTV 1P Credit cards ①③

GH Greenside 124 Clifton ☎(0904) 23631 Closed Xmas 6hc (2▥) (2fb) CTV in 1 bedroom TV in 1 bedroom ♨ CTV 4P 1▲

GH Hazelwood 24–25 Portland St, Gillygate ☎(0904) 26548 Closed 16 Dec–Jan 15hc (2⇄6▥) (1fb) CTV in all bedrooms ✕® ♨ 10P Credit card ③

GH Heworth 126 East Pde ☎(0904) 426384 7hc (1fb) LDO2pm Lic ♨ CTV 1P 1▲

GH Inglewood 7 Clifton Gn ☎(0904) 53523 7hc (3▥) (2fb) CTV in all bedrooms ✕♨ CTV 1▲

GH Linden Lodge Nunthorpe Av, Scarcroft Rd ☎(0904) 20107 Closed Dec 9hc (3fb) ® LDOnoon Lic ♨ CTV

GH Mayfield Hotel 75 Scarcroft Rd ☎(0904) 54834 7hc (2⇄4▥) (3fb) CTV in all bedrooms ♨ LDO7.15pm Lic ♨ ♩ Credit cards ①②③

GH Minster View 2 Grosvenor Ter ☎(0904) 55034 8hc (3⇄1▥) (4fb) CTV in all bedrooms ® LDO 5.30pm Lic ♨ CTV 6P

GH Moat Hotel Nunnery Ln ☎(0904) 52926 9hc (1fb) ✕CTV 10P Credit cards ②③⑤

GH Orchard Court Hotel St Peters Gv ☎(0904) 53964 11hc (1⇄6▥) (4fb) CTV in 7 bedrooms ® LDO7.30pm Lic CTV 11P Credit cards ①③

GH Priory Hotel 126 Fulford Rd ☎(0904) 25280 Closed Xmas week 20hc (2⇄18▥) (5fb) CTV in all bedrooms ® LDO9.30pm Lic ♨ CTV 24P Credit cards ①②③⑤

GH St Denys Hotel St Denys Rd ☎(0904) 22207 Closed Xmas 11hc (7⇄4▥) (4fb) CTV in all bedrooms ® LDOnoon Lic ♨ CTV 9P

GH St Raphael 44 Queen Anne's Rd, Bootham ☎(0904) 645028 7hc (1fb) CTV in all bedrooms ✕♨ CTV nc8yrs

GH Sycamore Hotel 19 Sycamore Pl ☎(0904) 24712 6hc (2fb) CTV in all bedrooms ® LDO9.30am Lic ♨ 3P nc5yrs

GH Town House Lodge 112–114 Holgate Rd ☎(0904) 34577 Closed 24 Dec–1 Jan 12hc (3⇄6▥) (7fb) CTV in all bedrooms ® ♨ 18P Credit cards ①②③⑤

SELF CATERING

F Abbey House 2 St Mary's *for bookings* Mrs M l'Anson, Littlethorpe Hall, Littlethorpe, Ripon, North Yorkshire HG4 3LP ☎Ripon (0765) 5133 & York (0904) 707211
Three flats located in a Victorian terraced property, near to the town centre. Two of the flats accommodate two people the other flat up to four. They all comprise lounge, separate dining room and kitchen plus bathroom/WC.
All year MWB in season 1night min, 6mths max, 3units, 1–4persons ◆ no pets ◎ fridge Electric Elec metered ⌁ inclusive ☎ Iron & Ironing board in unit [Launderette within 300yds] ☺ CTV ☻3pin square 1P

F Bainton House 6 St Mary's *for bookings* Intermain Leisure Ltd, 7 St Mary's, Bootham, York YO3 7DD ☎York (0904) 36154 (am) & 707211 (pm)
Four flats, two of which sleep four people in one double-bedded room with two bed-chairs in the lounge, the other two flats sleep five people in one double and one single bed plus two bed-chairs in the lounge, each have shower/WC.
All year MWB in season 1night min, 6mths max, 4units, 1–5persons ◆ ◎ fridge Gas fires Gas/Elec inclusive ⌁ inclusive ☎ Iron & Ironing board in unit Launderette within 300yds ☺ CTV ☻3pin square 1P 1▲

F Birch House 5 St Mary's, Bootham *for bookings* Mrs M l'Anson, Littlethorpe Hall, Littlethorpe, Ripon, N Yorks HG4 3LP ☎Ripon (0765) 5133 or York (0904) 707211
Four flats within a Victorian town house near the town centre. The ground-floor flat sleeps two in twin beds (double beds in the other three flats), two have double bed-settees in the lounge, and two have single folding beds available. All have combined bathroom/WCs and well fitted kitchens.
All year MWB 2nights min, 6mths max, 4units, 1–4 persons ◆ ◎ fridge Electric Elec metered ⌁ inclusive ☎ (10yds) Iron & Ironing board in unit [Launderette within 300yds] ☺ CTV ☻3pin square 4P

F 1 Bootham Terrace (Flats 1–5) *for bookings* Mrs Felicity Walker, 52 North Lane, Haxby, York YO3 8JP ☎York (0904) 768460
Five flats situated in an Edwardian town house near the centre of the city. They offer different types of accommodation.
All year MWB out of season 3days min, 3mths max, 5units, 1–5 persons ◆ no pets ♢ fridge Electric & gas fires Gas & Elec inclusive ⌁ inclusive ☎ Iron & Ironing board in unit [Launderette within 300yds] ☺ CTV ☻3pin square 6P

F Carlton House *for bookings* Intermain Leisure Ltd, 7 St Mary's, Bootham, York, N

Yorks ☎York (0904) 36154 (am) & 707211 (pm)
Three flats located within a Victorian terraced house, near the town centre. The ground-floor flat has a twin-bedded room, the first-floor flat sleeps six people and the second-floor flat has two bedrooms. All comprise bathroom/WC, kitchen and lounge.
All year MWB in season 1night min, 6mths max, 3units, 1–6persons ◆ ◆ ◎ fridge Electric Elec inclusive ⌁ inclusive ☎(20yds) Iron & Ironing board in unit Launderette within 300yds ☺ CTV ☻3pin square 1P 1▲

F Dale House 13 St Mary's *for bookings* Mrs M l'Anson, Littlethorpe Hall, Littlethorpe, Ripon, N Yorkshire HG4 3LP ☎Ripon (0765) 5133 or York (0904) 707211
All year MWB in season 1night min, 6mths max, 4units, 1–6 persons [◆] ◎ fridge Electric Elec metered ⌁ inclusive ☎ Iron & Ironing board in unit Launderette within 300yds ☺ CTV ☻3pin square P ▲

C 58 Dale Street *for bookings* Mr & Mrs W D Kimberling, 17 Ashbourne Way, Woodthorpe, York YO2 2SW ☎York (0904) 704844
All year MWB out of season 3days min, 3wks max, 1 unit, 6persons no pets ◎ fridge Gas inclusive Elec metered ⌁ inclusive ☎ TD in unit Iron & Ironing board in unit ☺ ☻ TV ☻3pin square P ▲

F Mrs West-Taylor The Flat Dalham House, Heslington, York, North Yorkshire YO1 5DX ☎York (0904) 411617
A self-contained first-floor flat in a converted farmhouse. Accommodation is for two to four people in a twin-bedded room and on divans in the living/dining room. There is a bathroom/shower/WC and a separate kitchen.
All year 1wk min, 1unit, 1–4 persons, nc5 no pets ♢ fridge ♨ Elec inclusive ⌁ inclusive ☎(¼m) SD in unit Iron & Ironing board in unit ☺ CTV ☻3pin square 2P ▥

H St Saviours House St Saviours Place *for bookings* Mr T P Marks, 34 St Saviourgate, York ☎York (0904) 27230
Spacious three-storey Victorian house close to the town centre. Accommodation comprises lounge, dining room, kitchen, utility room, two bathrooms and a cloakroom, two double-bedded rooms, one twin-bedded, one with bunk beds and a single room.
All year MWB out of season 1wk min, 1mth max, 1unit 9persons [◇] ◆ ◆ ◎ fridge Gas inclusive ⌁ inclusive ☎ WM, SD & TD in unit Iron & Ironing board in unit ☺ ☻3pin square 1P ▥

WHERE TO EAT:

The AA's choice:

✕**Tony's** 39 Tanner Row ☎(0904) 59622
This charming little restaurant has a cosy aperitif bar, and a warm, homely atmosphere.
Closed Sun & 2 wks Feb Lunch not served Sat 𝄞Greek 24 seats Last dinner 10.30pm ✇

other recommended restaurants:

Bettys 6 St Helens Square ☎(0904) 59142
An all-day menu provides plenty of choice. Yorkshire specialities like spiced

teacakes and rarebit with ham are firm favourites. Imaginative children's menu. Non-smoking area. Closed 1 Jan & 25 & 26 Dec

Gillygate Wholefood Café
Millers Yard, Gillygate ☎(0904) 24045
An appealing little vegetarian restaurant in a courtyard of shops selling local craftwork. The adjoining bakery prepares a regular supply of yummy cakes and slices, and from noon there are savoury pies and daily specials such as vegetarian lasagne or cheese and vegetable bake. Unlicensed. No smoking. No dogs. Closed Sun, 1 Jan & 25 & 26 Dec

Mulberry Hall Coffee Shop
Stonegate ☎(0904) 20736
With its elegant mulberry decor and fine china on polished tables, this coffee house above a china shop is a most civilised place to stop for refreshment. Delicious light bites range from sandwiches served with pickles and a salad garnish, Welsh rarebit and quiche to lovely home-made cheesecakes – and a fruit cake accompanied by a slice of cheese. Unlicensed. Closed Sun, Mon, 1 Jan, Good Friday & 25 & 26 Dec

St William's College Restaurant College Street ☎(0904) 34830
This fine old timbered building has a charming courtyard for summer eating and a pleasant restaurant where you help yourself to cakes, scones and pastries to enjoy with tea or coffee. At lunchtime, there are soups and salads, pâté and cold meats, as well as more substantial offerings like savoury raised pie and vegetables. Homely puds to finish. Non-smoking area. Closed Good Friday & 25 & 26 Dec

Taylors Tea Rooms Stonegate ☎(0904) 22865
Three pleasantly relaxing rooms above a splendid tea and coffee shop. An all-day menu is in operation, providing a good choice of snacks both sweet and savoury: chocolate and fruit cakes, tea loaves and Yorkshire curd tarts, sandwiches, rarebit variants, omelettes, even full grills. Sweets include some tempting ice cream creations. Unlicensed. Non-smoking section. Closed 1 Jan & 25 & 26 Dec

York Wholefood Restaurant
98 Micklegate ☎(0904) 56804
Part of a wholefood co-operative, this pine-furnished restaurant offers a tasty line in vegetarian food. Choose from quiches in imaginative combinations like mushroom and rosemary or leek and tomato, nourishing soups such as cream of courgette, crunchy salads, plus a vegan dish of the day. Super sweets, too. Booking is possible in the evening, when there's even greater choice. Unlicensed. No smoking. Closed Sun, Bank Holidays (except Good Friday) & 10 days Christmas.

For more details on the establishments listed here, please see the current editions of the AA guides, *Guesthouses, Farmhouses and Inns in Britain, Holiday Homes, Cottages and Apartments in Britain,* and *Hotels and Restaurants in Britain,* where the AA hotel and restaurant symbol rating system is explained.

DIRECTORY

Tourist Information

Stonegate, a street of fine old buildings, was the route by which stone for building the Minster was transported from the river bank

---

ANTIQUE DEALERS

Acomb Antiques, 3 West View Close *Tel York 791999*

Barker Court Antiques & Bygones, 44 Gillygate *Tel York 22611*

Bishopgate Antiques, 23 Bishopgate Street *Tel York 23893*

Blenheim House Antiques, 47 Holgate Road *Tel York 22905*

Brian Thacker Antiques, 42 Fossgate *Tel York 33077*

Burr S K, 2 Melrosegate *Tel York 425757*

Carter Toll Antiques, 15 Grape Lane *Tel York 29090*

Clifford K F, 181 Boroughbridge Road *Tel York 792322*

Crown Forge, 5 Station Road, Haxby *Tel York 768273*

Hardcastle Henry, 46 Parliament Street *Tel York 23401*

Holgate Antiques, 52 Holgate Road *Tel York 30005*

Longley B & T, 3 The Village, Haxby *Tel York 764698*

Miscellaneous, 9 Lord Mayor's Walk *Tel York 641710*

Morrison Robt & Son, 131 The Mount *Tel York 55394*

Ruddock G, 36 Stonegate *Tel York 22822*

Thornton John D, 1 Pulleyn Drive *Tel York 23264*

Vickers G, 29 Gillygate *Tel York 24936*

Yates I M P, 5 The Shambles *Tel York 54821*

Yon Antiques, Whip Ma Whop Ma Gate *Tel York 27928*

York Antique Centre, 2 Lendal *Tel York 641445*

AUTOMOBILE ASSOCIATION

AA Centre, 6 Church Street *Tel York 27698*

BANKS

Barclays:
54 Acomb Road
50 Clifton
11/12 Main Street, Heslington
1/3 Parliament Street
2 St Helen's Square
46 The Village, Haxby

The York Livestock Centre, Murton
York District Hospital, Wiggington Road

HFC Trust & Savings:
1 Bootham

Lloyds:
12 Lendal
Main Street, Heslington
2 Pavement
21 Front Street, Acomb
28 Hawthorne Grove, Heworth

Midland:
80 Clifton
Main Street, Heslington
13 Parliament Street
The Green, Upper Poppleton
88 The Mount
37 The Village, Haxby
York Livestock Centre, Murton
19 York Road, Acomb

National Westminster:
14 Coney Street
119 East Parade
Main Street, Heslington
1 Market Street
4 Osdal House, Front Street, Acomb
41 The Village, Haxby
York Livestock Centre, Murton

Royal Bank of Scotland:
Ousegate House, 6 Nessgate

TSB England & Wales:
130 Haxby Road
5 St Helen's Square
73 York Road, Acomb

Yorkshire Bank PLC:
46 Coney Street

BOAT TRIPS

Castle Line Cruises *Tel York 702240*
Departure point for self-drive hire: North side of Skeldergate Bridge

Hills Boatyard *Tel York 23752*
Departure point: South side of Lendal Bridge

White Rose Line Cruises *Tel York 28324*
Departure point: South Esplanade, about 150 yards south east of Ouse Bridge on eastern bank

---

BOOKSELLERS

Automobile Association, 6 Church Street

Barbican Bookshop, 24 Fossgate

Blake Head Bookshop, 104 Micklegate

Blue Star Publications, 93 Nunnery Lane

Forum Books, 45a Blossom Street

Godfrey T C Ltd, 32 Stonegate

Leisure Books, 1 Odeon Buildings, Blossom Street

McDowell D, 3 Grape Lane

Minstergate Bookshop, 8 Minster Gates

Penguin Bookshop, Coppergate

Pickering & Co, (York's oldest bookshop) 42 The Shambles

Stonegate Bookshop (SPCK), 42 Stonegate

Story Edwin Ltd, 9 Minster Gates

University Bookshop (York) Ltd, New Bookshop University of York, Heslington

W H Smith & Son Ltd, 39 Coney Street

York Community Bookshop Ltd, 73 Walmgate

BUREAU DE CHANGE – *see also Banks*

Deak International (UK) Ltd, De Grey Rooms, Exhibition Square *Tel York 54229*

Opposite: still Shambles by name but not by nature, York's one-time butcher's quarter is considered one of Europe's finest Medieval streets

Deak International (UK) Ltd, York Railway Station *Tel York 24528*

Thomas Cook, 33 The Shambles *Tel York 647557*

CAR HIRE – SELF DRIVE

Budget Rent-a-Car, Foss Islands Road *Tel York 644919*

Economy Car Hire, 12 Gregory Close, Skelton *Tel York 470009*

Fitton Robert (Car Hire), 37 Heworth Green *Tel York 426868*

Godfrey Davis Europcar, Leeman Road *Tel York 20394* 32 Lawrence St *Tel York 414969* York Station *Tel York 59790*

Kenning Car Hire, Micklegate Bar *Tel York 59328*

Polar Self Drive, Fulford Road, York *Tel York 25371*

Reynards Rent a Car, 21 Piccadilly *Tel York 24277*

Russell's Garage (York), The Stonebow *Tel York 55118*

Stan-Hire, Lynsey Croft, Pidgeon Cote Lane, Malton Rd, *Tel York 726922*

Walbers Garage, 17b Bewlay Street *Tel York 55040*

Wills & Ellis, Poppleton Garage, Boroughbridge Road, Poppleton *Tel York 792651*

CAR PARKS

All the car parks listed below are pay car parks and many in the City Centre are short stay and therefore not suitable for tourists.

Bishophill Senior – Small car park on western side of River Ouse

Bootham Row – Small car park near Bootham Bar.

Castle – Large car park in centre of York. Recommended for Castle Museum, Cliffords Tower and Jorvik Viking Centre

Coppergate Multi-storey Car Park – City Centre car park recommended for shopping visits, Jorvik Viking Centre, Castle Museum

Esplanade – Elongated car park beside river Ouse – easy access to National Railway Museum

Foss Bank Multi-storey car park – Located outside city wall with easy access to Minster and surrounding area

Haymarket – Small car park within city walls

Heworth Green – Large car park on north east side of city on A1036. Also coach park and 'park and ride scheme'

Kent Street – Car park just outside city wall on southern side

Kings Staith – City Centre car park beside river. Very small and usually full

Leeman Road –Adjacent to National Railway Museum and recommended for National Railway Museum

Marygate – Large car park on west side of city – recommended for Museum Gardens, Yorkshire Museum, Art Gallery

Monkgate – Medium size car park on north east side of City. Access to Minster via Monk Bar

Nunnery Lane – Elongated car park just outside city wall on south west side of city

Paragon Street – Large car and coach park adjacent to Barbican Swimming Baths. Located outside city wall on south east side of city

St George's Field – Large car park between Rivers Ouse and Foss. Recommended for Castle Museum, Clifford's Tower

St John's – Medium size car park on northern side of city

Tanner Row – Multi-storey car park on western side of River Ouse. Access to City Centre via Ouse Bridge

Union Terrace – Medium size car park on north side of city. Access to Minster via Bootham Bar

Streets that were never meant for cars can be explored by bicycle

CHEMISTS

Badger Hill Pharmacy, 35 Yarburgh Way *Tel York 414912*

Blass & Fisher (York) Ltd, 151 Beckfield Lane *Tel York 798796*

Boots The Chemist, 48 Coney Street *Tel York 53657*

Boots The Chemist, 41 York Road, Acomb *Tel York 798109*

Brack C & A, 67 Front Street, Acomb *Tel York 791502*

Brooke O Chemists Ltd, 28 York Road *Tel York 798271*

Bulmer J R, The Green, Upper Poppleton *Tel York 781022*

Burton Pharmacy, Intake Avenue *Tel York 23472*

Cuckston Roy S, MPS, 412 Huntington Road *Tel York 23415*

Gillygate Chemists, 2b Gillygate *Tel York 642557*

Heaton H Philip, 66 Clarence Street *Tel York 22829*

Hepworth Michael (Chemists), 71a Main Street, Fulford *Tel York 33458*

Hutchinson B & T, 18 Bishopthorpe Road *Tel York 23509*

Johns Pharmacy, 57 Blossom Street *Tel York 22761*

Marks Allan J (Chemists) Ltd, 18 Allerton Drive, Nether Poppleton *Tel York 794854*

Minster Pharmacy, 16 Goodramgate *Tel York 56382*

Mitchell W B, 103 Green Lane, Acomb *Tel York 791997*

Nixon P M, MPS, 69 Fulford Road *Tel York 22652*

Riley J S, MPS, 24 Acaster Lane, Bishopthorpe *Tel York 707169*

Robinson D W, 126 Hull Road *Tel York 410365*

Solomon Jos B, 275 Melrosegate *Tel York 410987*

Thompson G, 8 Boroughbridge Road *Tel York 793440*

Trevor Gordon W, 1 Wains Grove *Tel York 706923*

Wood F W & Son (York) Ltd, 10 East Parade *Tel York 424375* 5 Heworth Village *Tel York 423760* 153 Tang Hall Lane *Tel York 413285* 68 The Village, Haxby *Tel York 768911* 72 Clifton *Tel York 24507*

Wright G H, 71 Monkton Road *Tel York 422913*

Wroe's King Square Pharmacy, 29 Colliergate *Tel York 54771*

CINEMAS

Odeon Film Centre, Blossom Street *Tel York 23040*

CYCLE SHOPS

3A's, York Road, Acomb *Tel York 798208*

Boswell Tony, 133 Tang Hall Lane *Tel York 410405*

Cycle Scene, 2 Ratcliffe Street, Burton Stone Lane *Tel York 53286*

Duckworth C H, 46 Haxby Road *Tel York 54835*

Halfords, Feasegate *Tel York 22632*

Ian White Cycles, 64 The Village, Haxby *Tel York 763302*

Peddle Power, Chestnut Grove, New Earswick *Tel York 763188*

Riverside Cycle Repairs, B15, Parkside Commercial Centre, Terry Avenue *Tel York 645727*

Russell C S (York), 1 Clifford Street *Tel York 22744*

Shannons Cycle Centre, 171 Boroughbridge Road *Tel York 791610*

Trotter Bob, 18 Monkgate *Tel York 22868*

York (Cycle Wholesale), 79 Beaconsfield Street, Acomb *Tel York 799368*

York Cycleworks, 16 Lawrence Street *Tel York 26664*

DEPARTMENT STORES

Boots, 48 Coney Street
British Homes Stores, Coney
Street
Debenhams, 5 Coney Street,
Davygate
Marks & Spencer, 9 Pavement
Victoria House, George Hudson
Street
W H Smith & Son, 39 Coney St
Woolworth, 2 Spurriergate

EMERGENCY

Automobile Association, 6
Church Street *Tel York 27698*
Dental Service (emergency)
Tel York 30371 (Bank Holidays
only)
Samaritans, 89 Nunnery Lane
Tel York 55888/9
The Health Centre, Monkgate
Tel York 30351
York District Hospital 24-hour
Accident & Emergency *Tel York
31313*

HOSPITALS (MAIN)

City, Huntington Road *Tel York
31388*
Clifton, Shipton Road *Tel York
36661*
Naburn, Naburn Lane *Tel York
28955*
York & District General,
Wigginton Road *Tel York 31313*

LAUNDERETTES

Bendix Launderette, 5 Matmer
House, Hull Road
**Circle Washeteria, (Hyde &
Kelly),** 54 The Circle, Green
Lane, Acomb
**Clifton Coin Op Laundry & Dry
Clean,** 1 Clifton
Glenn T, 113 Millfield Lane
Haxby Road, Washeteria,
124 Haxby Road
Launderama, Mill Garth,
Harcourt Street
Launderette & Sweetshop,
83 Heworth Road
Lockwood W, 148 Bishopthorpe Rd
Monarch Coin Launderette,
114 Gale Lane
Spic Launderettes,
2a Bishopthorpe Road
Walmgate Bar Laundromat,
39 Huby Court

LIBRARIES

Bishopthorpe Library, Main
Street, Bishopthorpe
Clifton Library, Rawcliffe Lane,
Clifton
Dringhouses Library, Tadcaster
Road, Dringhouses
Front Street Library, Front Street
Fulford Library, Social Hall
School Lane, Fulford
Haxby Library, Station Rd, Haxby
Huntington Library, Garth Road,
Huntington
New Earswick Library, New
Earswick
Strensall, 19 The Village

*York archaeologists have learned
from the litter of centuries – but
above ground there wages a constant
battle against today's contributions*

Tang Hall, Fifth Avenue
Upper Poppleton Library, Upper
Poppleton
York Library, Museum Street
Yorkshire Law Society (Library),
23 Stonegate

LOCAL ADMINISTRATION

York City Council, Guildhall
Tel York 59881
Tourism Dept., De Grey Rooms,
Exhibition Square *Tel York 28666*

LOCAL RADIO

BBC Radio York, 20 Bootham
Row *Tel York 641351*

NEWSAGENTS

Atherton D & M, 77a Bootham
74 Haxby Road
5 Nessgate
14 Tadcaster Road
45 York Road, Acomb
Fishergate Newsagency,
32 Fishergate
Forbuoys, 45 Crichton Avenue
Fox Wood News Agency,
2 Beagle Ridge Drive
Hartley's News Agency,
175 Osbaldwick Lane
Haxby News Agency, 19 Front St
Heslington Road News Agency,
26a Heslington Road
Holly Tree News, 39 Oak Tree
Lane, Haxby
Johnson E, PO Broadway
Martins the Newsagent, The
Circle Green Lane, Acomb
Maynews, 27 Oak Tree Close,
Strensall
Maynews, 23 Parliament Street
Mills (North British) Ltd,
16 Stonegate Arcade
Monk Bar Newsagency,
10 Goodramgate

Newshaws Newsagents,
43 Front Street, Acomb
Nixons News, 70 Fourth Avenue
123 Bad Bargain Lane
198 Fulford Road
Piccadilly News, 5 Piccadilly
**Saville Barker Newsagents
(Northern) Ltd,** 101 Main
Street, Fulford
South Bank Newsagents,
2 Queen Victoria Street
Stead G, PO, Eastholme Drive
Tilstons Newsagents, 6 Garfield
Terrace
Towler G E & E & Son, 14 York
Street, Dunnington
West John, The Kiosk, Leeman Rd
W H Smith & Son, New Station
Shop, Railway Station
**Wilkins Newsagents & Off
Licence,** Clifton Green

OPTICIANS

Berry & Nutton, 28 Colliergate
Tel York 55866
J Black & Son, 4 Church Street
Tel York 22465
Co-operative Optical Service,
5 Davygate Centre *Tel York 38819*
**Coverdales Ophthalmic
Opticians,** 12 Colliergate
Tel York 31793
Dolland & Aitchison (North),
12 Market Street *Tel York 52896*
13 New Street *Tel York 23854*
23 Parliament Street *Tel York
23293*
Humphreys A E, 17 Micklegate
Tel York 53297
Pearle Vision Centre,
11 Coppergate Walk *Tel York
32472*
Pheasey Frank C, 74 Petergate
Tel York 53582
Row & Sadler, 44 York Road,
Acomb *Tel York 791688*
Terry R B, 15–17 Bootham
Tel York 52231
6 Ryedale Centre, Haxby
Tel York 761216
Viewpoint Contact Lens Centre,
1 Church Street *Tel York 646425*

PHOTOGRAPHY

Coverdale & Fletcher,
22 Colliergate
Dixons, 20 Market Street
Jessop of Leicester, 2 Piccadilly
Sanderson Keith,
20 Bootham
Saville Photo Hi-fi,
7 Goodramgate
York Camera Mart, 18 Church St
York Photo Audio Centre,
51 Fossgate

POLICE STATIONS

Bishopthorpe *Tel York 706022*
Clifton *Tel York 24977*
Copmanthorpe *Tel York 706464*
Huntington *Tel York 26088*
New Earswick *Tel York 761525*
Sand Hutton *Tel York 490673*
Shipton *Tel York 470222*
Strensall *Tel York 490221*
York *Tel York 31321*

Sport

POST OFFICES

Crichton Avenue PO, Intake
Avenue
Melrosegate Sub PO,
204 Melrosegate
Naburn PO, Front St, Naburn
Upper Poppleton PO, Station
Road, Upper Poppleton
Woodthorpe PO, 61 Moorcroft Rd
York Main PO, 22 Lendal

THEATRES

Arts Centre York, Micklegate
Tel York 27129
Theatre Royal, St Leonards Place
Tel York 23568
Youth Theatre Yorkshire,
54a Nunthorpe Rd *Tel York 39707*

TOILETS

Clarence Street
Coppergate Shopping Centre
(behind Fairfax House)
Fossbank Car Park (disabled
facilities)
Heworth Green Car Park
(disabled facilities)
Low Ousegate (adjacent to Ouse
Bridge)
Monkgate Car Park (disabled
facilities)
Museum Gardens (near Lendal
Tower) (disabled facilities)
Nunnery Lane Car Park (disabled
facilities)
Paragon Street Car Park
Parliament Street (south-eastern
end) Men only
Parliament Street (north-western
end) Women only
St George's Field Car Park
(disabled facilities)
St Leonard's Place (adjacent to
Bootham Bar) (disabled facilities)

TOURIST INFORMATION CENTRES

**York Tourist Information
Centre,** De Grey Rooms,
Exhibition Square *Tel York
21756/7* (General enquiries –
York and District.
Accommodation Finding
Service: 'Book-A-Bed-Ahead'
Service: Bureau de Change.)
**Yorkshire and Humberside
Tourist Board,** 312 Tadcaster
Road *Tel York 707961*
Also:
**Historic Buildings and
Monuments Commission
for England (DoE),** English
Heritage, Crown Buildings,
Duncombe Place *Tel York 22902*
**National Trust Shop and
Information Centre,**
32 Goodramgate *Tel York 59050*

TRANSPORT

British Rail Enquiry Bureau
Tel York 642155
West Yorkshire Road Car Co,
Rougier Street *Tel York 24161*
York Pullman Bus Co, Exhibition
Square *Tel York 22992*

CRICKET

York Cricket Club, Clifton Park,
Shipton Road *Tel York 23602*

FOOTBALL

York City Football Club,
Bootham Crescent *Tel York 24447*

GLIDING

Ouse Gliding Club, Rufforth
Aerodrome (on B1224 4 miles
west of York) *Tel Rufforth 694*
(Saturdays & Sundays only)
Yorkshire Gliding Club, Sutton
Bank (off the A170 7 miles east
of Thirsk) *Tel Thirsk 597237*
(Flying on most days of the year)

GOLF

There are four golf courses within
easy reach of York city centre.
Fulford, Heslington Lane (2m
SE of York) *Tel York 412882*
18 hole, 6779 yds, Par 72, SSS 72.
Visitors welcome.
A flat, parkland, moorland course,
well-known for the superb quality
of its turf, particularly the greens,
and now famous as the venue for
some of the best golf tournaments
in the British Isles.
Heworth, Muncaster House,
Muncaster Gate (1½m NE of
city centre on A1036) *Tel York
39110*
18 hole, 6091 yds, Par 69, SSS 69.
Visitors welcome. Parkland course,
easy walking.
Pike Hills, Tadcaster Road,
Copmanthorpe (N side of village
on A64) *Tel York 706566*
18 hole, 5718 yds, Par 69, SSS 68.
Visitors welcome. Parkland course
surrounding nature reserve.
York, Lords Moor Lane, Strensall
(6m NE of city, E of village)
Tel York 490304
18 hole, 6225 yds, Par 70. Visitors
welcome.
A well-designed, heathland
course with easy walking.

HORSE RACING

Flat racing and National Hunt:
York Racecourse, The
Knavesmire, York. Flat race
meetings between May–October
Beverley Racecourse, Flat Race
meetings April–September
Catterick Racecourse, Flat Race
meetings March–October
National Hunt meetings
November–March
Doncaster Racecourse, Flat Race
meetings March & May–July
& September–November
National Hunt Meetings
October & December–March
Pontefract Racecourse, Flat Race
meetings, April–October

Redcar Racecourse, Flat Race
meetings May–November
Ripon Racecourse, Flat Race
meetings April–August
Thirsk Racecourse, Flat Race
meetings April–July &
September
Wetherby Racecourse, National
Hunt meetings September–May

HUNTS

Most hunts have regular meets
on Saturdays between November
and April. Local hunts include
Bramham Moor (south west of
York), the Holderness (south east),
the Middleton (north east), the
York and Ainsty North (north
west) and the York and Ainsty
South (south).

MOTOR-CYCLE RACING

Oliver's Mount, Scarborough,
one annual national and one
international road race meeting
Harewood – Speed hill climbs
held during Spring & Summer
Castle Howard – Speed hill climbs
April & October

POINT-TO-POINT-COURSES

Charm Park, Wykeham, nr
Scarborough, Derwent Hunt,
March
Stainton Dale Hunt, Easter
Monday
Sinnington Hunt, late February
Duncombe Park, Helmsley, April
Easingwold, York and Ainsty
Hunt, Spring
Hornby Castle, nr Bedale, Bedale
and West of York Hunt, April
Hutton Rudby, nr Stokesley,
Hurworth Hunt, Spring
Little Ayton, nr Stokesley,
Cleveland Hunt, Spring
Wetherby, Badsworth Hunt, May
Braham Moor Hunt, April
South Durham Hunt, end of
February
Whitwell-on-the-Hill, nr Malton,
Middleton Hunt, May

ROWING

Regattas are held on the Ouse at
York each May and June

RUGBY LEAGUE

**York Rugby League Football
Club,** Wigginton Road *Tel York
24252*
**York Rugby Union Football
Club,** Clifton Park, Shipton
Road *Tel York 23602*
Season September to April

SWIMMING

There are swimming baths at the
following locations:
Barbican Swimming Pool,
Paragon Street *Tel York 30266*
Edmund Wilson, Thanet Road
Tel York 793031
Yearsley, Haxby Road *Tel York
22773*

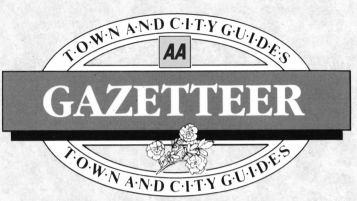

TOWN AND CITY GUIDES
AA
GAZETTEER
TOWN AND CITY GUIDES

Places of Interest
around York

*Surprising little features like this charming statue are
to be found in the grounds of Harewood House, one of
many interesting places to visit in the York area*

Map references marked with an asterisk in this section of the gazetteer refer only to the maps on pages 114 and 115. All other places can be found on map pages 112 and 113

ALDBOROUGH

SE4065
This pretty village stands on the site of *Isurium*, the northernmost town to be built without any military motives during the Roman occupation. Remains (AM) revealed through excavation include sections of a boundary wall, two tessellated pavements, and a wide variety of coins, pottery, and artefacts on display in the small site museum. In the village itself are a striking maypole and a cross that probably commemorates the Battle of Boroughbridge, which was fought here in 1322.

ALDBROUGH

TA2338
About 1½ miles from this small village is a pleasant sand and shingle beach backed by small eroded cliffs. In the village itself is the 13th- to 15th-century St Bartholomew's Church with a Norman arch and a sundial bearing a Saxon inscription.

AMPLEFORTH

SE5878
Perched upon a shelf of the Hambleton Hills, this village was chosen in 1802 as the site of a Roman Catholic school by English Benedictine monks who had fled from France to escape the French Revolution. The college and abbey of St Lawrence stand at the eastern end of the street along which most of the stone-built houses of the village are ranked, overlooking magnificent views to the south. Within the college library are some of Robert Thompson's earliest pieces of furniture. His much sought-after work is easily recognisable by the handcarved mouse he always hid somewhere on his furniture as his signature.

APPLETREEWICK

SE0560
On the east side of Wharfedale two miles below Burnsall, and locally called 'Aptrick', the village prospered from 1300 when Bolton Priory acquired its manor with its extensive sheep ranges and valuable lead mines.
Stone houses line the steep, attractive main street. The Tudor-style High Hall was restored by Sir William Craven, Appletreewick's own 'Dick

Whittington', who became Sheriff and Lord Mayor of London at the beginning of the 17th century. Monks' Hall was largely rebuilt in 1697 on the site of Bolton Priory's grange.

AYTON, EAST AND WEST

SE9884
Situated on either side of the River Derwent, the twin villages of East and West Ayton are linked by an attractive four-arched bridge of 1775. The ruined pele tower of Ayton Castle makes a good counterpoint to the tower of East Ayton's church, on the other bank.

BATLEY

SE2424
This once-booming woollen town has undergone many changes, owing to the run-down of its major industry. The town's buildings have had a facelift, and around the market place a conservation area has been declared. In Wilton Park is the Bagshaw Museum, housed in a 19th-century building. It contains a museum of local history. North of Batley is the Oakwell Hall and Country Park complex. The Elizabethan moated manor house dates from 1583 and was 'Fieldhead' in Charlotte Brontë's novel *Shirley*.

BEDALE

SE2688
This mainly-Georgian town features an old stepped market cross in the main street, and an unusual church whose first floor is reached by a stair guarded by a portcullis. These elaborate precautions were taken against the very real possibility of Scottish raids. Opposite the church is Georgian Bedale Hall, a fine house with a museum and a complete ballroom wing.

BEMPTON

TA1972
North of the village are the famous chalk Bempton Cliffs rising a sheer 350 feet. The cliffs are a Royal Society for Protection of Birds reserve and comprise the only location in England where there is a gannet colony. Many species of birds can be seen, including kittiwakes, guillemots, puffins, fulmars and razorbills.

BENINGBROUGH HALL (NT)

SE5159
Completed in the first half of the 18th century, this fine house is largely intact and original.
William Thornton, a carpenter-architect from York, is thought to have been the builder, but certain exterior features have been credited to a better-known architect, Thomas Archer. Thornton gave Beningbrough its chief glory; the quite superb decorative woodcarvings which have been compared to those of Grinling Gibbons. Throughout the interior — and especially in the great staircase and two-storey hall — there is evidence of unusually high standards of craftsmanship. The house is therefore a fitting home for a permanent exhibition of nearly 100 17th- and 18th-century portraits, placed here by the National Portrait Gallery in 1978.
The house stands in a 375-acre wooded park.

BEVERLEY

TA0339
The gothic completeness of Medieval Beverley Minster has won its acclaim as one of the most beautiful churches in Europe. Its lovely twin bell towers can be seen for miles across the flat Humberside pastures, and its interior is packed with the monumental art of some 700 years. Here can be seen the full blossoming of the 14th-century stonemason's skill in the magnificent Percy Tomb, the

Interior of Beverley Minster, one of Europe's finest churches

ingenuity of 15th-century glassmakers in the great east window, and the craft of local men in the rich extravagance of carved wood. At the far end of the Main Street is St Mary's Church, a beautiful building that was started in the 12th century as a chapel for its more famous neighbour. One of its more notable features is a 15th-century ceiling painting of the English kings. In early times the town was an important market centre and the capital of the East Riding of Yorkshire, a status that it had to defend with a stout wall pierced by five gates. Subsequent periods saw the community outgrow these confines, and all that remains today is the 15th- century North Bar. Evidence that much of the expansion was in the 18th and 19th centuries can be seen in the many Georgian houses and shopfronts that survive. The ornate market cross dates from *c*1714, and the Guildhall of 1762 displays woodcarving by local men. Inside 18th-century Lairgate Hall, which houses the council offices, is a Chinese Room with hand- painted wallpaper. Beverley's Art Gallery and Museum displays pictures and relics of local interest.

A unique collection is displayed at the Museum of Army Transport.

BINGLEY

SE1039

This old woollen town situated in the Aire Valley has a mixture of old and new buildings, ranging from the historic White Horse Inn, 16th-century All Saints' Church and old woollen mills to the modern Bradford and Bingley Building Society Headquarters. The Leeds and Liverpool Canal was of great importance to the town — it brought in the coal and raw materials to its grand mills. The number of wharfs in Bingley testifies to this. The Three and Five Rise Locks raise the water level of the canal by nearly 100 feet by a man-made staircase which was constructed in the 18th century.

The River Wharfe's serenity at Bolton Abbey (top) is contrasted by sudden turmoil at the nearby Strid

During the summer a waterbus runs along the canal between Bingley and Shipley. Near by is the St Ives Country Estate, comprising woodland, moorland and a championship golf course.

BISHOP BURTON

SE 9839*

A large wayside pool reflects this attractive black-and-white wold village, with picturesque cottages set around its green. For centuries it belonged to the Archbishops of York, and one of their palaces is said to have stood in a nearby field called Knight Garth. Bishop Burton's parish church contains a bust of John Wesley, in elm.

BOLTON ABBEY

SE0754

Woodlands and pastures in a bend of the River Wharfe make a fittingly peaceful setting for the remains of this once-powerful 12th-century priory. Most of the structure lies in ruins, but the nave has served as a parish church for hundreds of years and the old gatehouse was incorporated into a mansion during the 19th century. The little river can be crossed by stepping stones or a footbridge here, and attractive riverside walks extend from the ruins to The Strid.

The modern translation of this old English word is Turmoil, which is an apt description of the way in which the River Wharfe boils through a 12-foot constriction of its gorge at this point. Farther north are the picturesque ruins of Barden Tower, a 12th-century structure that was restored by Lady Anne Clifford of Skipton Castle in 1659.

An intriguing window at 17th-century Bolling Hall, Bradford

BOLTON PERCY

SE5341
This pleasant village probably takes its name from William de Percy, who held the manor during the 11th century. The Church of All Saints is early 15th century; standing alone beyond the churchyard is a half-timbered 15th-century gatehouse with delicately carved woodwork.

BOROUGHBRIDGE

SE3966
Before the bypass was built, Boroughbridge, lying halfway on the Great North Road between London and Edinburgh, was a familiar posting point in coaching times. The bridge overlooks a Salmon Leap and near by are the three 'Devils Arrows' gritstone monoliths – approximately 20 feet high. They are thought to be of the mid Bronze Age; however, alternative tales of their origin abound.

BRADFORD

SE1633
Bradford's growth and rise to fortune came with the industrial revolution. It was the woollen capital of the world, and many of the grand Victorian buildings have survived the considerable redevelopment that has swept away the more unsavoury aspects of its Victorian legacy.

Bradford became a cathedral city in 1920 and the Institute of Technology became a university in 1966.

There is plenty for the visitor to see and do. Among older features are two buildings of which Bradford is particularly proud — the great 'iced-cake' creation of City Hall, built in 1873, and the dignified Wool Exchange of 1867.

Before attaining cathedral status St Peter's was a parish church whose foundation is thought to go back as far as the 7th century. The present building is probably the city's oldest and dates from the 14th century.

One of Bradford's most dramatic buildings is the Cartwright Memorial Hall, a large and ornate structure standing in the 53-acre Lister Park. It was purpose-built as a museum and gallery in 1904.

In complete contrast is the up-to-the-minute National Museum of Photography, Film and Television.

Also concerned with visual images is the Colour Museum, in Perkin House.

An old spinning mill in Moorside Road is the appropriate home for Bradford's Industrial Museum, which traces the development of the worsted textile industry through advances in its technology. Adjacent is the mill owner's house.

Bolling Hall is a fine example of West Yorkshire manor-house construction dating mainly from the 17th century (though its earliest parts are of 15th-century origin).

BRAMHAM

SE4242
In the days when stagecoaches travelled the Great North Road, two inns stood on the village square – one, the Red Lion, still a public house today, and the other now identifiable by a bas-relief of a carthorse on its wall. Two miles south-west is Bramham Park, built in the Queen Anne style, and with gardens reminiscent of Versailles, by the first Lord Bingham in about 1700. It was damaged by fire in 1828 and restored early this century, but the exterior remains unaltered. The house contains fine furniture, pictures, and porcelain.

BRIDLINGTON

TA1766*
Bridlington has lost some of the 'genteel' Yorkshire resort atmosphere of days gone by, but it is still a very popular seaside town boasting an attractive and historically interesting centre. The main point of interest in old Bridlington is the Priory Church of St Mary, which is particularly noted for its nave — the remains of an Augustinian priory founded here in the 12th century. The richly-decorated north porch, the 14th-century south aisle and the beautiful west doorway are also of note. Across the green is the priory's Bayle Gate which was built in 1388 and has, at various times since, served as the prior's courtroom, a sailors' prison, a barracks and a school, before being used in its present rôle of museum. Stones from the old priory were used in the building of two piers in the harbour, which still services a small fishing fleet. The long stretches of fine sandy beach to the north and south of the harbour, on Bridlington Bay, enjoy a sheltered location.

BRIMHAM ROCKS (NT)

SE2165
Brimham Rocks have been a popular attraction since the 18th century. People come in their thousands to enjoy the views and to marvel at the curious rock formations which crown Brimham Moor. Over millions of years, outcrops of millstone grit have been eroded to form fantastic shapes. Some huge stones are perched so precariously that they look as if the touch of a hand would topple them.

BURNSALL

SE0361
Wharfedale's landscape changes at Burnsall. Above the village are the distinctive limestone uplands; below Burnsall the valley becomes more wooded. The village has many mellow stone houses of 17th- and 18th-century date. St Wilfrid's church is approached through a 17th-century tapsel gate — a lychgate with a revolving 'turnstile' entrance. It was largely rebuilt during the reign of Henry VIII but shows some 14th-century work, including a beautiful, sculptured Adoration of the Magi.

BURTON AGNES

TA1063*
The sleepy village of Burton Agnes is one of the most attractive in the Wolds. The main attraction is Burton Agnes Hall, built by Sir Henry Griffith more than 380 years ago and still owned by his family. It stands among smooth lawns and clipped yews, its red brick mellowed by time, and its semi-octagonal plan echoed in the octagonal towers of the gatehouse (built slightly later). The interior is splendidly furnished and has a fine collection of Impressionist and 20th-century paintings. The

Norman church, containing a fine alabaster tomb, stands next to the hall, and near by is a restored Norman manor house (AM).

BYLAND ABBEY (AM)

SE5478
In 1177, a colony of Cistercian monks settled here and established the community that was to last until the Dissolution. The site has been excavated, and the plan of the church and monastic buildings can be seen, as can well-preserved green and yellow glazed floor tiles. Most of the great west front of the Abbey stands, topped by a single turret and the broken circle of a rose window 26 feet in diameter.

Weathered gritstone at Brimham

CARLTON

SE6423
The Duke of Norfolk's Yorkshire home, Carlton Towers, was built in 1614 on property owned by the Duke's ancestors since the Norman Conquest. It was remodelled in the 18th and 19th centuries and now presents a mainly Victorian appearance. The staterooms by John Francis Bentley, architect of Westminster Cathedral, contain interesting paintings, furniture, silver and exhibitions.

Castle Howard has the first windowed dome to be incorporated in an English private house

CASTLE HOWARD

SE7170*
Castle Howard is one of the largest houses in the country, and was built in 1670 of pale yellow local stone by Sir John Vanbrugh and Hawksmoor.

Inside is particularly magnificent, although most of the rooms are surprisingly small – which gives the house a pleasant atmosphere. The marbled entrance hall is lit by a multi-windowed dome — the first to be put on an English house. Near the main staircase hang tapestries by John Vanderbank depicting the four seasons, and paintings by Rubens, Canaletto, Van Dyke and Holbein adorn the walls. The beautiful staterooms are vast and luxurious and are filled with magnificent examples of Sheraton and Chippendale furniture and many fine pieces of porcelain.

In the stables is Britain's largest collection of 18th- to 20th-century costume, including beautiful period-dress lavishly embroidered and trimmed, and costumes belonging to famous artistes.

The grounds surrounding the house extend for some 1,000 acres and sparkle with lakes and fountains, while peacocks strut about the parkland. Scattered around the gardens are elegant ornamental structures such as Hawksmoor's circular Mausoleum, and Vanbrugh's charming domed Temple of the Four Winds.

CAWOOD

SE5737
Cawood village is pleasantly situated on the River Ouse, high on the river bank of which stands the church, with its fine perpendicular tower. An impressive, tall gateway, dating from the 15th century, is all that remains (AM) of the palace of the Archbishops of York.

CLEVELAND WAY

SE6183
After nearly 16 years of planning, the Cleveland Way was eventually opened in 1969 as the second long-distance footpath established in England and Wales. It stretches 93 miles from Helmsley in the south-west, along the western escarpment to Roseberry Topping in the north. From there the path cuts east to join the Heritage Coast at Saltburn-by-Sea, then follows the sea along the cliffs southwards to Whitby, Scarborough and on to Filey, where it links with the Wolds Way. It is entirely contained in the North York Moors National Park and passes many historic sites, offering some magnificent and varied moorland and coastal scenery.

COXWOLD

SE5377
One of the most picturesque villages within the North York Moors National Park, Coxwold's broad main street is lined by warm-toned, stone cottages, set back behind the wide green verges so often found in rural Yorkshire. In the 18th century the village was fortunate to have as its clergyman the eccentric and writer Laurence Sterne, whose comic masterpiece, *The Life and Opinions of Tristram Shandy* had been published just before his appointment to

Writer Laurence Sterne was clergyman at Coxwold village

Coxwold. He named his house Shandy Hall and it now belongs to the Sterne Trust, who have preserved and renovated both it and the garden.

CRAYKE

SE5670
This mostly brick-built hilltop village affords fine views across the vale to York Minster. The 15th-century Church of St Cuthbert is a short way down the hill. Cobblestoned small lanes off the main street enhance Crayke's charm. At the highest point of the village is the battlemented house (not open) of Crayke Castle, built in the 15th century on the site of a Norman castle.

EASINGWOLD

SE5269
An unusual bull ring can be seen in the market place of this pleasant town of red-brick houses and cobbled lanes. The local church, itself an attraction, contains an ancient parish coffin.

Hooked summit of Roseberry Topping, on the Cleveland Way

EAST RIDDLESDEN HALL (NT)

SE0742
A mid-17th-century manor house on Keighley's northern edge, East Riddlesden Hall has fine panelling, plasterwork and furnishings, with two splendid examples of rose windows in the north and south porches — they were regarded in Yorkshire then almost as architectural badges of rank. Across the fishpond are two barns, the larger of around 1640–50, stone-built, with two round-arched cart entrances and a superb timber-framed interior.

ELVINGTON

SE6947*
Elvington is a large riverside village in the Derwent Valley, with several attractive cottages overlooking the green. It is also the location of the Yorkshire Air Museum (see page 107), which has a restored World War II Flying Control Tower as the centrepiece. The Watch Office within the tower has been accurately recreated from archive film.

FILEY

TA1180*
Filey is now a popular holiday town, standing mostly on the cliff tops overlooking the bay. The old village has quaint streets and several houses dating from the 17th century, and the modern town boasts a fine promenade, a sandy beach and well-kept gardens. A lovely wooded road called the Ravine leads down to the beach, and at the top of it stands St Oswald's Church.

FLAMBOROUGH

TA2270*
About 1,000 years ago the area around Flamborough was taken by the Vikings, and is still sometimes called 'Little Denmark'. The sprawling village stands two miles inland from Flamborough Head and the lighthouse, and boasts the much restored but delightful St Oswald's church. There is also a monument of a man with his heart bared; he is Sir Marmaduke Constable who died in 1520, because, it is said, a toad which he swallowed ate his heart. Flamborough Head is where the Yorkshire Wolds meet the sea in glistening white 400-foot cliffs. From here onlookers watched John Paul Jones, the Scottish-born American sailor who performed a number of daring naval exploits during his career, win a sea battle with two British men-of-war. The cliffs between Flamborough and Bempton are famous as a valuable breeding ground for seabirds, and here the only mainland gannetry in Britain is to be found.

FOUNTAINS ABBEY AND STUDLEY ROYAL COUNTRY PARK (NT)

SE2768
The largest, possibly the best preserved, and certainly the most famous ruined abbey in Britain is Fountains Abbey. Standing majestically beside the River Skell and part of the Studley Royal Estate, it was founded in the 12th century by a handful of monks who had split from their brothers at York. Devoted to a life of poverty, the Cistercians farmed the land and built the large, but austeré, Abbey. Ironically, their farming was so efficient that it eventually became the wealthiest abbey in Britain.

After the Dissolution the Abbey and its grounds were sold by Henry VIII to Sir Richard Gresham. It then gradually fell to ruin, some of the stones being used in the building of nearby Fountains Hall.

The park of Studley Royal was landscaped in the 18th century and features many of the conceits of the period, including a temple folly and various statues. Its lakes and woodland combine in a sylvan beauty enhanced by grazing deer.

GILLING EAST

SE6176
A charming village in mellow stone, Gilling East is dominated by its castle. After long associations with the Fairfax family, it is now owned by Ampleforth College. It dates from the 11th century but, after many alterations and owners,

White cliffs mark where the wolds and sea meet, near wild and exposed Flamborough Head

A glimpse of the magnificence enjoyed by boys attending school at Castle Gilling, Gilling East

it is now a preparatory school for about 120 boys.

The magnificent Elizabethan Great Chamber, used as a refectory, has superb oak panelling.

GOOLE

SE7423*
Some 50 miles from the North Sea, at the confluence of the Rivers Ouse and Don, this low-lying red-brick town is a port, one of the farthest inland in Britain. Since docks and a canal were built in 1826 the town has become a thriving centre.

GRASSINGTON

SE0064
The lovely area in which this Upper Wharfedale village stands has been settled since very early times. Many Iron Age camps and barrows survive, and during the Roman occupation the area was extensively mined for lead ore. The village itself is a popular tourist centre with a cobbled market square reached via a picturesque Medieval bridge. A National Park Interpretation Centre is based in the village.

GREAT DRIFFIELD

TA0257*
Driffield is a busy agricultural town on the edge of the Yorkshire Wolds, boasting an annual show and a regular Thursday cattle market. Anglers come to Driffield to fish for trout in streams which flow down from the Wolds.

Isolated farm cottage near Greenhow Hill, in the Dales

GREENHOW HILL

SE1164
Occupying a bleak and exposed situation at 1,300 feet, Greenhow Hill is one of Yorkshire's highest villages, developed solely as a lead-mining community from the early 17th century.

The scattered settlement is loosely centred on The Miners' Arms. Numerous small, isolated cottages, reached along narrow walled lanes, represent homes of former lead-miners. Old levels, workings and ruined smelt-mills survive on the moors and in the little valleys to the north of the road.

Greenhow Hill is just outside the Yorkshire Dales National Park, but within the Park boundary to the west are Stump Cross Caverns, a magnificent cave system discovered by lead-miners in 1858. The main cave has been developed into an impressive showpiece, floodlit to demonstrate the splendid stalactite and stalagmite formations.

HACKNESS

SE9690*
Set deep in the Derwent Valley, this is a village that is hard to rival in beauty and interest.

The poet William Mason described Hackness as *'A nest of sister vales, o'er hung with hills of varied form and foliage'*. Several valleys and streams converge here, such as the Whisperdales, while the surrounding hills boast acres of Forestry Commission conifers with splendid walks and a drive open to the public.

Hackness has a history too. The foundations of the present church of St Peter were laid in about 1050. It has a 13th-century tower, a 15th-century spire and a magnificent font with a tall oak cover carved in 1480. Hackness Hall, built in 1791, is the seat of Lord Derwent (not open to the public).

HALIFAX

SE0825
Old and new blend in this ancient cloth-manufacturing town, rising on steep hills from the Hebble Brook in the Pennine foothills. New flats and office blocks contrast with solid stone-built mills and their tall chimneys; old cobbled streets, with glimpses of the surrounding green hills, lead to modern pedestrian precincts.

The cloth trade was important to the town as long ago as the 13th century. Carpets and yarns are still manufactured in the town, and evidence of the past importance of cloth can be seen in the splendidly restored 18th-century Piece Hall. Here 315 rooms open off colonnaded galleries round a large quadrangle. In these rooms the cottage weavers once exhibited and sold their 'pieces' or lengths of cloth. Today they are occupied by a museum, exhibitions and a wide range of crafts, antique and souvenir shops, while twice a week there is also a busy open-air market. Bankfield Museum and Art Gallery also has a comprehensive collection of costumes and textiles among many other items of interest. Calderdale Industrial Museum has over 100 machines on display, representing Calderdale's industrial heritage during the past 150 years.

The story of town horses during the 19th and 20th centuries is exhibited at the National Museum of the Working Horse.

Britain's most ornate chimney must be Wainhouse Tower, completed as a dyeworks chimney in 1875, and overshadowing the district called King's Cross. It has a conventional circular brick flue surrounded by a stone casing, with a 403-step spiral staircase leading to balconies — intended as observation platforms — at the top, 250 feet above ground. Since the structure was never connected to the dyeworks, perhaps John Edward Wainhouse designed it as a folly.

Water-borne calcite formation known as The Organ, in Stump Cross Cavern, near Greenhow Hill

On the edge of the town, set in parkland, is the 15th-century Shibden Hall, which houses the Folk Museum of West Yorkshire.

HAREWOOD HOUSE AND BIRD GARDEN

SE3144
Home of the Earl and Countess of Harewood, this house was designed by John Carr and Robert Adam in the 18th-century.

The grounds, landscaped by Capability Brown, offer lakeside and woodland walks.

The interior is outstanding, offering a display of 18th-century craftsmanship which includes furniture by Thomas Chippendale, said to be the finest ever made in England. A fine collection of Sèvres and Chinese porcelain is also

94

to be seen in the elegant rooms.

Covering an area of some four acres is the Harewood Bird Garden, containing over 200 species of exotic birds. In these natural surroundings many of the birds wander freely.

HARROGATE

SE3055

Harrogate has the garden-city quality of an elegant spa resort — which it once was — with gardens stretching floral fingers between Georgian and Victorian streets. Had it not been for the coincidence of two powerful and ill-understood forces — geology and high fashion — it is possible that Harrogate as it is known today would never have existed.

That is because it owes its past reputation as a high-quality resort and its present fame as one of the North's leading conference centres to local mineral springs and the 18th- and 19th-century fad for taking the waters.

Deep beneath the foundations of the town, in the bedrock of the lofty 500-foot plateau on which it stands, are underground deposits of iron and sulphur that give rise to no fewer than 88 'spa' wells.

Although it is likely that the waters from these were valued for their curative properties from very early times, the real history of Harrogate begins in 1571 when a gentleman by the name of Sir William Slingsby rediscovered the Tewit Well. Still open and

marked by an elegant little domed shelter, the well head is on a 200-acre strip of well-tended greensward which rolls enchantingly into and around the town centre. This is known as The Stray, and is all that remains of the Forest of Knaresborough, the rest having been cut down or developed long ago. Its survival, albeit in a manicured form, is the result of protection for 'time immemorial' by the Enclosure Act of 1770.

Some 30 or so other springs rise in the relatively confined area of the beautiful Valley Gardens, but though different types are sometimes very close together there is no discernible mixing of chalybeate and sulphurous waters.

The wide green spaces, magnificent flower borders and pleasing mixtures of trees and shrubs in the Valley Gardens and elsewhere have made Harrogate internationally famous as England's Floral Town. But they also provide the spacious and elegant setting against which the town's earliest resort buildings are seen to best advantage.

Opulent reminder of Harrogate's resort past, in the Pump Room

It is difficult to judge which is chief amongst them, but the Royal Pump Room on Royal Parade must be a close contender. Built in 1842 and showing later additions, it now houses a museum in which there are costume, Victoriana and pottery collections.

The original sulphurous well head still bubbles forth in the cellars of the building, and any

visitor so inclined can sample its strong-smelling issue.

Opposite the fine Crescent Gardens are the old Royal Baths of 1897, which when opened were reputed to be the finest in Europe. Original facilities still available there include Turkish Baths, but these have been augmented by such 20th-century comforts as a sauna and solarium.

Varied programmes of events are arranged at the Royal Hall, which adjoins the town's most modern landmark — the new International Conference Centre. This building more than any other reflects the success with which Harrogate has transferred the 18th-century lessons it learned in hospitality to the needs of the 20th century.

Not actually in the town but accessible by a charming woodland walk from Valley Gardens are the Harlow Car Gardens —45 acres of borders, beds and arboreta.

HAWORTH

SE0337

To the south of the Aire Valley lies an area immortalized in English literature by the novels of the Brontë sisters.

At its centre in a valley on the edge of rugged moorland is Haworth, a small, bleak, grey West Yorkshire village. Its narrow streets still contain buildings dating from the 16th century, such as the Elizabethan Emmott Hall at the foot of the area called Old Kirkgate.

It was to the bleak Georgian parsonage that the Brontë family came in 1820 and the sisters lived and wrote here until 1849. Now the house is a museum containing the family's belongings, including Branwell's portraits of his sisters, Charlotte's sewing box and Mr Brontë's spectacles.

The tower is all that remains of Haworth Old Church, in which the Brontës worshipped, as the rest of the existing church was rebuilt in 1881.

A Memorial Chapel was built for them in 1964, and beneath the base of one of the stone entrance pillars is the family vault.

In the village itself at the top of the hill is the Black Bull Inn, where Branwell Brontë was a frequent and (by all accounts) witty visitor.

Some two miles west of the churchyard on Haworth Moor, along a favourite footpath of the sisters, lies the Brontë Bridge and Waterfall.

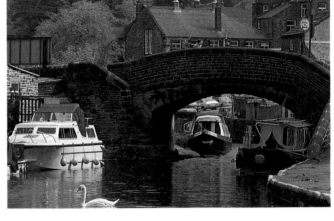

Mill town turned tourist centre – the success story of Hebden Bridge

HEBDEN BRIDGE

SD9927
Deep in the Pennines' Heart, Hebden Bridge was a mill town, but is now reborn as a tourist centre of the Calder Valley. Walkley's Clog Mill is the only surviving clog mill in Britain, and visitors can see the complete process of clog-making. Housed in a former textile warehouse is 'Automobilia', a collection of Austin Sevens and Morris cars, motor cycles and various items of motoring interest.

HEDON

TA1828*
At one time this small town was a major port connected to the Humber Estuary by canals. It was rich enough to start building the magnificent King of Holderness church in the 12th century, and subsequent work shows the prosperity to have lasted at least until the 15th century. Trade has long since filtered away to Hull, but the huge pinnacled tower of the 'King' remains in all its glory. Near by, the Ravenspur Cross commemorates a long-vanished village of that name, where Bolingbroke (later Henry IV) landed in 1399 to claim the English throne for the House of Lancaster.

HELMSLEY

SE6183
Nestling in a corner of Upper Ryedale, Helmsley is one of the prettiest of North Yorkshire's country towns. It is a magnet for visitors because roads from Cleveland, Thirsk and York converge upon its market square. Helmsley's friendly atmosphere persuades motorists to stay. Market day is Friday.

The town's handsome houses and inns are built of local yellow stone with red pantile roofs, although a Tudor house (Canon's Garth) behind the church and an extension to the Black Swan Inn are half-timbered.

Some interesting walks leave the town, including the long-distance Cleveland Way and Ebor Way. Helmsley also contains the headquarters of the North York Moors National Park Committee, and the Tourist Information Centre is in Claridge's Bookshop.

Helmsley Castle (AM), a ruined 12th-century stronghold with domestic buildings added in the 14th century, sometimes called Furstan Castle, is close to the market square.

The imposing bulk of the parish church contains one of 19th-century explorer David Livingstone's letters, from Africa.

Duncombe Park, with its 600 acres of parkland and fine mansion built by Vanbrugh, is to become a new attraction for visitors to Helmsley. Ancestral home of the Earls of Feversham, the great house served as a school for girls until 1985. The present Lord Feversham hopes to open the

Central and unspoiled, Helmsley is popular with visitors

gardens and the house after renovation.

Helmsley's summer festival of music and arts is now part of the Ryedale and Helmsley Festival.

HORNSEA

TA2047*
Hornsea has become very well known through its fine pottery, which is made in Rolston Road and can be bought from a seconds' shop. More can be learned about the processes and skills involved from a conducted tour, and the company has a special playground and mini-zoo for children. The resort itself is popular with families and offers excellent sands separated from gardens and amusements by the fine Promenade. Behind the narrow streets and clustered houses of the old village is Hornsea Mere, a two-mile lagoon formed during the Ice Ages. Today it is a popular boating venue with a reserve for wildfowl and a walk.

HOVINGHAM

SE6675*
The stone cottages of this lovely little village cluster round the green under the Saxon tower of All Saints' Church and Hovingham Hall.

The latter is an unusual building in distinctive yellow limestone. Built in the mid-18th century, its entrance is an archway leading off the village green into the riding school and stables. Sir Thomas Worsley, the builder, loved horses and this design enabled them to be exercised out of the rain. The lawn of the house is actually the village cricket field, and an annual festival of cricket is held there which attracts some of the country's finest players.

*Hull's Guildhall and Law Courts
survived World War II bombing*

HULL (KINGSTON UPON)

TA0929*
This major industrial and
commercial centre is an
international port and a fishing
base for deep-sea vessels. As such
it suffered badly in World War II,
but its rebuilding has included a
fine shopping precinct scattered
with flowerbeds and interspersed
with parks and gardens. Docks
stretch for a full seven miles along
the north side of the Humber,
joined here by the little River
Hull. The Humber Bridge is one
of the world's longest suspension
bridges at 4,626ft/1410m. Despite
these extensive new developments
the city centre still has a few old
buildings untouched by bombs or
town planning, including the
largest parish church in England
and 18th-century Maister House
(NT). An early 17th-century
mansion in which the MP and
anti- slavery campaigner William
Wilberforce was born in 1759 is
now preserved as the William
Wilberforce Historical Museum.
Paintings, sculptures and visiting
exhibitions of work can be seen in
the Ferens Art Gallery. The Town
Docks Museum relates to fishing
and shipping. The Transport
Museum has a collection of
vehicles including a steam train
locomotive of 1882. The
Archaeology and Natural History
Museum has several interesting
displays and contains the biggest
surviving prehistoric logboat in
the country.

Since May 1983, masts and sails
have restored the city's skyline to
something of its glory 170 years
ago, when Hull merchants and the
Corporation completed their
ambitious dock projects. Until
recently, the old docks and their
Victorian warehouses were
redundant, but a con-
tinuous conservation
programme has been
restoring the core of
the 'Old Town'.

Most of this Conser-
vation Area lies south
and east of Queen's
Gardens, itself created
from the 18th-
century Queen's
Dock.

HUTTON-LE-HOLE

SE7090*
This attractive village was built
randomly around a wide green
dissected by two becks and various
picturesque bridges, at the foot
of a limestone escarpment. Grey-
stone houses with red pantiled
roofs complete the showplace
effect. Ryedale Folk Museum is one
of the main attractions here.
Bygones from the area are
displayed in a range of buildings
which include a number of
reconstructions. Craftsmen's tools,
farm implements, an ancient dairy,
Roman pottery and an Elizabethan
glass furnace are among the
exhibits.

ILKLEY

SE1147
During the 1840s the spring water
here was found to have medicinal
properties and Ilkley became a
popular spa town. Most of its
buildings date from the 19th and
20th centuries, but there is a
nucleus of older houses around the
church. One of these, Manor
House, is an Elizabethan house
built on the site of a Roman fort
and has Roman material on display.

Near by, Heber's Ghyll is the
site of the Swastika Stone, a unique
carved relic believed to have been
instrumental in ritual fire-worship.

JERVAULX ABBEY (AM)

SE1885
The ruins of this 11th-century
Cistercian monastery lie in a
magnificent garden setting on the
edge of the Yorkshire Dales.

The monastery was founded
in 1156 by an order not allowed to
eat meat, although many bones
were found here. Fifteen masons'
marks are discernible on remaining
stones, and the best feature is the
wall of the monks' dormitory, with
its high lancet windows.

Until it was dissolved by Henry
VIII in 1538, the Abbey thrived
and was particularly noted for its
cheese-making. Although little
remains of its former grandeur, the
mellowed ruins scattered amidst
the trees and shrubs
which abound here,
are enough to indi-
cate the original plan
of the Abbey
buildings.

Kilburn's White Horse is a relative newcomer of around 1857

KEIGHLEY

SE0641
The Brontë girls used to walk to this pleasant 19th-century town from Haworth to do their shopping.

A great attraction nowadays is the Keighley and Worth Valley Railway. Vintage trains, all restored by Society members at their workshops in Haworth, travel the line at regular intervals. Its main terminus is Keighley, where the restored Midland Railway Building of carved stone, gothic gables and wrought iron has been a star of film and small screen.

Other stops are Damems, once the country's smallest station; the Victorian country halt of Oakworth, which has been voted the best-preserved station in Britain, and was chosen for the filming of *The Railway Children*; then Haworth and the end of the line, Oxenhope, where there are retired locomotives, rolling stock and an exhibition shed.

Just north-west of the town on the A629 is Cliffe Castle, really a mansion dating from 1878 and now a museum which contains collections of natural and local history, craft workshops, and rooms with French furniture from the Victoria and Albert Museum.

KILBURN

SE5179
On the almost sheer side of one of the Hambleton Hills is the Kilburn White Horse, which took its shape in 1857. In the foothills is the pretty little beckside village of Kilburn,

Carving the mouse 'legacy' of wood craftsman Robert Thompson

home of Robert Thompson, a woodcarver whose trademark was the mouse. Examples of his work can be seen throughout the country, including York Minster and Westminster Abbey. The Medieval chapel of St Thomas has been refitted with oak furniture as a memorial to Robert Thompson, who died in 1955. His grandsons carry on the business, the workshop and a showroom being within a half-timbered Elizabethan house.

KIRBY MISPERTON

SE7779*
Within the 350 acres of wooded parkland at Kirby Misperton Hall is Flamingoland, containing over 1,000 birds, animals and reptiles.

Probably the most spectacular sight is the flock of pink flamingos standing in a handsome lake edged by willow trees. Many species of animals roam in large paddocks. Other attractions include a funfair, Gnomeland, a model railway, an adventure playground, a jungle cruise — a raft-ride through jungle scenes and Zulu villages — and a pottery workshop. For children there is a real working farm.

KIRKBYMOORSIDE

SE6986*
Lying at the southern edge of the North York Moors, Kirkbymoorside is a charming market town and the headquarters of one of the oldest hunts in the country, the Sinnington Hunt. It is associated with George Villiers, the notorious 2nd Duke of Buckingham, who died in the house next to the King's Head Inn.

KIRKHAM PRIORY (AM)

SE7365*
A ruined Augustinian priory standing beside the bank of the picturesque River Derwent, Kirkham was founded by Walter Espec, Lord of Helmsley, in 1125

and enlarged during the 13th and 14th centuries. A magnificent 13th-century gatehouse is set amongst the remains of the priory, which also include a lavatorium, (the monks' washroom), and a Norman doorway.

KNARESBOROUGH

SE3557
Knaresborough is an attractive town with narrow streets of Georgian houses, steep steps and alleyways. The area is full of caves, the most famous being that named after Mother Shipton, the 15th-century seer. The most interesting phenomenon is the Dropping Well, where drops of water containing a lime deposit are gradually petrifying a curious assortment of objects placed beneath them

by locals and visitors. On a cliff-top high above the river stand the remains of the 14th-century castle, including the keep, two baileys, gatehouse and the Court House Museum.

LEEDS

SE3034
Third largest city in England and regional capital of Yorkshire, Leeds was originally a wool town. From the mid-19th century it developed into a world centre for ready-made clothing and remained so until well into the 1970s. Today engineering and retail trade provide the main sources of employment.

Probably the most dramatic building in the city is the Town Hall, with its impressive continuous rows of giant Corinthian columns and pilasters, the building's centrepiece a baroque clocktower rising some 255 feet. Built in 1853 by architect Cuthbert Brodrick, who also built the Corn Exchange, the interior is one of Victorian opulence. Some fine carvings and ornamentation have been revealed as a result of the stonework being cleaned. The Town Hall is venue for the city's International Concert Season. Next to the Town Hall, the Italianate Municipal Building houses the City Museum, which has a collection of artefacts and natural history.

Another showpiece of Leeds is the magnificent Civic Hall, headquarters of the city's administration. Built in 1933 of Portland stone, its twin towers are surmounted by two owls in gold leaf. A gallery and centre of Henry Moore's sculptures form part of the City Art Gallery. The many works of art include watercolours by Turner and his contemporaries, plus a collection of French paintings.

Apart from still being the market for the sale of corn, the Corn Exchange is also used for the city's exhibitions and shows. The huge structure built in 1861 has a glass domed roof which allowed traders over the years to see the quality of the grain they were buying.

Leeds has a network of covered shopping arcades, mostly built in the late Victorian period. There is much of architectural interest here as well as specialist shops.

Mineral-rich water percolating through the limestone at Knaresborough (left) can 'petrify' even bears and hats at the town's famous Dropping Well

Leeds Town Hall is known for its impressive baroque Ivanhoe Clock

The cultural life of Leeds is strong and offers much from the classics to the more light-hearted entertainment. Music has a well-established prominent position and the theatre's associations may be remembered by *The Good Old Days* from the City Varieties Theatre. A major opera centre is currently housed in the Grand Theatre and the Leeds Playhouse has one of the most successful repertory theatres in the country.

West of the city centre, on the banks of the River Aire, are the ruins of Kirkstall Abbey. Founded by Cistercian monks in 1152, the remains are considered the finest of early monastic sites in the country. The 12th-century gatehouse of the abbey is now an interesting museum of folk studies. A series of reconstructed full-size Victorian streets with shops, cottages and workshops typical of those common to old Leeds is probably the main attraction of Abbey House.

The 16th- and 17th-century Temple Newsam House, east of the city, is a fine example of the architecture during this period. The house, which contains an important collection of decorative art, is surrounded by 900 acres of grounds designed by Capability Brown. An addition to the estate is Home Farm, an interpretation centre and farm museum with a collection of rare breeds.

Authorised by an Act of Parliament in 1758, a short stretch of railway line at Middleton, to the south of Leeds, claims to be the oldest in the world. First to succeed with steam locomotives in 1812, the Middleton Colliery Railway operates steam trains during the summer.

LINTON

SD9962
Scenically and architecturally one
of the finest villages of the
Yorkshire Dales, Linton has a
layout which probably dates from
Anglo-Saxon times. Houses are
informally grouped round a green,
with Linton Beck chuckling by. It
is crossed by stepping stones, a
clapper bridge, a packhorse bridge
and a modern road bridge.

Dominating Linton is the
Fountaine Hospital of 1721, one of
the first examples of classical
architecture built in the Dales.

Half a mile away, is Linton's
church, with Norman features.

LONDESBOROUGH

SE8645*
The Wolds Way, a long distance
footpath, runs through parkland
created by the 3rd Earl of
Burlington in the early 18th
century. Sample it by walking from
the park gates in Londesborough
village southwards for a mile.

LONG MARSTON

SE5051
This is the nearest village to
Marston Moor, where one of the
most important and decisive battles
of the Civil War was fought in the
evening of 2 July 1644. An
obelisk, commemorating victory
under Cromwell, stands on the site.

*Spacious cobbled market place at
Masham, home of Theakston's
Brewery and Old Peculier ale*

LOTHERTON HALL

SE4436
Lotherton Hall, with its
outstanding collection of European
works of art, furniture and
porcelain, was given to the city of
Leeds by the Gascoigne family and
is now a country-house museum.
In addition to the Gascoigne
collection, there are superb Chinese
ceramics, 20th-century pottery and
a fascinating display of historical
costumes, including examples of
the best of the fashion designs of
modern times.

MALTON

SE7871*
Old Malton and New Malton are
separated by the site of a Roman
station, finds from which are kept
in the museum in the old town
hall. The £500,000 Eden Camp
museum, a former prisoner-of-war
camp for Germans and Italians,
reflects wartime experiences.
Exhibits include the replica of a
German U-boar. New Malton was
built in 1138 when the old village
was largely burnt down. Its wide
market square is the centre of
activity for the surrounding
farming district. The quaint old-
fashioned cottages and inns of Old
Malton lie a mile north-east of the
town.

MASHAM

SE2280
The great Market Place, partly
cobbled, is Masham's outstanding
feature. Surrounded by hotels,
inns and houses of grey-brown
stone, it retains a degree of dignity.

Masham is the home of
Theakston's, an independent family
brewery since 1827, whose most
potent brew, *Old Peculier*, has
brought new distinction to the
town, and in its name
commemorates the fact that
Masham was a 'peculier' from
Roger de Mowbray's time, when
the Archbishop of York freed it to
have its own 'Peculier Court' — an
ecclesiastical body with wide
powers.

MIDDLEHAM

SE1287
Middleham used to be the capital
of Wensleydale. Now, it is a small
but pretty village. The castle (AM),
in ruins, was once known as
'the Windsor of the North', when
the great Neville family owned
it. Richard III acquired it in 1471,
and his eldest son was born there.
The 13th-century chapel and the
14th-century gatehouse survive.

NEWBURGH PRIORY

SE5576
This is essentially an 18th-century
hall built on a site where
Augustinian canons settled in 1150.
It is set amid pleasant gardens
featuring a pond and striking
ornamental hedges. At the
Dissolution Henry VIII gave the
property to Anthony Belayse, who
rebuilt the house. In time it passed
to Lord Fauconberg, who, (it is
said), married a daughter of Oliver
Cromwell's, who brought her
father's heart to Newburgh and had
it bricked up in an attic room to
save it from desecration.

NEWBY HALL AND GARDENS

SE3567
Newby is a late 17th-century house
with additions and interior by
Robert Adam, containing an
important collection of classical
sculpture, Gobelin tapestries and
selections of fine Chippendale
furniture. The gardens cover some
25 acres, and include a miniature
railway and adventure gardens for
children.

NORTH YORK MOORS NATIONAL PARK

SE6587*

The sixth of the National Parks in England and Wales, the North York Moors National Park was created in 1952.

The Park covers an area of 533 sq miles (1,438 sq km) and is broadly oval in shape, the North Sea marking the eastern boundary with a coastline of high fretted cliffs and some tiny, pleasant and picturesque coves. To the north and the west, the boundary follows the steep scarp faces of the Cleveland and Hambleton Hills, looking over the fertile farmlands of the Vale of York and Stokesley Plain. The southern boundary meanders from the back slopes of the Tabular Hills by Pickering and Helmsley to Scarborough.

The topography of the park is generally an uplifted plateau with a sequence of steps or scarps of northerly aspect. The underlying rock, mostly of the Jurassic era, is mainly limestone, gritstone and chalk with a shallow overlying layer of soil. Generally, the park experiences a relatively drier and cooler Continental climate, with occasional intrusions of cold, moisture-bearing air from the North Sea giving an average rainfall of around 30 inches inland and slightly less nearer to the coast. The tabular appearance of the moor has been intersected by a number of streams running north to south. Understandably, given the physical constraints of its position, soil, drainage conditions and climate, the North York Moors National Park has few expanses of forest. Essentially, it is a widespread expanse of windswept heather-clad moor interspersed with farming country and rich arable land in the dales. Of the forested areas, perhaps the most picturesque and most accessible to the tourist is the Dalby Forest. About 10 miles of well-surfaced roads pass through beautiful woodlands of conifers and deciduous trees, which are a vast haven for many species of wildlife. Planned amenities include numerous parking places, picnic sites and forest trails.

As in any of the other National Parks in England and Wales, man has had a profound effect on maintaining an equilibrium in the park. Evidence has traced settlements back to the Palaeolithic period, around 10,000 BC. But it was not until the introduction of agriculture that permanent settlements and farming were

established in the more fertile areas. The open-field system continued to flourish through the Medieval period, when monastic foundations, especially Rievaulx, established large-scale sheep farming on the moors.

The introduction of railway made more accessible not only the moors but also the resorts along the coast. The advent of the car brought the moorland even closer to the urban man through his demand for wider recreational facilities, and as a result a better network of communications developed. Varied landscape, nature trails and walks, pony trekking, gliding clubs, sailing on numerous reservoirs and off the coast, forest drives and game shooting are only some of the recreational activities that have made the North York Moors National Park so attractive and well used.

The privately-operated North Yorkshire Moors Railway runs through some of the county's most spectacular countryside

NORTH YORKSHIRE MOORS RAILWAY 'MOORSRAIL'

SE7988*

The North Yorkshire Moors Railway operates over 18 miles of track between Pickering and Grosmont, taking in some superb panoramic views along the way. The private company which runs the railway was founded in 1967, and became a trust in 1972. Steam and diesel locomotives pull the trains, and at Grosmont there is a loco shed, viewing gallery, gift shop and catering facilities. At Pickering station there is an excellent bookshop and also a National Park information and audio-visual centre.

Memorial at Otley Church to 30 men who died building a local rail tunnel

NUNBURNHOLME

*SE8548**
The small, attractive cottages of this village are strung out along a road bordering a clear chalk-stream in a sheltered valley. Named after a former convent for Benedictine nuns, the village was home for Victorian ornithologist, the Reverend F O Morris, rector from 1854 to 1893. In the house by the church he wrote his six-volume *History of British Birds*.

NUNNINGTON

*SE6679**
Nunnington Hall (NT) is a large 16th–17th-century manor house situated on the banks of the River Rye. Nunnington's most cohesive architectural feature is undoubtedly its south front, with its classical doorway and beautifully-carved stone window surrounds. This was the work of Lord Preston, who remodelled the south side of the house in the 1680s and also laid out the formal walled garden. The house is noted for its fine tapestries and china, and the Carlisle Collection of Miniature Rooms, fully furnished in different periods.

OTLEY

SE2045
Although largely dominated by modern industry, this old market town on the River Wharfe retains several good buildings as reminders of its long history. Above the town is the 925-foot summit of Otley Chevin, from which panoramic views over the lovely countryside of Lower Wharfedale can be enjoyed.

Exquisite example of Palladian decor, part of the Carlisle collection of miniature period rooms at 16th- and 17th-century Nunnington Hall

PARCEVALL HALL GARDENS

SE0862
Beautifully sited south of Grimwith Reservoir and east of the main Wharfedale valley, the fine Elizabethan house of Parceval (Percival) Hall is famous for the splendid gardens which complement its attractive setting.

PATELEY BRIDGE

SE1565
Since ancient times this pleasant market town has been a focus for the everyday life of Nidderdale, but nowadays its steep main street is busy as much with tourists as with local traffic. The picturesque ruins of Old St Mary's Church occupy a lofty hillside site, and the Nidderdale Museum displays over 3,000 items relating to life in the Yorkshire Dales. Of particular note are the Victorian Room and a replica cobbler's shop.

PICKERING

*SE7983**
This ancient market town, situated amidst beautiful countryside, is known as the Gateway to the Moors. The market place façades are mainly Georgian or Victorian, but older structures are often concealed behind them. The 12th century is evoked in the robust towers and ruined remains of Pickering Castle (AM), where Richard II was confined after his abdication. The Church of St Peter and St Paul, which stands above the main street, has retained fragments of a similar date. Its main attractions are the fine 15th-century wall paintings, depicting Bible stories with the figures in the daily costumes of over 500 years ago. The Beck Isle Museum of Rural Life is housed in a fine Georgian house, formerly the home of William Marshall, a noted agriculturalist, and displays folk exhibits of local interest. Pickering is also the terminus of the North Yorkshire Moors Railway.

POCKLINGTON

*SE8048**
A little market town in the shadow of the Yorkshire Wolds, with many attractive houses and a Medieval church, Pocklington is sometimes called the Cathedral of the Wolds. On the outskirts are the beautiful water gardens of Burnby Hall created by Major Stewart. He gathered rare plants on his travels around the world and brought home one of the finest collections of water lilies in Europe. Specimens of more than 50 varieties of lily bloom here all summer. Near by, in the Stewart Museum, is his collection of hunting trophies.

PONTEFRACT

SE4522
Liquorice-flavoured Pontefract cakes became famous at the turn of the century, and although the liquorice is no longer grown here, two local firms still produce them. There are several attractive 18th- and 19th-century buildings in the town and the local history museum in Salter Row provides a good background to Pontefract and its historically important castle — now in ruins in a public park.

All Saints' Church has an octagonal lantern tower that survived the Civil War.

RIEVAULX ABBEY (AM)

SE5785
Pronounced 'Reevo', the abbey was founded in 1132 as the first Cistercian house in Yorkshire, later becoming the mother church of the Order in England.

The most imposing of the Cistercian houses, it has the earliest Cistercian nave in Britain (1140), while the aisles of the chancel and the triforium were not completed until 1240. The choir is one of the finest remaining examples of 13th-century work in England.

At the Reformation the walls were razed to the ground and many local buildings are constructed with material taken from them. Lead from the roof was buried; nearly 400 years later it was found and used in the restoration of the Five Sisters Window at York Minster.

Looking down upon the abbey is Rievaulx Terrace (NT), a beautiful example of landscape gardening completed in 1758. With a lawn ½ mile long, there are two classical temples and superb views.

RIPLEY

SE2860
Much of this attractive village was rebuilt during the 19th century, but it is largely unspoilt. Ripley Castle has been home of the Ingilby family since 1350, but the present castle dates from the 16th and late 18th centuries. The beautiful grounds were landscaped by Capability Brown and its gatehouse is a fine building of around 1450. The castle has Cromwellian associations, and Royalist armour and weaponry are on view.

RIPON

SE3171
Popularly known as the Gateway to the Dales, this attractive city stands at the meeting of the Rivers Ure, Skell, and Laver and boasts a small but impressive cathedral. The main features of this lovely 12th-century building include a Saxon crypt that may be the earliest Christian survival in England, a fine early-English west front, and a beautiful 15th-century screen. Excellent examples of local woodcarving are the finely-worked misericords and curious Elephant and Castle bench. Every night Ripon's market square is the scene of a 1,000-year-old custom, when the town Hornblower or Wakeman strides out in his tricorn hat and

sounds his ancient horn at each corner of a huge 18th-century obelisk. Years ago this sound indicated that the Wakeman had begun his night watch over the town, and that the townspeople could sleep secure in their beds. The half-timbered Wakeman's house, later used by the mayor, dates from the 13th century and now contains a museum. An interesting Prison and Police Museum is housed in the old prison building dating from 1686.

RIPPONDEN

SE0319
An old-world village set in the Ryburn valley, most of old Ripponden is now a conservation area, comprising a packhorse bridge of around 1654, the 650-year-old Bridge Inn, St Bartholomew's Church and many attractive cottages. Ryburn Farm Museum is set in an old farmhouse and barn,

featuring agricultural implements, kitchen and dairy.

RUDSTON

*TA0967**
In 1933 a ploughman uncovered a Roman villa at Rudston, and three fine mosaic pavements from the site are now on view in the Hull Transport Museum. The largest measures 13ft by 10ft 6in and depicts a voluptuous Venus with a mirror and surrounded by leopards, birds and hunters.

SALTAIRE

SE1338

Sir Titus Salt's ideal of an industrial community far from Bradford's smoke consisted of mills like Renaissance palaces, good-quality housing, opportunities for education and advancement, and care for the sick and old. The huge Saltaire mill was opened in 1853, and in the next 20 years 792 houses were built, together with almshouses, a school, a hospital, churches and chapels, public baths, Turkish baths, a steam laundry and a 14-acre park (with essential bandstand), all in a rural setting by the River Aire. Strangely, the visionary's statue shows him looking away from the town.

Ceiling (below) of an Ionic 'temple' that overlooks the ruins of Rievaulx Abbey (top) from landscaped Rievaulx Terrace

SCARBOROUGH

TA0388*
The Victorians described
Scarborough as 'the Queen of
Watering Places' and it is
England's oldest holiday resort.

There is literally something for
everyone; almost every taste and
age group is catered for. It has two
bays with golden sands separated
by a castle-topped headland; there
is the colourful bustle of the sea
front, the gracious splendour of
the Spa and the calm dignity of
parks and gardens.

Add to this a quaint old market
in the town centre, some very
modern shops and a surrounding
beautiful landscape and the result
is a place in which visitors can
always find something new.

The town's history is ancient. The
remains of very early man were
found near Scarborough in 1949
and Bronze Age relics have been
found at the castle. The Romans

*Tides of trees lap Scarborough Castle
while holidaymakers paddle in the
resort's real waves*

and the Vikings also settled here.

Invaders made use of nature's
fortress behind the harbour, and
on that site, in 1136, began to
construct the present castle (AM).

Scarborough's modern appeal
owes much to a Mrs Farrow. In
1620, she noticed that some spring
water was different from the usual,
with an acid taste, and soon its
health-giving reputation attracted
visitors from afar. In 1660 a Dr
Wittie of Scarborough strongly
recommended the beneficial
properties of sea-bathing and
attracted people to the town.

The Theatre in the Round hosts
the world premieres of plays by
local playwright Alan Ayckbourn.
There is an Open Air Theatre, a
Royal Opera House and a Floral
Hall with top entertainers, plus
dances in the Spa Complex.

SELBY

SE6132
Famous for its beautiful abbey
church, Selby is an ancient town
and port on the River Ouse, where

small ships still put in and out of
the small dock. When boats were
built here they had to be launched
sideways because the river was
too narrow for the usual method.
The abbey was founded in 1069
by a monk of Auxerre in France
who, following a vision, came to
England and sailed up the River
Ouse, stopping at a place where
three swans settled on the water.
Here he built a hermitage and
received permission from the King
to found an abbey. Unfortunately
he fell out with the authorities
before work could begin, and the
present church was started by
Hugh de Lacy in 1100. Building
finished in the 14th century.

SEWERBY HALL

TA2068*
Sewerby Hall was built in the 18th
century and is surrounded by a fine
park of 50 acres, which sweeps
down to striking cliffs overlooking
Bridlington Bay. The mansion has
been turned into a museum, and
included in this is the Amy
Johnson Room, where many of the
pilot's mementoes are kept. A
miniature golf course, croquet
lawns, a putting green and a
children's corner provide
entertainment.

SHERBURN-IN-ELMET

SE4933
Once the eastern capital of the
ancient Brigantine kingdom of
Elmete, Sherburn has a church –
built of local limestone – that was
the secret meeting place for loyal
Catholics during the Reformation.
They are said to have made their
way by night through
underground passages, to worship
according to their faith. The
Medieval Janus cross in the
church, so called after the double-
headed Roman deity because the
carved figures face opposite
directions, was buried for safety
during the 16th-century
Reformation.

SHERIFF HUTTON

SE6566*
The village, with its long main
street flanked by high grassy banks,
is dominated by the ruins of the
castle. Built by the Nevilles in the
1380s, the castle fell into disrepair
by the mid-17th-century and many
of the older buildings in the village
are built from the castle's stones.

Close look at the detail on one of Sledmere's fine war memorials

SKIDBY WINDMILL

TA0133*
Well-preserved Skidby Windmill was built in 1821 and is the only example to have remained intact north of the River Humber and east of the Pennine Chain. Its black-tarred tower and white cap form a striking combination that makes it a prominent local landmark. An agricultural museum has been established inside.

SKIPSEA CASTLE (AM)

TA1655*
Soon after the Norman Conquest, William I granted the lordship of Holderness to Drogo de Brevere, a Flemish adventurer who built a motte-and-bailey castle at Skipsea Brough. Its enormous earthworks remain, their outer ramparts, a 300-yard crescent, linked to the motte (36 feet high) by a grassy, raised causeway.

SKIPTON

SD9851
Attractively situated on the Airedale moorlands at the eastern edge of the Craven district, Skipton is dominated by a Medieval castle that was restored by Lady Anne Clifford in 1658. Founded in Norman times, the building was subsequently extended and was strong enough to resist a three-year siege before falling into the hands of Cromwell's Parliamentarian army in the Civil War. The Lord Protector dismantled the castle to make sure that it could never again be manned against him, but thanks to Lady Anne its six massive towers still punctuate the skyline of the town that grew beneath its walls. Opposite the massive castle gateway is the Craven Museum, where exhibits and displays illustrate the geology and folk history of the district.

SLEDMERE

SE9364*
This neat little village forms part of the Sledmere Estate, of which Sledmere House is the centre. A beautifully decorated house, it contains many handsome pieces of furniture. The estate is the property of the Sykes family, who were largely responsible for the development of the Wolds. Beside the main road in the village stand two remarkable war memorials.

Just outside the village, Garton Hill is a good vantage point from which to view the magnificence of the Wolds.

SPOFFORTH

SE3650
A quiet, attractive village beside the little River Crimple, Spofforth's main feature is the remains of Spofforth Castle (AM). A 13th-century fortified manor, which had long associations with the Percy family, only its hall and the solar wing are left.

SPROATLEY

TA1934*
Burton Constable Hall is a fine Elizabethan house, home of the Constable family for hundreds of years, set amidst 200 acres of parkland landscaped by Capability Brown. The great house dates from 1570, although the interior was remodelled in the 18th century by craftsmen such as Robert Adam, Wyatt and Lightoler. The superb staterooms, the drawing room with its rare Chippendale furniture and the Chinese room are particularly notable. In the Alice in Wonderland room is a collection of dolls.

STAMFORD BRIDGE

SE7155*
In 1066 at the Battle of Stamford Bridge, King Harald of Norway, who had sailed up the Humber and the Ouse and sacked York, was decisively beaten by King Harold of England. The battle took place on the flats above which now stands a fine 18th-century bridge. As everyone knows, immediately after the battle, Harold and the English army had to race south to meet William of Normandy and defeat at Hastings.

STEETON HALL GATEHOUSE (AM)

SE4832
Across the woods and meadows from the village of South Milford is this 14th-century gatehouse of a Medieval castle, once owned by the Fairfax family. A forbear of the famous Cromwellian general is said to have ridden out from here to escape with his sweetheart, a wealthy heiress.

Patterns of stone and sun in the Conduit Court, Skipton Castle – a huge fortification with six massive towers and a strong gateway

SUTTON BANK

SE5182
Sutton Bank affords the finest view in Yorkshire, if not in England. The view stretches from The Pennines in the west, into Cleveland in the north and across to York and West Yorkshire in the south. There is a large car park, a telescope and a guide to the points in sight. A National Park Information Centre is here.

SUTTON-ON-THE-FOREST

SE5864
Sutton-on-the-Forest is a beautiful conservation village and the location of Sutton Park. This early Georgian house, built in 1730, has fine examples of English and French furniture and is surrounded by beautiful gardens and parkland.

TADCASTER

SE4843
Tadcaster is the home of traditional Yorkshire ales, and the scent of the breweries pervades old streets which are famous for the large number of public houses. A restored 15th-century house called the Ark has been converted into a museum with a unique collection of fascinating relics associated with the British beer drinking habits.

THIRSK

SE4282
Thirsk and the surrounding countryside have become known as Herriot Country, thanks to the books of James Herriot, and the television series.

But there is a good deal more in Thirsk. It is a busy town in two parts, the old and the new, with the Cod Beck flowing through it. The new has a fine cobbled market place surrounded by shops, restaurants, and some fine coaching inns.

The old part of Thirsk is centred around St James' Green, which was once the market place.

The parish church of St Mary is magnificent, known as 'The Cathedral of the North' because of its splendour. The tower was started in 1410 and it took 50 years

Colour and bustle in old Thirsk

to complete the church. There is an impressive roof and some delicate tracery in the battlements which furnish the walls. One of its bells came from Fountains Abbey. The altar stone is from Byland Abbey. There are many other treasures.

In Kirkgate, on the approach to the church, is the town museum. It was once the home of Thomas Lord, born in 1775, founder of Lord's Cricket Ground in London.

Thirsk Racecourse, opened in 1854, is one of the finest in the north of England.

TOP FARM AGRICULTURAL MUSEUM

SE4518
Over 2,000 items are on show at this small Museum set in an existing farmyard, ranging from steam threshing equipment and traction engines to hand tools, mostly in their original setting. Also on display are some farm animals representing the art of husbandry.

TOWTON

SE4839
One of the most savage battles in English history took place near this peaceful little village in wooded Wharfedale. A stone cross just outside Towton marks the place where more than 30,000 men were slaughtered on Palm Sunday, 1461, during the Wars of the Roses. The bodies were interred in a mass grave in a field near by, and for centuries after, ploughmen would often turn up bones.

WAKEFIELD

SE3320
Wakefield was the capital of Yorkshire's woollen industry for more than 700 years, but when the factory age arrived the wool trade moved north to Leeds and Bradford. Cloth manufacture still plays a part in Wakefield's life, but the town has diversified into chemicals and engineering.

The cathedral-church of All Saints stands in the city centre where the old streets of Kirkgate, Warrengate, Northgate and Westgate meet. Parts of the nave and chancel date from the 14th century, and its lovely 247-foot spire is the tallest in Yorkshire.

The city of Wakefield incorporates the old towns of Pontefract and Castleford. Above

Pontefract rise the ruins of one of England's most famous castles. It changed hands three times in the Civil War, and was partly demolished in 1649.

South-east of Wakefield is Nostell Priory (NT), a mid-18th-century mansion, started by James Paine in 1733 and completed by Robert Adam. Almost every room contains fine examples of furniture.

WETHERBY

SE4048
Famous for its six-arch bridge over the River Wharfe, Wetherby is a charming market town in the attractive valley of lower Wharfedale. The 11th-century castle was built by the Knights Templar. Something else Wetherby is famous for is its racecourse, where National Hunt and point-to-point meetings are regularly held.

Just to the north of the town is the small country mansion of Stockheld Park. The house, in attractive gardens and grounds, is built in Palladian style and is one of the finest works of James Paine. Main features of the house are the central hall and staircase.

WOLDS WAY

*TA1180**
The most recent of the long-distance walks, opened in 1982, the 72 miles (115 km) route passes through some of the pleasant, low-level agricultural land of East Yorkshire. The path starts at Filey and follows a circuitous route across to Hessle Haven.

YORKSHIRE AIR MUSEUM

SE6947*

This Museum at Elvington opened in June 1986. Volunteers and a Manpower Services Community Programme have restored the World War II Flying Control Tower as the centrepiece of the Museum, a charity which will commemorate the allied air crews who served in the area. Sponsors include British Aerospace plc, Brough and among the patrons are Group Captain Leonard Cheshire and Lord Halifax. There is a unique Halifax Restoration Project.

The Museum opened with a fly-past of Jet Provosts from RAF Church Fenton, the launch of a book, *Halifax: Second to None*, and a fly-over from a Handley Page Victor tanker from RAF 57 Squadron — which was formed in Yorkshire and disbanded in 1986.

The interior of the Watch Office in the Control Tower has been accurately recreated from archive film taken there during the war. Many ex-air and ground crew have visited the Museum and help with its running. Groups from Canada and France are regular visitors, as so many were based in the area.

YORKSHIRE DALES

SE0574

Sweeping landscapes and a pattern of dry stone walls are essential components of the unique Dales character. Stone-built villages, farms and barns on valley sides and beside rivers are further elements in the composition. Dominating the western skyline is the backbone of

Aspects of the Yorkshire Dales – the rugged country of Buttertubs (inset) and gentler sparkle of Aysgarth Falls

England, The Pennines.

Stretching from Stainmore Forest — close to the old Roman road from Brough to Barnard Castle (now the A66 and A67) — down to Skipton in the south, and across from Sedbergh westwards to Great Whernside, is the 680-square-mile Yorkshire Dales National Park. It encompasses the finest of the Dales scenery.

Largest of the Dales is Swaledale, a good place to begin to understand the landscape, the character of the villages and the people. The pattern of farming life shapes the land throughout the Dales, and in Swaledale sheep graze the fells, with cattle in the fields along the valley floor.

Made of the material that is easily available, all the buildings in the Dale are of stone and blend beautifully with the landscape.

The road through the Dale stays close to the River Swale from its

birthplace on Birkdale Common in The Pennines, near Keld, all the way to ancient Richmond.

Progress along Swaledale is by way of the seemingly evenly spaced villages.

High above Swaledale on the road from Thwaite over the moors to Wensleydale, is a series of deep holes known as the Buttertubs. Back in Swaledale itself is Gunnerside. The gill which gives the village its name can be followed northwards up through a beautiful little valley. High up the valley are many remains of the lead-mining industry which was once so important here. Men have lived and worked in the Dales for thousands of years, and evidence of that is to be seen in the huge earthwork called Maiden Castle, on the fell-side near Reeth.

Over the ridge to the south lies Wensleydale, completely different in character from its northern neighbour. Wensleydale is a broad farming Dale with very little history of lead-mining. The river that has carved its way out of The Pennines here is the Ure, so perhaps the Dale derives its name from the former importance, in Medieval times, of the village of Wensley.

Further on in Wensleydale, is Aysgarth, an attractive village given added beauty by Aysgarth Falls. Wensley itself is a lovely little place with a delightful green.

The River Wharfe has its source in several becks high up on the moors of Langstrothdale Chase. For its first mile it flows through remote Langstrothdale, entering Wharfedale at Buckden. It flows south past Kettlewell and the limestone crags at Kilnsey and on down through Strid Gorge to leave the National Park just beyond Bolton Priory. Littondale can be followed along unclassified roads leading north-westwards from Wharfedale to the north of Kilnsey. It is one of the most secluded of the Dales; at its head is Halton Gill, from where strenuous paths lead across to Pen-y-ghent.

Limestone dominates the land formation in the Park and this is most evident in the west. Perhaps the best known of the natural features, and the most spectacular, is Malham Cove, a huge natural amphitheatre. Farther west again lies Ribblesdale, curving its way between Pen-y-ghent and Ingleborough. Apart from the infant River Ribble, the Dale carries the Carlisle to Settle railway line, one of the most spectacular rail journeys in Britain.

Selby and the Western Wold

Famous vet James Herriot's surgery, reconstructed at the Yorkshire Museum of Farming

Leaving the suburbs of York, the tour follows a secondary road along the shallow valley of the River Ouse to Cawood. The river is crossed here before proceeding to Selby, famous for its abbey church. The drive re-crosses the Ouse by a toll bridge and heads eastwards through level agricultural countryside to Holme-on-Spalding-Moor, where the Yorkshire Wolds can be seen in the distance.

After visiting the town of Pocklington, a byroad route is taken to climb on to the Wolds. There is a fine viewpoint at Garrowby Hill before the descent into the Vale of York to reach Stamford Bridge — the scene of King Harold's pre-Battle of Hastings victory in 1066. The drive crosses the River Derwent and returns to York.

From the Inner Ring Road on the south side of the city centre follow signs Selby to leave by the A19. In about 2 miles turn right on to the B1222 signed Sherburn-in-Elmet to reach Stillingfleet. A stream from the River Ouse runs through the village; to the north of this lies the interesting parish church, featuring all the styles of Medieval architecture.

At the T-junction turn right and in 2½ miles cross the River Ouse and enter **Cawood**. The village fits well into its situation on the River Ouse, and high on the river bank is a church with a fine 15th-century tower. An impressive gateway is all that remains of the castle (see page 92). *Here turn left on to the B1223 signposted Selby for* Wistow.

Standing not far from the River Ouse, Wistow Church — noted for the fine, 14th-century window in its chancel — is prominent in the flat landscape. *Continue with the B1223 and in 2½ miles at the T-junction turn left signed Town Centre, then turn right through the square into* **Selby**. Located on the River Ouse, Selby is renowned for its beautiful abbey church. In contrast, near by lies the site of an extensive, new coalfield development (see page 104). However, the town is no stranger to industry, since it was once a flourishing shipbuilding centre. Small sea-going vessels still put in and out from its riverside dock. *At the main road turn left on to the A19 (no sign) then follow signs York and cross the River Ouse (toll) to enter* Barlby. *At the end of the village turn right on to the A163 signposted Market Weighton for* Bubwith.

The bridge crossing the Derwent here was built at the end of the 18th century. There are a few pretty houses in the village and the church stands high above a loop of the river. *Continue on the A163 to reach* Holme-on-Spalding-Moor. The church lies to the east of the village on the top of an isolated hill from which there are superb views of the Wolds and the surrounding countryside. *At the end of the village at the mini-roundabout take the first exit, and 2½ miles further at the roundabout take the first exit on to the A1079, signposted York. Pass through Shiptonthorpe and Hayton. In 1 mile turn right on to the B1247 for* **Pocklington**.

This pleasant little market town sits snugly in the shadow of the Wolds, and there are many attractive houses. A diversion can be made here to visit the outstanding Burnby Hall Gardens, which lie about 2 miles to the southeast (see page 102). In the attractive water gardens is a collection of water lilies acclaimed by many as being among the finest in Europe. *At the roundabout keep forward signposted Malton and in ½ mile turn right on to an unclassified road (Garth Ends) signposted Millington. In ¼ mile at the roundabout turn left and 1¾ miles farther keep forward signposted Givendale. Ascend to the Wolds and pass the hamlet of Givendale. In about 2 miles turn left on to the A166 signposted York and descend Garrowby Hill (1-in-6) to reach* **Stamford Bridge**.

The first of two decisive battles was fought near this village on the River Derwent, in 1066. It was here that King Harold inflicted a crushing defeat on the invading Norseman (see page 105). *Cross the River Derwent and in 4¾ miles pass a road on the right which leads to the* **Yorkshire Museum of Farming**. Set in eight acres of country park, this fascinating museum uses modern displays, reconstructions, veteran agricultural machinery and actual livestock to relate the social and agrarian history of the English countryside from early times (see page 63). *At next roundabout take the third exit on to the A1079 for the return to York.*

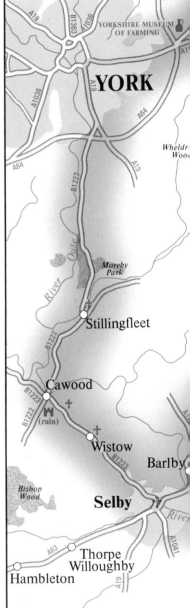

Almost all places in **bold type** are fully described in this guide's second gazetteer section, which starts on page 87; a minority appears in the first gazetteer, beginning on page 37. Both are organised alphabetically (by name).

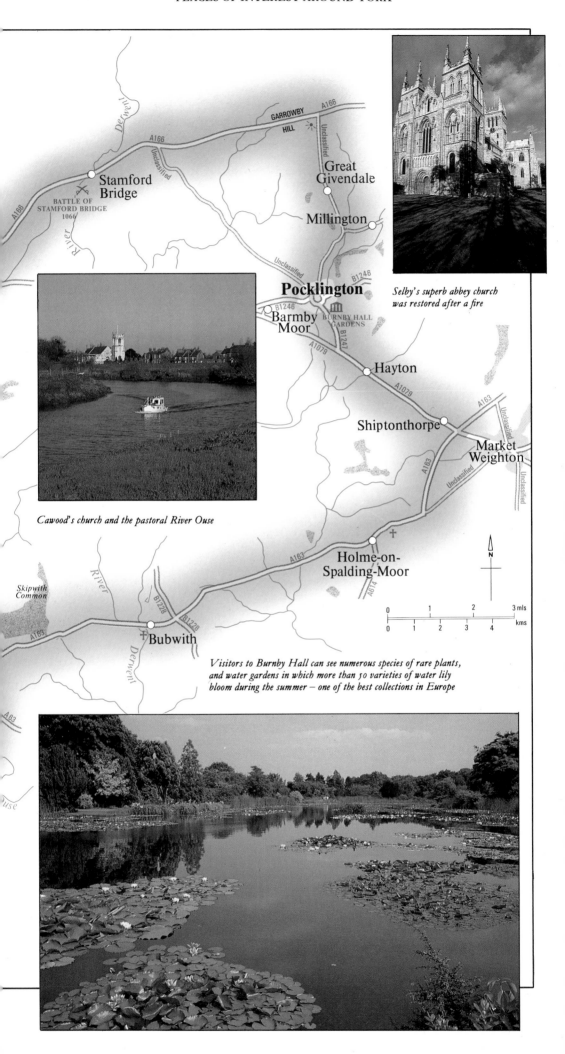

Selby's superb abbey church was restored after a fire

Cawood's church and the pastoral River Ouse

Visitors to Burnby Hall can see numerous species of rare plants, and water gardens in which more than 50 varieties of water lily bloom during the summer – one of the best collections in Europe

The Vale of York and Howardian Hills

After the agricultural Vale of York, this route becomes more undulating as it nears Sheriff Hutton and enters the Howardian Hills. A picturesque stretch crosses the grounds of Castle Howard, then the drive passes attractive villages before re-entering the Vale of York at Easingwold. Subsequently, there are places of interest at Boroughbridge, Aldborough and Newton-on-Ouse.

From the Inner Ring Road on the north side of the City Centre follow signs Helmsley to leave by the B1363. The drive passes through agricultural country in the Vale of York to reach **Sutton-on-the-Forest**. In the village are the house and grounds of Sutton Park (see page 106). *At the T-junction turn right and pass the entrance to Sutton Park and at the end of the village turn left signed Helmsley and continue to the attractive village of Stillington.* The 18th-century writer Lawrence Sterne (see **Coxwold**, page 92) was vicar here and the lovely old church in which he served features a 12th-century priest's door. *At the T-junction turn right and near the end of the village turn right on to an unclassified road signposted Sheriff Hutton. Pass through Farlington to reach the outskirts of* **Sheriff Hutton**. Of interest are the impressive remains of the 12th-century castle (see page 104). *Go over the crossroads signed Bulmer. In 2¼ miles descend then ascend (1-in-6) for Bulmer. One mile further at a crossroads turn left signed Castle Howard. Keep forward at the gateways through the grounds of* **Castle Howard** — a magnificent 17th-century mansion designed by Vanbrugh (see page 91).

At the obelisk keep forward passing the entrance to the house to arrive at the outskirts of Slingsby. From here a short detour can be made to visit the village, where there is a castle ruin. *Here turn left on to the B1257 signposted Helmsley to arrive at* **Hovingham** (see page 96). *Forward through the village and in 1½ miles a detour on the right can be made to visit* **Nunnington**. The 16th and 17th-century Nunnington Hall with its panelled hall and staircase, contains the Carlisle Collection of miniature rooms (see page 102).

Continue with the B1257 for Stonegrave — a small village with a magnificent church. *In 2¼ miles turn left on to the B1363 signposted York and descend through the edge of Oswaldkirk to reach* **Gilling East**. To the west of the village lies Gilling Castle, dating from the 11th century and now a preparatory school (see page 93). *Cross the Howardian Hills and in 4 miles descend (1-in-7) to Brandsby. Here turn right on to an unclassified road signed Crayke to reach the pleasant village of* **Crayke**. The castle was built in the 15th century on the site of a Norman castle (see page 92). *In the village turn right signposted Easingwold. After 2 miles keep left signed Market Place into* **Easingwold** (see page 92).

Here join the one-way system, then at the T-junction turn right on to the A19 (no sign) and at the end of the main street turn left on to an unclassified route signed Boroughbridge. At Raskelf, the 15th-century church tower is made of wood and is said to be unique in Yorkshire. *Keep left, then bear right to reach the outskirts of Brafferton.*

At the Oak Tree PH turn right signed Boroughbridge and in 1 mile cross the River Swale and turn left. After 2½ miles keep left, then bear right and in another 1 mile at the T-junction turn left, then at the roundabout take the first exit on to the B6265 to enter **Boroughbridge** (see page 90). Three large monoliths known ominously as the Devil's Arrows stand to the west of the town. *Here turn left signposted York, then left again through the Market Place to reach the edge of* **Aldborough**. The Roman Town and Museum lie to the left (see page 88). *Continue with the B6265 and in 3 miles turn left into an unclassified road signed Great Ouseburn. About ½ mile beyond Great Ouseburn turn left and in another 1½ miles cross Aldwark Toll Bridge (River Ure) then turn right signed Linton/Newton-on-Ouse. Continue through Linton-on-Ouse to reach* Newton-on-Ouse. A detour to the right leads to **Beningbrough Hall**. The present hall was completed by 1716 (see page 88). *In the village keep left signed Shipton and York and in 1½ miles at the T-junction turn right. After 2 miles cross the railway bridge and turn right signed York and in another ½ mile turn right again on to the A19 for the return to* York.

This rare City of Troy turf maze, near Bransby, is thought to date from the Middle Ages. Its original purpose is unknown

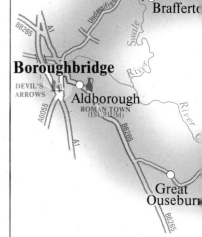

One of three colossal Bronze Age monoliths, known as the Devil's Arrows, which stand in a line running north–south on the outskirts of Boroughbridge. Fashioned from millstone grit and standing from 18 to 22ft high, the stones form one of Yorkshire's most famous ancient monuments and have been curiously fluted by weathering

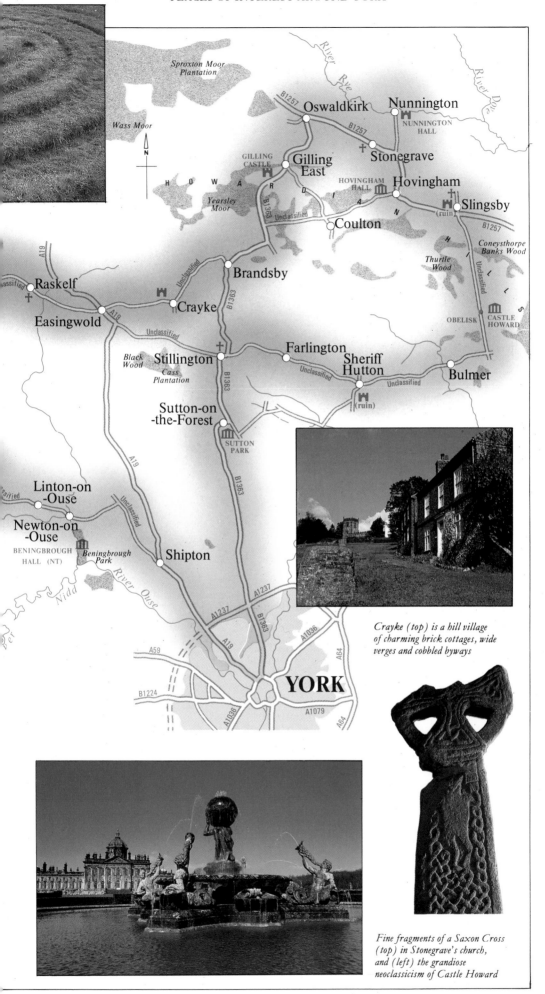

Crayke (top) is a hill village
of charming brick cottages, wide
verges and cobbled byways

Fine fragments of a Saxon Cross
(top) in Stonegrave's church,
and (left) the grandiose
neoclassicism of Castle Howard

Acknowledgements

The Automobile Association wishes to thank the following photographers, organisations
and libraries for their assistance in the compilation of this book. Many of the photographs
reproduced are the copyright of the AA Photo Library.

M Adleman 57 Plaque Guy Fawkes, 89 Beverley Minster, 96 Hebden Bridge, 105 Conduit Court. *P & G Bowater*
4/5 Treasurer's House, 67 Minster from the walls. *J Allan Cash Photolibrary* Cover view of York from
Kleisers Court. *Castle Museum* 10 Seals of York, 15 Terry's Shop, 45 King William Hotel, Corsets. *C. Kightly*
31 Sword Dancing. *L P Sports* 96 Helmsley Village, 111 Castle Howard. *The Mansell Collection* 13 Monk
Bar, Bootham Bar, Micklegate Bar, 15 Stage Coach, 24 North Eastern railway station, 26/7 York from
the Ouse, 28, Seal, Edward IV, 29 Frederick, Henry VIII, Prince Edward, Prince George, 32 Wm Etty,
77 Anne Boleyn, 80 Thomas Percy. *Mansion House* 5 York Coat of Arms. *Mary Evans Picture Library*
24 George Hudson crash. *S & O Mathews* 69 Shambles, 81 Shambles, 88/9 Strid Gorge, 89 Bolton Abbey,
91 Brinham Rocks, 94 Greenhow Hill, Stump Cross Cavern, 100 Masham, 106/7 Aysgarth. *C. Molyneux*
107 Buttertubs. *Rich Newton* 1 Ironwork, 13 Former Debtors Prison, 14 Assembly Rooms, 15 Black
Swan Inn, Dick Turpin's grave, 22 Terry's Shop, 24 Clock, Railway Station, 27 Skelderdale Bridge,
30 Sigismund's Sword, Cap of Maintenance, Great Mace, Chamber Pot, 32 Minerva, 34 Lady Peckitt's
Yard, 35 Pope's Head Alley, Printer's Devil, 36 Powell's Yard, lamp, 37 Terry's sweets, 38 All Saints',
North St, All Saints', Pavement, 39 Regimental silver, 40 Barker & Lendal towers, 41 Bishop's Palace,
Bootham Bar, 42 Clock, 43 The Street, 44 Clifford's Tower, Fairfax House, 45 Guildhall window, Herbert
House, 46 Holy Trinity church, Jacob's well, 48 King's Manor, Lendal Tower, 49 Merchant Adventurers'
Hall, Banner, 50 Window, Micklegate Bar, 51 Multangular Tower, 52 Railway Museum, Luncheon
basket, Nameplate, 54 St Leonard's Hospital, 55 St Margaret's, St Martin le Grande, 56 St Mary's window,
58 St William's, 60 Stonegate, Red devil, 61 Drawing Room, 62/3 York Story, 63 Gallion, 64 Museum
of Farming, 66 Rampart levels, 68 Walmgate Bar, 70 Gate sign, Judge's lodging, Marygate
Tower, 72 All Saints', North St, 73 Leeman statue, 73 Ouse Bridge, Water authority, 75 Castle Museum,
76 Raffles Tea Room, 77 Theatre Royal, 78 The Walls, St William's College, 79 Holy Trinity, 80 Stonegate,
82 Bicycle, 83 Litter bin, 87 Harwood House, 90 Bolling Hall, 91 Castle Howard, 92 St Michael's, 93 Gilling
East Castle, 97 Guildhall, 98 White Horse, Workshop, 98/9 Knaresborough, 99 Old Mother Shipton's
Cave, 101 Northdale Scar, 103 Rievaulx, 104 Scarborough, 105 Sledmere, 106 Thirsk, 108 Museum
of Farming, 109 Selby Abbey, 111 Crayke, Stonegrave Minster. *C Park* 27 Flood levels, 56 St Mary's
Abbey, 66 The Minster, 73 Bonding warehouse, 74 Tower of York Minster. *V Patel* 92 Roseberry Topping.
Rex Features 28 Duke & Duchess of York. *Rowntree Mackintosh* 22 Rowntrees cocoa, chocolates, inside
Rowntrees. *PWB Semmens* 25 Mallard in York Station. *Fred Spencer* 18 Window with Peter Gibson,
by kind permission of the Dean & Chapter, York Minster. *Spellman's booksellers* 10/11 Panorama of York.
R. Surman 92 Flamborough Head, 95 Harrogate Pump room, 99 Leeds clock, 102 Nunnington Hall,
103 Ionic temple. *T & R Theakston* 100 Label. *M Trelawny* 102 Brammel tunnel. *Tim Woodcock* 36 Coffee
Yard, 68 Ice House, 71 Treasurer's House, 111 Brandsby Turf Maze. *York Archaeological Trust* 12 Coppergate
Helmet, 12 & 49 Jorvik Viking Centre. *York City Art Gallery* 14 Grand Assembly Rooms, 32 Painting
by Mary Ellen Best. *York City Library* 33 Poster. *York Minster Archaeological Office*, by kind permission
of the Dean & Chapter of York. 16 York Minster, 17 Plan, 18/19 Chapter House, 18 Kneeler, 19 Jonathan
Martin, 20 Minster Fire 1840 & 1984, 21 Painted mask. *Yorkshire Museum* 11 Roman kitchen. *Yorkshire
& Humberside Tourist Board* 109 Burnby Hall Gardens, River Ouse at Cawood. *York Tourist Board*
33 & 59 Mystery plays.